COLLEGE OF ALAMEDA LIBRARY

610272

D0443146

LENDING POLICY
IF YOU DAMAGE OR LOSE LIBRARY
MATERIALS, THEN YOU WILL BE
CHARGED FOR REPLACEMENT. FAIL-
URE TO PAY AFFECTS LIBRARY
PRIVILEGES, GRADES, TRANSCRIPTS,
DIPLOMAS, AND REGISTRATION
PRIVILEGES OR ANY COMBINATION
THEREOF.

AUG 2 2 2001

WHERE MY HEART IS TURNING EVER

PS
217
.C58
W48
1992

WHERE MY HEART IS TURNING EVER

CIVIL WAR STORIES AND CONSTITUTIONAL REFORM, 1861–1876

KATHLEEN DIFFLEY

THE UNIVERSITY OF GEORGIA PRESS

ATHENS AND LONDON

© 1992 by the University of Georgia Press
Athens, Georgia 30602
All rights reserved
Designed by Betty Palmer McDaniel
Set in Linotype Walbaum by Tseng Information Systems, Inc.
Printed and bound by Braun-Brumfield, Inc.
The paper in this book meets the guidelines for permanence and durability
of the Committee on Production Guidelines for Book Longevity of the
Council on Library Resources.

Printed in the United States of America
96   95   94   93   92   C   5   4   3   2   1

Library of Congress Cataloging in Publication Data
Diffley, Kathleen Elizabeth, 1950–
Where my heart is turning ever : Civil War stories and constitutional reform,
1861–1876 / Kathleen Diffley.
p.   cm.
Includes bibliographical references (p.   ) and index.
ISBN 0-8203-1445-5 (alk. paper)
1. United States—History—Civil War, 1861–1865—Literature and the war.
2. American literature—19th century—History and criticism.   3. American
literature—20th century—History and criticism.   4. Popular literature—
United States—History and criticism.   5. War stories, American—
History and criticism.   6. Narration (Rhetoric)
I. Title.
PS217.C58W48   1992   92-7048
813'.409—dc20   CIP

British Library Cataloging in Publication Data available

For Jude

CONTENTS

CODA

ACKNOWLEDGMENTS

AFTER YEARS OF QUIET respiration, it is a pleasure to thank both those who have made my solitude possible and those who have graced my days with talk, my work with care. I thank the National Endowment for the Humanities for two fellowships that have seen me through the writing of this book; the University of Iowa for summer grants and a developmental leave that have sped my research; Iowa's Center for Advanced Study for a room of my own; and the American Association of University Women for the fellowship with which this project began.

I am indebted as well to William Cain and Dale Bauer for their kind attention in reading the entire manuscript and their generosity in offering comments; to Werner Sollors, Nina Baym, Albert Stone, and Gordon Hutner for their encouragement and intellectual support while this project was gestating; and to Tom Lutz, Kenneth Cmiel, Timothy Sweet, and Geraldine Murphy for their incisive suggestions and unbounded friendship while the book coalesced. May they all forgive the errors and infelicities that remain.

I am also beholden to those in various archives who have willingly given of their time: Keith Rageth, Ann Ford, and Helen Ryan at the University of Iowa Libraries; Daniel Bearss at the Supreme Court Library; and a staff too numerous to mention at the Library of Congress. A special and personal thanks to my research assistants at various stages: Stan Sherwood and Stan Tag, Sarah Witte and Loretta Collins, Tim Gustafson and Dallas Liddle, and, above all, Mary-Jo Miller and Jan Carolus. All were smart and forthcoming; I appreciate their help.

I would also like to thank Oxford University Press and *American Literary History* for their permission to reprint a large section of chapter 1.

For my husband, Jude Heaney, gratitude is too little, words are too much. He is the rock on which I found myself.

Popular Narratives
and Civil Crisis

THE GUNS THAT OPENED on Fort Sumter have echoed for historians since April 1861, when South Carolina rebelled and the Civil War began. For literary critics, however, those first reverberations have long been so faint that the Civil War has seemed largely "unwritten," at least until the Centennial in 1876 guaranteed a more perfect union. During the years after the Federal retreat from Charleston harbor, the waning of morale on both sides of the Mason-Dixon line, while families disintegrated and brothers drew a bead on one another across the corpses of their friends, is thought to have sapped the imaginative will to remember, not only in the wake of Antietam and Gettysburg but throughout the Reconstructive years when ailing survivors turned resolutely toward the future. In the contemporary flight from the front lines, no writer of supposed genius arose to turn the national tide toward recollection, with the result that the "real" war of thrust and recoil apparently evaporated into the thin air of American amnesia and the postwar return to business as usual. Without the grit of a Hemingway or the urgency of a Wiesel, conventional wisdom runs, firsthand accounts were ultimately vitiated by the delicate priorities of a feminized cultural ethos, which closed the shutters of national reckoning against the shock of civil war.

Contemporary writers were not, however, silent about the crisis. Surveying the major magazines on hand during the Civil War and Reconstruction, this book and the trilogy it inaugurates recover the short war narratives that a burgeoning magazine trade delivered to its readers between 1861 and 1876 and examine where popular scenarios gave way, irrevocably, when historical crisis strained their customary resolutions. At issue is the assumption that the Civil War imaginatively vanished, that the tensions it released were suppressed or ignored by contemporary writers and the publishing industry they fueled. Not so in more than three hundred stories from sixteen magazines of the period, originating in the South and West as well as the culturally dominant Northeast. Not only did the conflict find its way into fiction, but domestic rhetoric and narrative strategies tried to contain its disruption, most precariously when they took up matters of race, political section, and gender.

Concentrating on these literary magazines and the stories they circulated, I begin in this volume to enlarge the territory that previous scholarship has surveyed, an endeavor that is overdue. Earlier critics of Civil War literature have tended, for example, to reinforce canonical authority by shunning the popular press, and they have consequently mistaken the opinions of an elite for those of "American" writers at large. That is a problem for Edmund Wilson in his otherwise insightful *Patriotic Gore* (1962), which examines the wartime records left by some thirty men and women. The scope of Wilson's interest permits him to range over genres (novels, journals, poetry, memoirs, speeches, political tracts, and public addresses) and to combine Lincoln and Grant in the North with the diaries of Southern ladies and the myth of the Old South in Civil War poetry, before considering postwar novelists of every stripe. But while he declares that war is a wholesale "power drive" meeting with resistance, his emphasis on literate accounts and his concluding praise for Justice Oliver Wendell Holmes and a soldier's duty make the war unexpectedly personal and idiosyncratic. Taking his title from the familiar Confederate song that became Maryland's anthem, Wilson nonetheless neglects popular wartime writers in favor of the articulate, and he ignores what was widely read in favor of those whose character and prose style have caught his imagination.

So, too, George M. Frederickson has chosen well-schooled though less well-circulated observers in *The Inner Civil War: Northern Intellectuals and the Crisis of the Union* (1965), a study that begins in Boston with Emerson, the Adams and James families, and the abolitionists of various creeds before moving south with the Sanitary Commission to Lincoln and Whitman. Principally concerned with American intellectual life, Frederickson draws connections between the experience of "collective trauma" and the shifts in thought that later encouraged both muscular Christianity and American imperialism. But his disdain for "the many who speak in clichés" and his narrow faith in an elite to chart American conflict are open to question, as is his preoccupation with a national "Eden" that few antebellum Americans really had to lose.

In marked contrast is that champion of neglected best-sellers Leslie Fiedler, whose *Inadvertent Epic: From "Uncle Tom's Cabin" to "Roots"* (1979) challenges established opinion about Civil War literature and finds in popular culture a "counter-tradition dominated by women and domestic values." Taking Stowe's *Uncle Tom's Cabin*, Dixon's *The Clansman*, Griffith's *Birth of a Nation*, Mitchell's *Gone With the Wind*, and Haley's *Roots* as a single collective work, Fiedler replaces the subversive male tropes elucidated by Wilson and Frederickson with a domestic emphasis on family and social coherence. Both in cementing a popular epic and in questioning the established criteria for critical judgments, he promotes the claims that "invisible" literature should rightly have on cultural critics today, quixotic as this compact study may appear and slack as a feminized ethos may seem by the turn of the century. Fiedler's aim is to restore literary awareness rather than to chart cultural norms, but he opens the channels that more culturally laden studies may navigate.

Contributing further to interest in what was popularly applauded is Rosemary L. Cullen's *The Civil War in American Drama Before 1900* (1982), an exhibition catalog she has designed to correct the impression that the issues of the Civil War did not figure on the American stage until after 1900. Cullen points out that the problems of slavery, secession, family collapse, competing loyalties, and rebuilding were all taken up in the popular theater, as were the war's actual events and their implications. Where battlefield spectacles in the 1860s replaced earlier slavery dramas, pageantry in turn gave way to military chronicle plays after the war and then to Civil War romances in the mid-1870s, all centering on union and the conflict between love and duty. Cullen's examination of plots, characters, and reception is brief, as is her attention to formal play, but the material she has gathered suggests how much can be learned from popular fare that has otherwise been overlooked.

Likewise attuned to popular tastes is David Kaser's *Books and Libraries in Camp and Battle: The Civil War Experience* (1984), which considers the role of reading among Civil War soldiers. Drawing upon letters and memoirs as well as regimental histories, accounts of prison life, and the output of army field presses, Kaser surveys the reading of American men in 1860, what soldiers then read, how reading figured in wartime settings, and where soldiers found reading material. His conclusions focus on soldierly habits rather than the newspapers and magazines most often circulated; in fact, he credits Civil War camp life with providing stretches of free time in which officers and enlisted men alike first discovered reading for entertainment. Kaser's attention to the increase in publishing, the drop in book prices, the advent of leisure time, and the new public library movement after the war provides fertile ground for a more thoughtful examination of the specific stories that carried growing numbers of American readers through Reconstruction.

In the light of such recent challenge and diversity, it is time to reconsider Daniel Aaron's *The Unwritten War: American Writers and the Civil War* (1973), which seeks the "real" war outside the polite circles that women were said to prefer. Once again, the focus is on men of established literary standing like Hawthorne and Melville, James and Howells, Cable and Faulkner, with allowances made for less luminous writers like De Forest, Bierce, Tourgee, and the Southern enthusiasts. Acknowledging that such writers were engaged with war issues at

least in passing, Aaron nonetheless regrets that no "epic" emerged from
their efforts and identifies their reluctance to consider racial tensions
as the most significant cause. His further claim that blacks remained
"docile children" or "putative racists" in wartime accounts is well supported in the familiar works he enlists, but the pages of contemporary
magazines tell a fiercer story that no critic thus far has brought to light.

Establishing the territory that commercial culture staked out is,
therefore, my first task. Equally important in the study of magazine fare
is the corollary emphasis on shorter narratives. Generally speaking, literary critics have also ignored popular stories in favor of Civil War
novels, as Robert A. Lively does in *Fiction Fights the Civil War* (1957)
with results worth testing. An analysis of more than five hundred novels
about the sectional conflict, Lively's book investigates the historical
understanding such narratives have fostered among millions of American readers. He concludes that the striking images of novelists reveal
more of historical truth than a dispassionate treatment of data alone; he
also maintains that these Civil War novels spawn American traditions
in a way that few scholars have recognized, even though Lively himself
ignores the immediate tensions channeled through the Reconstruction
press. At his shrewdest, Lively proves the merits of a comprehensive
canvass and a willingness to consider how popular memory is shaped,
useful lessons for literary scholars who need to look beyond celebrated
writers and into the shorter magazine fiction that Lively's work does
not incorporate.

Ernest E. Leisy has broadened the context of Civil War narratives in
The American Historical Novel (1950), where he progresses from white
migration westward to the Civil War and Reconstruction before considering postwar expansion. In Leisy's view, historical fiction invigorates
the historical record through its attention to peculiar detail and human
relationships, a technique conducive to the "realism" that finally replaced "conventional romance" after the Civil War. Leisy's scope is
so wide, however, that his coverage is hasty: he slights the fiction that
appeared during and just after the Civil War to dwell upon fratricidal
themes, though these were not widely invoked until well after 1876. In
addition, he only considers novels, largely by way of plot summaries

and spotty aesthetic judgments. The same brief treatment characterizes Albert J. Menendez's more recent *Civil War Novels: An Annotated Bibliography* (1986), which notes the factual bent of novels immediately following the war but only undertakes a cursory guide to the novels themselves.

Like Fiedler and Cullen, William R. Taylor has expanded his field of study to include more of the literature that Americans actually bought in *Cavalier and Yankee: The Old South and American National Character* (1961), which concentrates on whose needs were satisfied in the 1820s, 1830s, and 1840s. Drawing largely on the work of popular writers like James Fenimore Cooper and John Pendleton Kennedy, William Gilmore Simms and Sarah Josepha Hale, he traces the emergence of the plantation myth and the fundamental conflict between Southern and Northern cultures, a strategy that allows him a firmer grasp of national character and the regional traits that economic differences set more and more at odds. But Taylor's survey leaves off too early, and thus leaves the pattern of Southern "stability and Old World grace" that he sees as part of a larger "Northern introspection" without the further attention it deserves.

That is one reason to appreciate Paul H. Buck's *Road to Reunion, 1865–1900* (1937), a seasoned account based on more than sixteen hundred sources in official documents, newspapers, periodical articles, published books, and pamphlets. Commencing with sectional divisions, Buck follows them through postwar economic and social contacts, a catalog of Northern and Southern literature, the perspective of veterans, and "the Negro problem" to their ultimate political resolution. His emphasis on "divergent nationalisms" north and south of the Mason-Dixon line remains provocative, as does his claim for the "union of sentiment" that sectionalism only temporarily disrupted. But his devotion to late-century harmony and national integration, together with his tepid interest in "wearying" racial complaints, makes his progress suspect and opens this period to renewed examination.

The only study that includes short narratives is Rebecca Washington Smith's *The Civil War and Its Aftermath in American Fiction, 1861–1899* (1937), a limited survey of material from nineteenth-century magazines. Unfortunately, Smith offers little more than an annotated bibliography of "trite tales" and their plots, whose sentimental excesses she regrets. That bias leads her to conclude that the hope for a newly realistic war fiction sponsored by magazine fare never finally emerged, a conclusion that should be challenged. Still, Smith remains one of the few critics to direct attention to short wartime fiction, and the beginning she has made invites a more rigorous grounding in historical crisis and its impact on narrative design.

Ample in their number and enviable in their wide distribution, Civil War stories in the contemporary press actually offer little to support these miscalculations and even less to bolster the critical habit of examining individual careers. Charting narrative redundancies and revelations, I have arrived instead at a more expansive view of cultural dynamics than a respect for authorial purpose alone would have encouraged. Rather than Emerson's window or Hawthorne's manse, competitive industry strikes me as the key model for understanding cultural work as less individually inspired than collaboratively produced. Helping to dismantle the assumption that the gifted few create paradigms for the docile many to consume by way of cultural diet, popular narratives emerge as the consequence of joint production dictated by the magazine trade and thus as the site of converging interests, the field on which writers, editors, and readers dickered. At best theirs was a mutual activity bound by conventions, but it was an activity that bred resistances to which popular narratives also give play. In these negotiations brought on by the magazine trade, writers can generally be seen as the most venturesome, editors as the most normative, and readers as the most traditional in their perceived expectations.[1]

Gaining ground on writers as the definitive agents in a model of cultural production are magazines themselves, particularly when they are cast as editorial institutions rather than authorial outlets. During the early days of the literary press, in fact, home office control was firm and magazine circulation was scarcely a direct conduit to the public. While Hawthorne might testify in *The Scarlet Letter* to the magic of moonlight and the imagination in spiritualizing the familiar, contemporary magazine editors routinely undertook to familiarize the spiritual for their readers; the Church brothers at the *Galaxy*, for example, insisted that Rebecca Harding Davis cut large sections from *Waiting for the Verdict* when it was serialized in 1867, just as Henry Mills Alden edited out large chunks of Hardy's *Jude the Obscure* some years later on behalf of the family circles to which *Harper's Monthly* was sent. Although some writers like Thoreau and Higginson resisted such high-handedness with their work, others acknowledged an editor's skill at anticipating the magazine's readership and thereby safeguarding circulation, a pressing concern in the volatile periodical marketplace.

Significantly, readers also made demands and occasionally exercised their muscle to an editor's dismay: Harriet Beecher Stowe's "The True Story of Lady Byron's Life" so scandalized readers of the *Atlantic Monthly*, for instance, that the magazine's circulation dropped by fifteen thousand after Stowe's revelations of incest and insanity appeared in September 1869. Readers of the *Overland Monthly* also made Bret Harte's "Plain Language from Truthful James" (familiarly known as "The Heathen Chinee") what biographer Richard O'Connor calls "the most quoted and recited verse of post–Civil War years" when it came out in 1870, in spite of Harte's hasty preparation, his public opposition to harassment of the Chinese, and his usually savvy judgment as creator of the magazine. All the more reason for deliberate mid-century editors to regulate their copy, trespassing with impunity on the creative license that has more recently belonged to writers protected by copyright.

In addition to foregrounding the collaborative process by which both popular texts and national memory have been engendered, my attention to nineteenth-century commercial culture underlines the role of popular narratives at a time of civil crisis: to experiment with provisional resolutions for the political drama under way. In that respect, I have found that Civil War stories were less reflective of the immediate past than constitutive of the immediate future, what Michael Schudson has called "a performance in society's subjunctive mood." Articulating the "Negro question," the prostrate status of the South, or the political rights of ex-slaves as dramatic encounters, for example, stories in the *Lakeside Monthly* or the *Southern Magazine* prodded the Union's

potential futures out of its contested pasts by helping to set the stage for
popular debate, a crafty maneuver. For guiding that performance in the
making were generic conventions, which bound writers and readers to
the editorial preference for reducing commercial uncertainty, as Clinton Sanders has pointed out. While magazines cum institutions were
thus most likely to control cultural production, writers were instrumental in plotting the events worth remembering and readers were at
liberty to chart their significance, especially when it was time to resub-
scribe. Under the auspices of production conventions, then, popular
narratives helped to codify the events of significant social drama for a
growing audience and thereby oriented the normative national culture
that was taking shape. Particularly as the claims of settlers to the con-
tinent grew, the magazine industry in the nineteenth century was sin-
gularly positioned to articulate how the Civil War would be recollected
and national citizenship would thereafter be defined.[2]

The cultural territory that individual magazines staked out varied,
naturally, and for that reason I have taken into account their declared
intentions, as well as other factors that contributed to the context in
which stories were read: circulation, political tack, and willingness to
cover the Civil War. Mindful, too, of both regional claims and economic
pressures, I have founded this project in reading the past upon a survey
of the following magazines: the *Atlantic Monthly* and the *Continental
Monthly* in Boston; *Harper's Monthly* and *Harper's Weekly*, *Putnam's*,
n.s., and the *Galaxy* in New York; *Godey's Lady's Book* and *Lippincott's*
in Philadelphia; the *Southern Literary Messenger* and the *Southern
Illustrated News* in Richmond; the *Southern Monthly* in Memphis, the
Land We Love in Charlotte, and the *Southern Magazine* in Baltimore;
the *Overland Monthly* in San Francisco, the *Lakeside Monthly* in Chicago, and Frederick Douglass's *New National Era* in Washington, D.C.
As literary journals, these magazines aimed broadly at white middle-
class values and tastes, with the exception of *Godey's* in its more narrow
focus on women and the *New National Era* in its appeal to "the colored
people." Mainstream though they were, most did not survive both the
Civil War and the postbellum era. Some failed during the war years
(the *Continental Monthly*, the *Southern Literary Messenger*, the *South-*

ern Illustrated News, and the *Southern Monthly*), some were founded thereafter (the *Galaxy* and *Lippincott's*), while some were born and died between the war and the American Centennial (*Putnam's*, n.s., the *Land We Love*, the *Southern Magazine*, the *Lakeside Monthly*, the *Overland Monthly*, and the *New National Era*). Only the powerful *Atlantic Monthly*, *Harper's Monthly*, *Harper's Weekly*, and *Godey's Lady's Book* published continuously from 1861 to 1876, as well as before and after that period.

Absent from this canvass are cheaper working-class sources, which I set aside because archives were distant and microfilm copies were expensive. Fortunately, the domestic rhetoric that was early on a hallmark of mainstream literary miscellanies was not limited to comfortable firesides in its appeal, although the rhetoric of home and family served to shore up bourgeois authority. Even before the war, as David Paul Nord has demonstrated in his study of the *New-York Magazine* and its eighteenth-century subscription lists, male readers of a "middle-class" literary journal included sea captains and bakers, shopkeepers and cabinet makers, while female readers spanned an even broader economic spectrum. For them as for other readers both more and less well-to-do, the institution of the family had come by midcentury to exemplify fireside values even after the corporate family, as Mary Ryan has shown, fell apart for want of unimproved land to farm. Surviving that breakdown, what Ryan has called the "privatized home" emerged in Victorian America to shelter the industrious paterfamilias, the selfless mother, and the tractable children who would appear in subsequent popular narratives about as often as family households of any class appeared on magazine subscription rolls.[3]

That the servants of such households might have preferred the more affordable New York *Ledger* to *Harper's Monthly* does not seem to have mattered a great deal in the stories that were subsequently told of the war: Sylvanus Cobb, Jr., and Amy Randolph supplied much the same captains and nurses, amputees and steadfast romances to clerks and cooks that *Harper's Monthly* supplied at somewhat greater length to its readers. To be sure, there was more evidence of sharply pressed seamstresses and of captains aboard whalers in two-dollar magazines than the Harpers were likely to recognize, but girls could still weary of sable stoles and twelve o'clock suppers without costing the *Ledger* much of its phenomenal circulation (four hundred thousand in 1860) or tilting protagonists and their likely fates to iconoclastic angles that would challenge the norms set by more august magazines.

Cheaper periodicals also confirmed the tendency of middle-class communications channels to radiate from the Northeast and, increasingly, from New York. As waterways were extended through canal projects and railroad lines opened in the first half of the nineteenth century, preeminence in the production of culture went to those cities and those publishers that could control the routes of distribution and thus enlist the consumers who would in turn boost the power and drawing appeal of magazines. By the eve of the Civil War, a handful of Northern publications could already claim a national audience, *Harper's Monthly* and *Godey's Lady's Book* among them. But as nationalizing agents, even they were a curious mixture of the local and the cosmopolitan or of the urban local cum cosmopolitan, to paraphrase James Carey. The resulting ascendancy of Boston, New York, Philadelphia, and even Richmond in defining a national profile was therefore undeniable, as a closer look at market dynamics reveals. Yet the control that such publishing centers assumed was never monolithic, for urban rivalries grew as did the checks to their farflung dominance from the smaller but persistent journals that also found markets during and after the war.[4]

PROMINENT IN COLONIAL affairs from the moment John Winthrop stepped off the *Arbella* in 1630, Boston actually entered the nineteenth century as a publishing center hampered by its virtues. A literate resident public, competition from numerous small-town presses nearby, and the want of a significant inland river contrived to keep the city more parochial than mid-Atlantic publishing hubs. As a result, accomplished writers in Cambridge and Concord profited mainly from the retail trade that made them renowned on the Charles but less popular elsewhere; Emerson, for example, never learned the good sense of sizable wholesale discounts that would have extended his reputation to Cincinnati and beyond. But the advent of railroad lines in the 1830s and 1840s enabled the publishing house of Ticknor & Fields to market New England talent more widely, just when the founding of William Lloyd Garrison's *Liberator* in 1831 forced educated Bostonians to begin looking beyond Beacon Hill and Harvard Yard. Receptive to Republican politics, which Massachusetts Senator Charles Sumner helped to launch in the 1850s, Boston's intellectuals joined the enthusiastic crowds that sent the first black regiment to South Carolina in 1863, where even elitist Boston journals like the *Atlantic Monthly* and the *Continental Monthly* were familiar enough to be reviled.[5]

From its inception, the *Atlantic Monthly* (1857–present) was Olympian, for in mid-nineteenth-century America there was no question that the literary gods resided in Boston. Edited until 1861 by James Russell Lowell, the journal boasted of contributions from Emerson, Hawthorne, Bancroft, Thoreau, Higginson, Whittier, and Holmes, the man who gave the magazine its name. Such writers quickly made the *Atlantic* the premier forum for American literature in the country, and they were paid at the handsome rate of six dollars a page, sometimes as much as ten dollars; Lowell himself received an unprecedented twenty-five hundred dollars a year for the shrewdness of his editorial eye and the intelligence of his taste, which rarely extended far from Boston. Throughout the 1850s and 1860s, the magazine remained superbly provincial: about two-thirds of its writers were from New England, even after publisher James T. Fields replaced Lowell in 1861. Though circulation climbed to thirty thousand by 1860 and to fifty thousand by 1870, many of the readers who welcomed the magazine's commitment to "Freedom, National Progress, and Honor" also lived in the New England states.[6]

They did not generally live in the South, where the *Atlantic* was attacked from its first issue. The *Southern Literary Messenger* declared in 1857 that the new journal's purpose was "to wage war upon Southern society," and so it was. Initially guided by Lowell's abolitionism and his founding aim to create "the new literary and anti-slavery magazine," the *Atlantic Monthly* in its first decade published Julia Ward Howe's "Battle-Hymn of the Republic," Edward L. Pierce's comments on the freedmen at Port Royal, Ralph Waldo Emerson's reflections on the Emancipation Proclamation, and Senator Charles Sumner's essay on the country's domestic relations. Some thirty-five Civil War stories also appeared before Federal troops retired from the South in 1876, and they too explored race relations where less exacting literary journals did not. When William Dean Howells assumed the editor's post in 1871, he capitalized on the *Atlantic*'s longtime Republican zeal by adding a column on politics and publishing essays on nationalism, free trade, John Brown, and currency reform. At the same time, however, he began at last to entertain contributions from the South and West; after 1874, writers like George Cary Eggleston and Mark Twain were likely to speak for regions that previously the *Atlantic* had preferred only to visit. The magazine continued to join literary and political ends as the Centennial approached, but attention to commerce and the railroads struck a more conciliatory note than the sectional assaults of 1861. Backed by Brahmins from the outset, the *Atlantic Monthly* gradually came to enjoy the wider popularity that Republican politics also courted after 1870, by which time improved channels of communication had increased Boston's share in cultural traffic.

Less openhanded because shorter lived was the *Continental Monthly* (1862–64), which was established upon the double principle of Union and Emancipation. Founded by James Roberts Gilmore and edited first by Charles Godfrey Leland, both committed Republicans, the wartime journal outstripped even the *Atlantic Monthly* in its suspicion of the South and its support for Lincoln once emancipation was proclaimed. Leland challenged the "Bobadil bluster" of Southern newspapers and the "old serpent of treason and disunion" hissing even in Copperhead New York; in his hands, the *Continental Monthly* responded with essays like Congressman George C. Boutwell's "Our Danger and Its Cause," Horace Greeley's "Southern Hate of the North," F. D. Stanton's "The Freed Men of the South," and Robert J. Walker's "Flag of Our Union." Appealing mainly to well-placed Republicans, the magazine upheld a triumphant nation, brave and democratic, in which the war's dangers and duties were fully compensated by an abject South.[7]

Unfortunately, such a message was not widely enough approved, especially as the war pushed up publishing costs. Leland was appar-

ently never paid for his services; in 1863, Gilmore sold a half-interest
in the magazine to former Senator Walker, whose sister then took over
the editor's desk. Under Mrs. Martha Elizabeth Duncan Walker Cook,
the journal's political invective diminished somewhat; where Leland
had written essays on the Knights of the Golden Circle and what to do
with the "darkies," Mrs. Cook instead contributed poems like "Autumn
Leaves" or "Clouds," occasional tales, and translations of Polish drama.
Otherwise the magazine showed a preference for damaged romances
and battlefield stories from the front, publishing twelve Civil War narratives before it failed just shy of the war's conclusion and Boston's
greater leverage in postwar cultural affairs.

Immediately to the south, the powerful literary journals of New York
were less sectarian and politically orthodox than their Boston rivals, in
large measure because the city was energetically committed to trade.
The completion of the Erie Canal in 1825 guaranteed that New York
could deliver goods west of the Hudson and into the Ohio Valley where
Boston publishers had no foothold and even the closer Philadelphia
houses had to hurry to compete. By 1840, New York was the leading
port in the country with a host of water and rail channels into the interior, already and forever what James Carey has termed "the center of
American communication." But the channels that brought more New
York periodicals to Cincinnati and Louisville ran two ways; as William
Charvat has observed, New York's success in tapping interior markets
made the city's journals more beholden to the readers they enlisted and
more receptive to diverging cultural tastes. Less insulated than their
Boston rivals, magazines like *Harper's Monthly* and *Weekly*, *Putnam's*,
and the *Galaxy* were more broadly pitched, both socially and politically, just as the growing metropolis was increasingly defined by rapid
jumps in population and steadfast attention to commercial interests.
In early 1861, when war threatened, Mayor Fernando Wood suggested
that New York declare itself a free city, open for trade with both the
North and the South. Wood's proposal failed to persuade the city's residents, who met in April for a mass demonstration in Union Square
and who favored Democratic Governor Seymour's modest Unionism
throughout the war. But Wood's devotion to commerce sent him to

Congress for the better part of the period during and after the war, while Republican spokesman and *New York Times* founder Henry J. Raymond served only for the brief stretch between 1865 and 1867 when Wood was out of office. In such a political climate, popular magazines promoted their own editorial agendas with a marked respect for the distant readers that Boston publishers often failed to reach.[8]

No literary journal was more attuned to widespread antebellum preferences than *Harper's New Monthly Magazine* (1850–present). Undertaken to promote the business of Harper & Bros., the journal routinely pirated material from British magazines, just as the publishing house had for decades made British literature its stock-in-trade. Such international eclecticism coupled with a deliberate disregard for sectional debates made the magazine popular south of the Potomac and west of the Mississippi; by the eve of the Civil War, circulation had climbed to a remarkable two hundred thousand, a figure that dropped sharply only when Southern mails were interrupted by the military blockade and Northern readers began to look elsewhere for war news. Promising instead "to combine entertainment with instruction," *Harper's Monthly* published wartime essays like J. Ross Browne's "A Tour Through Arizona," John S. C. Abbott's "Military Hospitals at Fortress Monroe," J. R. Gillmore's "The Poor Whites of the South," and B. J. Lossing's "Privateering in the War of 1812" without registering a clash between the Democratic principles of the Harpers and the Republican convictions of editors like George William Curtis, who filled the prestigious "Easy Chair" from 1853 until well beyond the Centennial celebrations.[9]

The challenge to the magazine's overt nonpartisanship instead came surreptitiously, in the short American stories that were successfully competing with British serial fiction by the time the war began. Altogether, *Harper's Monthly* published some sixty Civil War narratives before 1877 by writers like Nora Perry, Elizabeth Stuart Phelps, John W. De Forest, and Constance Fenimore Woolson. At first their narratives were generically straightforward, usually simple romances in small Northern towns. But from the later years of the war until the later years of the war decade, the magazine's stories were increasingly complicated: thematically by death and dislocation in the South, topically by Northern disturbances like the draft riots, and formally by the sudden freedom of hitherto "silent" slaves. Events of the war thus dislodged narrative conventions and unsettled the seeming ease of the magazine's political neutrality. Though no legislative agenda coalesced and few Southern writers were welcomed to the magazine's pages until the 1880s and 1890s, the short Civil War fiction in *Harper's Monthly* served for a time to mark the shifting currents in mainstream periodical fare and the altered channels into which popular fiction would finally settle.

More politically opinionated and much less narratively complex was *Harper's Weekly* (1857–1916), founded to take up the divisive issues that the more literary *Monthly* avoided. Inspired by the *Illustrated London News* and *Frank Leslie's Illustrated Newspaper*, this second Harper venture aimed to be a "family newspaper" that would capitalize on the wood engravings that had made the *Monthly* a success. Energetically overseen by Fletcher Harper until his retirement in 1875, *Harper's Weekly* reflected his commitment to the Union and thus preferred a conservative disdain for abolitionists and slavery apologists alike, until the fall of Fort Sumter ended all hopes for national compromise. After 1861, Fletcher Harper's support for the Union was buttressed by Curtis's Republican fervor as political editor, Thomas Nast's graphic admiration for Lincoln and Grant, and the magazine's special artists on the Federal lines throughout the war. Their concerted effort produced the most impressive war coverage readers had ever known, a feat which sent weekly circulation past the hundred-thousand mark pretty much for the duration.[10]

Although *Harper's Weekly* emphasized news rather than literature, it was also designed to incorporate the extra available fiction that the *Monthly*'s popularity brought in. Most of these stories were shorter than was customary in the *Monthly* and they were generally published anonymously, as were almost all other items in the magazine. The stories were no less numerous as a result: in all, *Harper's Weekly* published about 115 Civil War narratives, more than one-third of the total number appearing in sixteen magazines. All but 4 of these stories came out before the end of 1866; thereafter, Civil War coverage in the newsmagazine virtually disappeared. While the appetite for war news remained intense, *Harper's Weekly* circulated as many as 5 stories a month, more often unalloyed romances than any other genre and most concentrated in the grueling middle years of the war.

When the troops came home, the magazine trade picked up noticeably in New York, where many new journals were founded and some older publications were revitalized. One journal that returned for a second chance was *Putnam's* (1868–70), which had originally folded during the panic of 1857 after five years of providing some of the freshest and most vigorous American literature that the antebellum press could claim. The new series promised a similarly "broad, generous nationality" under the renewed editorship of C. F. Briggs, who would again publish "original papers on Literature, Science, Art, and National Interests." For these, *Putnam's* was prepared to pay royally, from ten to twenty dollars and more a page, one reason why the magazine received over three thousand manuscripts during its three-year run in the 1860s. Although the new series never attained the sparkle of George Putnam's original venture and circulation never topped fifteen hundred, the magazine's early candor in discussing Republican politics was undiminished and remained healthy until *Putnam's* withdrew in 1870, as part of the move to found *Scribner's Magazine*.[11]

During its brief second tenure, *Putnam's* again bolstered native output by accepting only American stories. Of the shorter fiction that came from writers like Jane G. Austin, W. C. Elam, and Rebecca Harding Davis, only two stories invoked the Civil War, though differently enough to render the opposite extremes of what was likely to characterize popular recollections of the war. William Douglas O'Connor's "The Carpenter" (January 1868) traces the political tensions that divide a border family near Washington, until the lost Southern brother returns on Christmas Eve; under the kindly eye of a stranger who closely resembles Walt Whitman, the virtue of Christian forgiveness and the integrity of the home are promoted to support national recovery. By contrast, Ross Guffin's "A Night on the Mississippi" (April 1870) describes the fate of a Federal detail that leaves Tennessee's Fort Pillow to pursue smugglers, only to freeze to death on a river island in the snow. Instead of celebrating a national family now reunited on New Year's Eve, Guffin's story bears witness to dead Northern boys and the uncertainty of a national future a full year after the slaves were emancipated. The scope of these two stories demonstrates the variety which had long been *Putnam's* hallmark, as well as the Union sentiment that likewise informed the magazine's sketches of Lincoln and Greeley, Parke Godwin's essays on political degeneracy, and H. M. Alden's talk with incoming President Grant. Though not as intent as Republican magazines in Boston, the revived *Putnam's* continued to lobby for extending America's civil rights to women in the years following the war, as the magazine had earlier argued on behalf of the slaves.

More consistently literary if less politically outspoken was the *Galaxy* (1866–78), which was established in New York to rival the preeminence of the *Atlantic*. Founded and edited by the Church brothers, William Conant and Francis Pharcellus, the new magazine strove to be innovative where *Harper's Monthly* was prosaic, and receptive to regional writers where the *Atlantic* still favored New England talent. Only about a third of its contributions came from New England, many solicited from the Atlantic's roster; another third came from New York, and the remainder from both familiar and unknown writers across the country. Disdaining party politics, the *Galaxy* was still a magazine of opinion: Mark Twain railed against the treatment of the Chinese in his column "Memoranda," Eugene Benson championed French manners against Puritan morals, Richard Grant White provoked linguistic controversy with his series "Words and Their Uses," and General George Custer serialized *My Life on the Plains* as well as "War Memoirs," until the second series was cut short by his death on the Little Big Horn. Circulation peaked at more than twenty-three thousand in 1871 while Twain was writing his short-lived column; after that, readership dwindled year by year to about seven thousand in 1878, when the magazine sold its subscription list to the *Atlantic*.[12]

By that time the *Galaxy* had published roughly 270 short American stories, of which some 21 dealt with the Civil War. About half of these were straightforward adventures, several written by men like James Franklin Fitts and John W. De Forest who had served in battle and continued to watch events unfold in the South. On the whole, their stories were less complex than crisp and wide-ranging, a fair gauge of the magazine's general tenor and its undeniable boost to the growth of indigenous American fiction. Vigorous in its diversity and willing to pay at least a modest sum to writers without previous reputation, the *Galaxy* was an able literary magazine that for twelve stellar years failed to make a profit. In New York, as elsewhere in the postwar market, only the distributive resources and financial clout of a publishing firm like Harper's could absorb such reverses and survive.

The most serious challenge to New York's market dominance came from Philadelphia, America's foremost publishing center in the eighteenth century. Two factors assured the rival city's early ascendancy: its strategic position near the South as well as the wagon road over the mountains to the Ohio River, and the arrival of the young Irish bookseller Mathew Carey in 1784. Nobody surpassed Carey in working delivery schedules and freight costs to advantage; by 1790, he had extended his territory well beyond Philadelphia through a network of agents who sold his books wholesale throughout the South and West. Since Carey was thereby able to command markets for large printings, he could offer higher royalties to authors like James Fenimore Cooper, John Pendleton Kennedy, and, most conspicuously, Sir Walter Scott. Only after his death in 1832 did New York surpass Philadelphia in regional control, as Carey's firm lost business to the Harpers. By then, the Quaker city was well established in engraving and thus the trade in gift books, miscellanies, and magazines like *Godey's*; the early Sunday School movement provided further publishing opportunities in the 1820s and 1830s, especially the demand for Bibles and prayer books that J. B. Lippincott would meet before inaugurating his magazine in 1868. But the city's tradition of tolerance was undermined years before the war as more and more slaves escaped into Pennsylvania from the Upper South, while business and social connections still tied Philadelphia's moneyed families to the Southern interests that men like Carey had fostered. For two decades before Philadelphia sent favorite son James Buchanan to the White House in 1856, racial violence polarized local factions and kept Democrats, Whigs, and Know-Nothings in competition. Only after Lee retreated from Gettysburg did Republican candidates make headway in a city that almost straddled the Mason-Dixon line.[13]

Although civil order was thus as scarce in antebellum Philadelphia as brotherly love, *Godey's Lady's Book* (1830–98) reigned serene and made money from one end of the century to the other. Throughout the Civil War and Reconstruction era, the magazine was edited by Sarah Josepha Hale, who urged President Lincoln to commemorate Thanksgiving Day, rescued Mount Vernon for the nation in the 1850s, and wrote one of the first anti-slavery novels before moving to Philadelphia and *Godey's* in 1837. For forty years, she oversaw the magazine's literary department and published writers like Lydia H. Sigourney, William Gilmore Simms, Harriet Beecher Stowe, Caroline Kirkland, Metta Victoria Fuller, and Edgar Allan Poe, among many others who helped make the *Lady's Book* a literary force before competition arose in the 1850s. Short on politics (Louis Godey declared: "I allow no man's religion to be attacked or sneered at, or the subject of politics to be mentioned in my magazine") but profligate in the recipes, embroidery patterns, and hand-colored fashion plates that attracted female readers, *Godey's* sold approximately 150,000 copies a month in 1860 and claimed a readership close to a million, before nearly a third of its subscribers were forfeited in the South. Nevertheless, it remained indisputably the most successful magazine for women ever published and one of the biggest American magazines during the years of the Civil War.[14]

About the events that shook the country, however, *Godey's* was mute, one reason why its popularity began to wane. A single story concerning the Civil War and giving thanks appeared in 1863, the year in which Hale's long-term campaign for a national holiday succeeded. Otherwise, there were no essays on emancipation, no poems about the flag, no columns on current developments as in other magazines. When Hale entered the public forum during these years, it was most often on behalf of women's education, for which she was an ardent and early advocate. She and her magazine were stalwart in promoting Vassar College and the Centennial Fair in the 1870s; but about the slaves for whom Hale had spoken in *Northwood* (1827) and again in *Liberia* (1853), neither *Godey's* nor its fair and vocal readers said a word.

More forthcoming was *Lippincott's* (1868–1916), which aimed for "common ground" with Southerners as national reunification got under way. Edited by John Foster Kirk with a conservative eye toward Reconstruction policies, *Lippincott's* owed its relatively long life to the support of a major publishing house, the high quality of its print, the breadth of its contributors' roster, and the early success achieved in representing the South. In its pages before 1870 were Paul Hamilton Hayne, William Gilmore Simms, Bayard Taylor, and George Fitzhugh, as well as writers from Philadelphia, New England, New York, and the West. The Centennial festivities received ample coverage; later, the magazine would publish the work of Paul Laurence Dunbar, Grace King, and Lafcadio Hearn, serialize Mary Roberts Rinehart's first novel, and introduce American readers to Sherlock Holmes. Though never challenging the popularity of giants like *Harper's Monthly*, *Lippincott's* vied amiably with the *Galaxy* and even the *Atlantic Monthly*, remained a steady success for decades, and made Philadelphia once again competitive with Boston and New York on the literary scene.[15]

The key to its aplomb lay in its cordiality, encouraged by the early networks that J. B. Lippincott had developed in the South. Every month, editor Kirk provided a rambling "chat" with "fellow-citizens of the republic of letters" in a column that shied away from sectarian issues; elsewhere, the magazine considered the songs of the slaves, manifest destiny, the future of the freedmen, the coming woman, the echoes of Appomattox abroad, and the fate of the republic. In the years before Reconstruction ended, thirteen Civil War narratives appeared as well, many of them eccentric in their development and almost all of them set in the South. Taken together, the stories in *Lippincott's* were unsettling, as was much else in a magazine that was more alert than *Godey's*, more Southern than its competition in Boston and New York, more judicious than the periodicals in rebel strongholds, and thus more representative of the uneasy political compromises that Philadelphia had sponsored in the years following the Revolution.

The success of Philadelphia and later New York in supplying Southern markets suggests one reason why local publishing ventures were more fitful in Southern states and less likely to find regional support. Readers were also comparatively less well informed than in New York or Boston, and those who were educated tended to prefer the ancient classics. With little concentrated demand for recent literature, there was little regional call for the apparatus upon which publishers relied: the 1860 census reported 555 paper factories in the United States, for example, of which only twenty-four were in the South. But nine of these were in Virginia, which could also claim at least one typefoundry by the end of the war. As the state's capital and long its best deep-water port, Richmond attracted planters to the tobacco market, merchants to the milling industry, and professional men in law, medicine, and theology to the traffic in politics, education, and publishing that made the *Southern Literary Messenger* the premier journal of the antebellum South, especially via the system of canals that served Richmond by 1854. In a city that remained Whiggish by inclination, the magazine resisted the growing Democratic rancor of the state at large; but as abolitionist charges multiplied and sectionalism grew, the *Southern Literary Messenger* joined with newer journals like the *Southern Illustrated News* in approving the policies of Jefferson Davis and challenging the cultural hegemony of the North.[16]

Dextrous at surviving shallow pockets and regional malaise, the *Southern Literary Messenger* (1834–64) was an early champion of American letters throughout the republic: Simms and Griswold, Jefferson and Longfellow, Francis Scott Key and Nathaniel Parker Willis all appeared in its pages. Begun by printer Thomas Willis White, the journal was edited by Poe for a short period in the 1830s and by John R. Thompson in the 1840s and 1850s; in 1860, George W. Bagby, a Virginia physician and writer, took over and served until just before the printers were enlisted to defend the Southern capital and the magazine collapsed in mid-1864. By then the subscription rate had jumped from five dollars a year to eight dollars, ten dollars, and finally fifteen dollars, as wartime shortages and inflation pushed up publishing costs. With a peak circulation of fifty-five hundred, the magazine at its most expensive paid many contributors nothing and most of its staff little more; but it managed for decades to augment the Northern and British periodicals that sold well in the South and thus to promote Southern culture well before its rivals diversified their fare.[17]

Gentlemanly in its politics as well as in its prose and poetry, the *Southern Literary Messenger* began to defend slavery only after the abolitionist campaign accelerated, the new *Atlantic Monthly* opened fire on the South, and the magazine itself changed hands in the 1850s. From the beginning of the war, editorial policy was committed to secession, but with less fire in the belly than journals published farther south. The magazine's Civil War stories, five of them, were by turns lighthearted, meditative, and wistful rather than grim or violent, a measure of the greater erudition of its contributors and the extraordinary longevity of its prewar success. In its last months, after even Bagby had departed, the *Southern Literary Messenger* was publishing essays on Chaucer and Horace, the Italian novel, and Renan's *Life of Jesus*, in addition to the portraits of generals and the poetry of uplift ("Southrons, Yield Not to Despair") that had become a staple in the Confederacy. Poised even in its demise, the magazine simply vanished after June 1864, without fanfare or relocation but with a publishing history that few periodicals North or South could match.

Setting a less stately pace during the Civil War was the *Southern Illustrated News* (1862–65), which was determined to replace malignant Yankee fare with "Literary Novelties, Historical Legends, Biographical Sketches, the Latest Current News, and, indeed, every subject within range of polite literature." In the absence of periodicals from England and the North after the mails were suspended, publishers Ayres and Wade proposed a family newspaper that would enlist women as well as men in "the cause of our country in this trying hour when she is engaged in a terrible, but resolute and hopeful struggle for her liberty and independence." To news, literature, and reports from Confederate soldiers were added wood engravings, generally portraits of rough quality since fine engravers were never plentiful in the South. Still, public response was encouraging: within six months the journal was self-supporting, demand was up, and contributors like John Esten Cooke, Henry Timrod, Susan Archer Talley, and Paul Hamilton

Hayne were submitting their work. Their energy and the ambitions of Ayres and Wade in expanding their publishing house persisted through the tightening of the Northern blockade, the escalation of printing costs, and the infringements of military service on literary production, until the journal succumbed just before Richmond fell to Grant in April 1865.[18]

By that time, the *Southern Illustrated News* had published four war narratives, including one clipped from *Harper's Weekly* and revised. In tone these stories were more effervescent than the personal reflections in the *Southern Literary Messenger*, probably because the journal appeared in 1862 and 1863 after Richmond had rebuffed McClellan's peninsular assault. Their message nonetheless served a national cause, what Louise Mannheim in "The First Campaign of a Fat Volunteer" (17 January 1863) called "the disenthralment of their beloved South from the tyrant's grasp." Only "The Chaplain's Story" (11 October 1862) acknowledged the death toll after the battle of Seven Pines and weighed Southern independence against the cemetery, as would the journal itself in the final days of the war.

Contemporary journals across the South, together with postwar upstarts across the nation, could not claim the stature of the *Southern Literary Messenger* or the Richmond contributors that helped the *Southern Illustrated News* to flourish. But the appearance of literary magazines in the South and West after 1860 does signal the continuing vitality of regional publishing and the maturing networks that allowed local magazines to reach a wider audience, as well as the intricacy with which commercial interests, publishing enterprises, and political agendas were bound together when the magazine trade accelerated. Some Southern periodicals surfaced in commercial centers like Memphis and Charlotte, which the war and Federal troops hit hard; others arose in cities like Baltimore that had once contended for regional supremacy and lost. Late arrivals signaled newer markets in San Francisco and Chicago, towns that were still awaiting the railroad in the 1830s when *Godey's* and the *Southern Literary Messenger* put out their first issues. Even in older cities like the nation's capital, laid out before the turn of the century, the upheaval of the war severed commercial ties and transformed cultural life, most noticeably in opening the District to thousands of free blacks and newly emancipated slaves. For them as for those who defended the Confederacy or moved west, popular magazines provided an unusual forum for making historical crisis make sense, often in ways that publishing centers like Richmond and Philadelphia, New York and Boston, rarely foresaw.

Of those Southern journals that carried war narratives, probably the most vitriolic was the *Southern Monthly* (1861–62), founded and published in Memphis until the fall of Fort Donelson prompted a short-lived move to Grenada, Mississippi. During those early months of the war, Memphis operated as a Confederate center for trade in cotton and slaves and as the terminus of the only East-West route from Richmond to the Mississippi, before the port fell to Federal gunboats in June 1862. In the initial euphoria of secession, the *Southern Monthly* pledged to replace *Harper's Monthly* in the South and called for a faithfully Southern literature to counter the infection of "federalism, materialism, and abolitionism" spread by Northern magazines. In their opening note, publishers Hutton and Freligh invited articles on a variety of subjects, among them science, biographies, tales, and politics ("in an enlarged sense—not mere partisanship"), and encouraged readers to underwrite a self-consciously national literature. For nine months the magazine ran presses on Southern cotton seed oil and printed contributions on paper from Georgia with ink from New Orleans. "Handsomely got up" the *Picayune* called it, and the *Chattanooga Gazette and Advertiser* declared that "Southern literature is in the ascendant"; but the journal struggled with difficulties in securing paper and engravers for some months before Grant threatened Memphis and the publishers decamped.[19]

During its brief existence, the *Southern Monthly* did publish two stories that touched on the Civil War, one by "Izilda" and the other by "Montesano." Both are romances, though their protagonists discover less happiness in love than satisfaction in service to their country. Defaulting on the genre's promised joy, both stories call upon honor, memory, and retribution in what Montesano describes as "a war of defense." In a similar vein were essays like Judge Swayne's "The Sanctity of Law and the Duty of Obedience," Mary J. S. Upshur's "A Woman's Plea for the New Republic," and the composite "Poesy of the Revolution." Insisting that the Yankees were "too loathesome, too hateful, for us ever, under any circumstances, to be identified with them as one people," the *Southern Monthly* delivered for a short while the literature that could help transform a regional market into an independent nation.

Officially, all hope for the Confederacy had ended when the *Land We Love* (1866–69) was founded in Charlotte, a growing railroad center that escaped Sherman's advance through North Carolina but not the refugees that his march created. War's end for General Daniel Harvey Hill, the magazine's editor and co-publisher, was thus the point at which remembrance and preservation began. Establishing one of the first postwar Southern journals, Hill discarded the classical tradition manifest in the *Messenger* and substituted a broader and more practical program of literature, agriculture, and military history, with special attention to gathering battle accounts from Confederate generals and anecdotes from the rank and file. Aggressively committed to an independent Southern literature, the *Land We Love* backed its patriotism with cash; at a time when money was scarce, the magazine paid every contributor possible, in spite of the delinquency of its own subscribers. For three years, Hill and his business partner James P. Irwin maintained this uneven balance, eventually serving twelve thousand readers in the North as well as the South before merging with the *New Eclectic Magazine* in Baltimore.[20]

As a former soldier, Hill was disposed to reconcile with the military victors in the North, but he could sanction neither Sherman's late offensive ("house-burners, thieves, and marauders") nor the "odeur d'Afrique" in the nation's Capitol. Consequently, the magazine pledged reconciliation while publishing attacks on "Northern Prison Life" and "Demoralized Weeklies" and furthering the separatist cause of the South in verses like "Dixie," "Lines Dedicated to Those Who Have Been Southern Soldiers," and "The Mother, to her Son in the Trenches at Petersburg." Eight Civil War stories were also published, almost entirely sorrowing over homes destroyed and romances turned to grief. A single adventure, E.'s "Hospital Sketches, Number 1" (October 1866), recounts the events in a Richmond hospital ward just after the fighting started; but even set so early in the war, the story concerns a feverish patient, his unexplained vision, and his unavoidable death, and it is told in so few paragraphs that the simple moral is a respect for dying requests. On similar terms, the *Land We Love* likewise distinguished itself by keeping faith with a defeated cause despite the extreme poverty of the postwar South.

When Hill's journal ceased publication in 1869, the immediate beneficiary was the *Southern Magazine* (1868–75), which had come of age through merger, relocation, and shifts in title. The Richmond *Eclectic*, founded in 1866 and edited by Presbyterian ministers, moved to Baltimore in 1868 as the *New Eclectic*, the first incarnation of the magazine, edited by Lawrence Turnbull and Fridge Murdoch until William Hand Browne returned as co-editor in 1869. During the year of the move, the magazine lost five thousand dollars, but it was solvent enough in 1869 to absorb the *Land We Love* and to become the official organ of the Southern Historical Society. Under the ultraconservative Brown until 1873, the journal was rechristened the *Southern Magazine* in 1871, when original contributions from writers like Sidney Lanier, General P. G. T. Beauregard, and George William Bagby began replacing the reprints from abroad. Thereafter, the journal diversified considerably, taking up travel, women's rights, science, education, the character of the Negro, and the state of the South. The scope of the *Southern Magazine* after its move from Richmond bespeaks the perennial resurgence of Baltimore as a commercial center, even after Philadelphia seized control of the Susquehanna River and the book trade with the South. Site of the early riotous attack on Massachusetts troops posted to Washington in 1861 and a later magnet for displaced secessionists after the war, Baltimore maintained lively Confederate sympathies despite Maryland's wartime neutrality and the city's reliance upon water and rail corridors that led north. As a creation of the postwar era, the *Southern Magazine* had more spunk and less deference than the *Southern Literary Messenger*; but it was similarly capable and the most robust of contemporary Southern journals, until contributors found that they could be paid for their work in the North and the magazine folded at the end of 1875.[21]

William Hand Browne was no more reconstructed than General Hill and no less vocal than the incendiary *Southern Monthly*, particularly on the subject of Southern letters. As wartime passions eased, however, and Reconstruction entered a second phase in the 1870s, the tone of Southern response became less strident and the task of invigorating regional production claimed more attention. That shift was especially apparent when the Civil War was remembered in the magazine's seventeen stories. Thirteen of these are adventures, a striking departure from the crumbling homesteads and fractured love affairs of earlier Southern narratives. On the whole, they are stories about the ones who got away, from Northern prisons, Petersburg under siege, Federal troops, or naval engagements on the Atlantic. They are thus stories of a second chance, unexamined for the most part but equally undevastated by invasion, sorrow, or want. Like the magazine itself, these narratives suggest a resilience born from remembering rather than ignoring the past.

At about the same time further west, California was looking instead to the future, not so much from the other side of the tracks as from the other end of the line. In the wake of Fort Sumter's surrender, thousands of families had migrated to escape the fighting, and they discovered in San Francisco that theaters, operas, and newspapers were already thriving. On the edge of the war's orbit, the city was more prosperous than politically doctrinaire; Union feeling generally prevailed after Southern states seceded, although Copperhead sentiment was also open and particularly agitated during Lincoln's re-election campaign. By 1868, commercial interests were foremost when bookseller Anton Roman joined with fellow businessmen to found the *Overland Monthly* (1868–75), edited in its first heady years by Bret Harte. It was Harte who fashioned the magazine's logo by placing the grizzly bear of California astride the railroad tracks that were bringing Americans west, and he who combined Western material and nonregional contributions successfully enough to challenge the *Atlantic Monthly* from the West Coast. Under his supervision, the magazine published only original work by writers like Charles Warren Stoddard and Mark Twain,

Ina D. Coolbrith and Theodore F. Dwight, who were all paid in cash. As the *Overland Monthly* announced on its cover, the magazine was "Devoted to the Development of the Country," which from the outset meant essays on subjects like diamond making, immigration, bohemianism, restaurant life in San Francisco, American education, and railroads. During its early years, the journal made money and quickly rose to a circulation of ten thousand; but ill health forced Roman to sell in 1869, and Bret Harte left for the East in 1871. By 1875, the *Overland Monthly* had temporarily suspended publication.[22]

In its first extraordinary years, the magazine was remarkable for taking risks. When a wary proofreader objected to the swearing and sinning in "The Luck of Roaring Camp," Harte pushed his story through to win instant acclaim. Just as bold were some of the nine Civil War stories, which included women running the blockade, black soldiers standing picket, and Kansas abolitionists defying the mob. In Harte's magazine, where looking ahead was considered an American habit of mind (said Harte: "We make history too rapidly in this country, and are too accustomed to changes to notice details"), it was also possible to look back with an audacity that few contemporary magazines shared. While Reconstruction policy and political malfeasance made little show in the *Overland Monthly*, a more obstreperous Civil War was recalled in scenes that Eastern writers and magazines had failed to portray.

But for a mysterious social gaffe, much the same might have been said of Chicago's *Lakeside Monthly* (1869–74), which Harte was on his way to edit when he left California in 1871. A railroad mecca by the 1860s, Chicago had already supplanted Cincinnati as the most active distribution center for markets from the prairies to the Pacific, while the traffic in grain, lumber, hogs, and books multiplied. Undertaken to promote the "go-aheaditiveness" of midwestern enterprise, the *Lakeside Monthly* offered Harte thirty thousand dollars to join its staff, but failed to invite Mrs. Harte's cousins to a congratulatory dinner and apparently for that reason lost the editor's services for good. Instead, the journal continued to be overseen by co-proprietor Francis Fischer Browne, who decided to encourage literary contributions instead of business biographies and thereby made the magazine less provincial.

To publicize the shift in policy, he changed the journal's title from the drab "Western Monthly" to a suggestion of the beauty of the lake and the fertility of the land that he could see from his office window. Though the contributions he published retained a local flavor, they were also cosmopolitan enough to impress Eastern editors and to open Eastern journals to more regional fare. Doggedly surviving the Chicago fire that destroyed its new office building, the *Lakeside Monthly* boasted a readership of nine thousand in 1871, brought out its celebrated fire issue in January 1872, and achieved self-sufficiency and a peak circulation of fourteen thousand in 1873. Thereafter, the nation's economic panic and Browne's deteriorating health curtailed the journal's prosperity and it declined, failing in 1874 after Browne refused an attractive bid to abandon Chicago for New York.[23]

Where Bret Harte was daring, Browne was discriminating. In his hands, the booster spirit ebbed in the *Lakeside Monthly* to be replaced by essays on the "sable singers," Chinese labor, moving the national capital west, the free library movement, the Indian Territory, the Kaiser's resolve, and Civil Service reform. The twelve Civil War stories that also appeared are oddly ambivalent and quirky, ready with Helen E. Harrington in "The Palmy Days of Slaveholding" (July 1870) to acknowledge both the "patriarchal kindness" of Southern masters and their "tyrannical oppression" in the eyes of the slaves. The war such stories depict takes place out of the way: on an Ohio farm, on Kennesaw Mountain, on a Florida plantation, and on Capitol Hill when it was just a rise above the river in colonial hands. In much the same fashion, the *Lakeside Monthly* kept out of the literary mainstream that Eastern activity muddied and instead made a going proposition of the little-known writers and unacknowledged scenes of a more western war.

Of all these new regional journals bidding for popular support in the trade's postwar years, perhaps none was more sanguine than the *New National Era* (1870–74), founded in Washington, D.C., just as the Fifteenth Amendment to the Constitution was ratified. The home of the General Government and Howard University, which was established by the Freedmen's Bureau Commissioner in 1867, Washington was under Congressional jurisdiction and had thus been for decades a unique

testing ground for abolitionist fears and aspirations. In 1847, Gamaliel
Bailey of Boston founded the *National Era* and shortly thereafter began
bringing out installments of *Uncle Tom's Cabin* for the white readers
who would make Stowe's novel a best-seller. At the height of Congressional Reconstruction, however, Frederick Douglass and J. Sella
Martin addressed their new effort to "the Colored People of the United
States," whom the weekly journal was prepared to represent. Practi-
cally speaking, the readership that bought and encouraged the *New
National Era* was more likely to be the free-born blacks in prospering families than the ragged freedmen who had begun to congregate
in the nation's capital; but the new publication ignored class distinctions in its determination to become both "Advocate and Educator,"
furthering the Homestead Act of 1867 that granted claims to public
lands, organizing black laborers, and promoting public education during the liberating days of the black community's greatest hopes. Several
months after the journal first appeared, Frederick Douglass purchased
a half-interest to fend off debts and instituted the first of several slight
title changes; in 1872, he passed the tasks of editing to his sons Lewis
and Frederick, Jr. Neither they nor the investment of almost ten thousand dollars could keep the journal afloat, however, and it suspended
publication in 1874, the year in which the Freedmen's Bank failed.[24]

As Frederick Douglass observed in his autobiography, the *New National Era* was pledged to "the defence and enlightenment of the newly
emancipated and enfranchised people," and to that end published the
work of able black writers like Richard T. Greener, Harvard's first black
graduate, who went on to teach at the University of South Carolina
during Reconstruction, to become dean of the Howard Law School in
the late 1870s, and to serve as United States consul at Bombay in 1898.
Early in the journal's career, five Civil War stories were also published,
several of them reprinted from other periodicals like the *Galaxy* in
New York and the *Christian Register* in Boston. Those written expressly
for the *New National Era* tended to be anecdotal: an army captain in
"Glimpses of Sunshine Among the Clouds of War" (31 March 1870) recounts his adventures with the general's staff before his brigade leaves
Washington for Second Bull Run; a superstitious soldier on picket duty

in "Believe in Ghosts!" (3 November 1870) describes the specter that appeared to him one night in Virginia. Sometimes the protagonists are black; sometimes their race is never stated, a sign of the journal's willingness to couple distinctly racial concerns with a more general postwar enthusiasm for the industry and self-reliance which would characterize American citizenship in the popular press. Welcoming such responsibilities in his early dedication of the *New National Era*, Frederick Douglass appealed to both intelligence and patriotism in urging support for a "grand national organ" that would vindicate the new role of black Americans in the body politic.

WHO WOULD COUNT in the turbulence and upshot of civil war is one of the chief issues of this ongoing project in social archeology, much as Douglass pointed out more than a century ago. To ensure that little more has been lost in the act of recovery than in the tumble of the nineteenth-century magazine world, I have taken care that each of the 321 stories has been read by two people and that observations have been coded into a computer database, a procedure that I trust will be less wayward than conventional literary analysis and more likely to reveal the redundancies that signal cultural patterns rather than the irregularities that literary scholars have sometimes overemphasized. The three volumes of this trilogy thus aim for a surer reading of the cultural pulse than previous studies of popular narratives have engineered. To accommodate the wealth of material that has surfaced in these sixteen magazines, each of the chapters to come opens with a substantial assessment of wartime stories against the backdrop of legislative debates in and out of popular magazines. To illustrate rhetorical maneuvers and give the chapter its subtitle, one representative story then appears in its entirety, followed by a reading that links a single author's career to the wider cultural and formal patterns that the primary material reveals. Essential in this closer examination is the question of what happened to predictable emplotment when history fractured the assumptions that readers often anticipated, editors often encouraged, and writers often undercut.

As this project has grown, three distinct orientations have emerged in assessing the primary material, and thus three volumes have evolved. This volume, a cultural history, focuses on the three narrative genres whose disequilibrium in representing matters of race, political section, and gender paralleled Congressional wrangling about the postwar Constitutional amendments, which abolished slavery, guaranteed federal authority over state jurisdiction, and extended voting rights to black men. Uppermost when I fit generic conventions to Constitutional reform have been cultural knots, how potent they were in Congressional debate, and how revelatory popular narratives can be in providing the context for knots to unravel. Particularly significant is the narrative fate of freedmen within a domestic rhetoric attempting to mediate sectional clash, and so I have taken my title from Stephen Foster's familiar "Old Folks at Home" and my theme from the effort to sing the body politic in parlors nationwide.

The second volume, entitled *The Fateful Lightning* after a phrase in Julia Ward Howe's "Battle Hymn of the Republic," examines the formal developments and colloquial vitality that Civil War stories first provoked in American letters. The Civil War marked the first time that many Americans left the neighborhoods they knew well, the first time that many Northern boys saw slavery at all. The magazines they made popular bespeak a growing appetite for the idiosyncratic, the innovative, and the diverse in literature at a time when the American "household" was opening up. As a result, the narratives that contemporary writers produced catch at the things that readers found unusual and are therefore instructive in explaining the direction in which American literature moved after the antebellum ferment that only began with Melville and Poe. Undertaking a taxonomy of the stories themselves, this second volume also integrates the cultural quarrels that would transform the production of popular magazines as the trafficked intersections of literary experiment, historical moment, cultural innovation, and marketplace demand. In the first of five key nexes, I see the self-conscious role of the press illuminating the contemporary narrative development of character, particularly after the founding of the Government Printing Office in 1860 encouraged Lincoln's partisan use of the new Associated Press wires and a classbound measure of which news was fit to print. Next, I link the postwar emergence of the International Copyright Association to the greater marketplace support for American writers, who subsequently shifted the site of Civil War conflict from the open battlefields of the east to the no-man's-land of border territory further west. In addition, I tie the wartime reorganization of the postal service to shifts in the delivery of episodic events, a sign that both midcentury government and narrative design were subject to breakdown, miscarriage, and significant repair. I then reveal how the extension of railroad lines during and after the war led to complaints about monopolistic control and the need for greater competition, just when the representation of time was similarly tugged by a storyteller's conventional omniscience and a soldier's battlefield dismay. Last, I take up the new functions of photography and magazine illustration as they informed changes in narrative distance and perspective while contemporary scientific inquiry undermined traditional definitions of "truth." Given such interplay, there is every reason to reconsider the mysterious sea change in American literature from Hawthorne to Crane, a transformation in language, texture, and purview that wartime magazines cumulatively promoted.

The third volume, whose title *Look Away!* is taken from a phrase in Dan Emmett's "Dixie," concerns the weaning of an American reading public and the fashioning of national recollection. It is thus the project's summa: an analysis of narrators and implied readers in the process of constructing meaning, as well as an evaluation of how the spread of magazine stories affected public memory and the ways in which ordinary Americans would recollect the Civil War to this day. Engaged in the popular and professional functions of historiography, I also bracket the period by discussing narrative voice with the fall of Fort Sumter in 1861 and reader response with the American Centennial in 1876, an invitation to link destablizing narrative control to magazine commentary on events in South Carolina and the Congressional declaration of war while I tie expanding readership in a reconstructing nation to magazine coverage of the Centennial celebrations and Congressional debates about the new nation that the Philadelphia Exposition was meant to glorify. My final task is thus to trace the "fortunate fall" of an

American nation in the making and the rise of a literature in which the heaven and hell of ordinary lives would be closer at hand, a task that rightly leads to a tally of the stories that could never have accumulated in such number or attracted such an audience before.

Laying claim as they did to the hearts and minds of readers in parlors and campgrounds alike, popular magazines during the Civil War and Reconstruction were spurred by the earlier growth in American literacy, what William Gilmore has called an "age of reading" in the 1830s and 1840s that made possible the general magazines to come. As mass literacy spread from the Northeast to the South and West, a market coalesced for the small books that early magazines like the *Southern Literary Messenger* and *Harper's Monthly* were designed to be. In the process, boosting subscription lists also boosted the republican message of uplift, opportunity, and common purpose to which the advent of literacy had been bound since Revolutionary days. As a newly paramount national citizenship began to emerge from the Civil War's buttressing of union over independence, the magazine trade was well situated to articulate the scope and infractions of Washington's authority, if only to hold the readers north and south of the Mason-Dixon line who kept magazines solvent. Poised to turn readers into citizens on a national scale, popular magazines could sing the virtues of patriotism to the jingling accompaniment of cash in the till.[25]

For that reason, the particular songs they sang on their way to the bank warrant inspection, as do the strains of oratory that returned national representatives to Congress or cost them their seats. As exercises in persuasion, both stories in popular magazines and speeches on Capitol Hill shared a keen awareness of audience and an orientation toward symbolic operations in their rhetorical effort to fashion the public they desired. Examining their strategies thus amounts to examining social order in the making, for, as James Klumpp and Thomas Hollihan have observed, the effort to fashion order is caught up in words. "The forms that organize the behavioral patterns called culture are not *expressed* in language," write Klumpp and Hollihan; "rather social order is *performed* in language." That rhetorical performance, whether in the *Southern Monthly* or the *Congressional Globe*, has occasioned for me a concerted task: to evaluate the ways in which cultural paradigms are launched, meaning is produced, and collective action is engendered. What Celeste Condit has called "the relationship between governance and culture" is thus revealed as the logic of public address, whose systematic as well as peculiar emphases signal the spectrum along which contemporary sense would run. Scratch a domestic metaphor like "sister states," and shared assumptions about social relations are revealed even as they are put to work.[26]

Especially significant in this regard was the manner in which legislators proposed change, whether in the Constitution that bound the nation together or in the laws that governed the ordinary transactions of commercial culture. Although attuned to shifts that were unexpected and revolutionary, just as popular stories were caught up in the dislocations of the war, the making of law in the congresses under Lincoln, Johnson, and Grant tempered innovation with a respect for precedent and the communal beliefs that had hitherto been maintained. What literary magazines recognize as generic conventions, the law sanctions as the doctrine of *stare decisis,* whereby previous decisions are maintained so long as they are considered just. Perpetually unhinged by events and yet tied to the past, as were the genres of popular narrative, the law was thus reconstructive by intent, especially amid the civil turmoil of the 1860s and 1870s. How energetically both radical change and responsible inheritance were argued when legislation was debated is one of my decisive preoccupations, since the rhetorical tension between revolution and legacy is a measure of cultural anxiety in the face of unrest and of the terms on which civil disruption can be recognized and resolved. Commenting upon the consequences of such tension, James Boyd White has recently observed: "As the object of art is beauty and of philosophy truth, the object of rhetoric is justice: the constitution of a social world." With White's axiom as guide, it is my purpose in the upcoming pages to discover how social justice was parsed during the Civil War and thereafter, when Congress was as intent as the magazine trade upon extending its domain on terms that the public would accept.[27]

I confess that my examination of popular periodicals is also and finally motivated by an understanding of the word *civil*, by which I mean both the domain of citizens and the courtesy that was once their most telling attribute. In the mid-nineteenth-century forum that American magazines provided, it was the function of domestic rhetoric to revive the public claim to virtue by making war civil, largely by segregating the roles that men and women were to play as part of the contemporary drama of loss and reconstruction. In the journalistic test of a political constituency, for union in the North and independence in the South, Civil War stories served as exercises in configuration, caught between the wartime action they made meaningful and the reaction they helped to shape. They tended thereby to domesticate the demands of an emerging national citizenship, which was forged both by the war and by the Reconstruction amendments to the Constitution. During and after the political crisis, when the social order and legal apparatus of the Revolution were permanently transformed, popular narratives made war make sense by representing both the pull of older ties and the terms upon which a new nation could be imagined.

Where My Heart Is Turning Ever

INTRODUCTION

WHEN *Harper's Weekly* published Winslow Homer's *News from the War* in the summer of 1862, the Army of the Potomac was reported to be four miles from Richmond. Aloft in his balloon, the magazine declared, General McClellan could see the harried citizens of the Confederate capital gathering on the streets that they would shortly have to defend or evacuate. What readers saw in the magazine's composite centerfold was a bird's-eye view of different territory: the channels through which news was communicated after Fort Sumter fell. Sketched while Homer was with McClellan's army for the Peninsular Campaign, *News from the War* depicts the significance of both special artists and journals like *Harper's Weekly* in delivering information, with the help of letters and dispatches, placards and bugle calls. Illustrating their joint service, Homer relies upon a visual code that would also help to shape other views of the war, just as McClellan's cry "On to Richmond!" helped to shape what the general thought he saw on the city's distant streets.

At work in Homer's drawing are the organizing principles of segregation, confrontation, and circulation, which were well established in the popular press by the time McClellan took his army south. Beginning with the uppermost vignette of the woman seated before a closed window and a bleak prospect, the illustration for the most part separates its figures by gender, the sequestered woman at the center and the men around her defining the margins of what would be represented in the field. At the upper right, however, the principle of segregation is displaced in the single vignette where male and female figures are seen

"News from the War," *Harper's Weekly*, June 14, 1862

together, only to confront one another across a visual divide: their wary
glances are supplemented in *From Richmond* by a notable difference
in the spaces they occupy, a formal device that underlines their cultural competition. To segregation and confrontation is then added the
sweep of the unbordered vignettes that remain: men at the front in the
open air of military depot, regimental camp, and ship deck. That sweep
encourages circulation, as the eye moves from one vignette to another
much as the news passed from one person to another and from one
representational form to another during the Civil War. Where wood
engravings like Homer's left off, in fact, the war news was illustrated
in the popular press by a host of short prose narratives that relied upon
similar principles of organization, narratives that were once as readily
available as the journals Homer sends flying from the newspaper train
and that have since remained as hidden as the letters in a now forgotten
mail pouch for the fleet.[1]

In the years during and after the Civil War, when the ascendancy of
the General Government also inspired three amendments to the Constitution, popular magazines helped to illustrate the tension between
local affiliations and national allegiance, a wartime development that
strained the stability of settled compacts and altered narrative scenarios
as magazines circulated among markedly diverse readers in camp and
at home.[2] Running tandem with Homer's visual code, three different
narrative genres—Old Homestead, Romance, and Adventure—helped
to shape the emerging demands of national service in a figural "marriage" between North and South, a rhetorical strategy that would open
up a wider world to be represented outside the home and encourage a
"reconstructed" American literature to coalesce.

The central role of domestic rhetoric in this negotiation was secured
by the resounding antebellum success of *Uncle Tom's Cabin*, which
Harriet Beecher Stowe began serializing in the *National Era* in 1851.[3]
The parameters of that role are given visual dimension in *News from
the Front*, which centers on the interior and feminized spaces of the
home. Above all, such premises are represented in Homer's vignette
as apparently stable: the open sewing basket, the ivy that has in time
crept around the window, even the bulk of the woman's dress, the

screen before which she sits, and the table on which she leans suggest the security of home. Upon similar mainstays Old Homestead stories relied in guaranteeing that no change would topple household gods. Instead, such stories answered the generic question "Will we survive?" by promising continuity, safety, and ultimately restoration.

But in their very commitment to domestic order and the bonds of kin, these narratives stumbled over the new race relations inaugurated by the Thirteenth Amendment abolishing slavery. As a result, Old Homestead stories generally avoided incorporating freedmen into a national household and were instead more noticeably strained, like the homes and families they represented, before 1865. In these stories the Civil War figures less often as a house divided than as a house invaded; repeatedly, national events are seen as a threat to the domestic order that patriotism drew upon in print, for which the casualty report that Homer's woman holds may serve as a visible sign. It was also true, however, that domestic priorities were popularly aligned with the war's cause as early as 1861, just as the central vignette in the *Harper's Weekly* illustration is buttressed by scenes from the war served by woman's sacrifice. Like the rounder lines of her dress and the ivy circling her window, curves that are visually echoed in the hoop of the artist's barrel seat and the star-spangled banner that frames the central trumpet blast, homefront sacrifices became instrumental in translating ties to kin into ties to country, though they signaled the cost in domestic collapse.

More attuned to shifting relations than to homefront maintenance were Romances, since they had less need to monitor homogeneity through kin and less generic emphasis on restoration. Fundamental instead were the gender distinctions upon which courtship rituals had traditionally relied, though their emphasis on men and mating served to distract readers from other social relations as time went by. Homer's adjacent vignette, *From Richmond*, suggests how. Like the dress and scarf that partially obscure the slave woman standing behind her mistress, domestic rhetoric since the eighteenth century had tended to obscure distinctions of race and class in favoring the priority of gender roles, a cultural maneuver that Mary Poovey has read as both establishing and thwarting the assumptions clustered around separate spheres.[4]

Here, too, *News from the War* proves revealing. Where Homer could have underlined racial tensions by positioning the slave woman to confront the several white figures, or emphasized the apparent class differences that might separate the top-hatted gentleman in the background from the more dilapidated veterans, he instead arrays battlefield against homefront by arraying men against women, spare and truncated forms against voluminous dress and a cargo of vegetables, shallow space before a brick wall against the open space of the tree-lined street. If, as the magazine's text suggests, the men are meant to be "gallant Unionists in prison" or "wounded men in hospital," then the brick wall could serve as a reminder of Richmond's Libby prison and thus, for Northerners, the startling inverse of everything that domestic precincts were meant to ensure.[5]

In a similar strategy of inversion, Romances written between the fall of Fort Sumter and the advent of the American Centennial sometimes faltered in their anticipated guarantee that change would be desirable and easy, when Johnny did not come marching home again or Johnny Reb died in the arms of his Northern sweetheart. Such stories rescinded the genre's promise of compassion, improvement, and regeneration, together with the paradigmatic "marriage" between North and South. Their narrative failure reveals that the romance of national union was sometimes rocky in popular stories, as it was in Fourteenth Amendment debates when Southern states would not acquiesce to federal protection of civil rights. Most likely to come to grief during the period of Congressional Reconstruction that ended in 1870, Romances customarily asked "Will I become we?" and thus their failed resolutions during the period of military occupation in the South are disturbing. The look of discomfort between Homer's wounded men and the misgivings expressed by his Southern women, white and black, anticipate a postwar era of civil confrontation and subterfuge that in 1862 was still some years away.

The depth of field given to the slave mistress also contrasts provocatively with the contained interior of Homer's central vignette, emblematically so when the bare trees of the Richmond street are set against the bird cage above the knitting needles at home. But how freely would women, white or black, be thought to circulate outside domestic precincts? Although Homer repeatedly gives them ample space in their command of the Richmond avenue, the visual spread of their clothes and cargo, and the potential room for their dog to run, his women at their most capacious are still separated from the male freedom on horseback that the "CAVALRY" placard introduces; in addition, only the wounded soldiers rest before a brick wall supporting the telegraph lines that the illustration officially celebrates. To horse and telegraph the women have no visual claim, and they are wholly unrepresented at the military depot, in the tents of the First Maine regiment, and aboard ship with the fleet. In dresses like theirs, they would never climb into the saddle with the commissioned staff. No matter how regularly the curve of domestic instincts was discovered in camp life, the freedom of women to move is rendered doubtful in *News from the War* by their enormous hoops, perversely the mark of their local weight.

In a similar fashion, Adventure stories more easily invoked their generic promise of service, courage, and invention on behalf of men, particularly when they asked "Will I survive?" and when they intimated that change would be necessary and irreversible. After 1870, when the disorientation of Romances diminished with their numbers, Adventure stories were in the ascendant and on their way to becoming the most prevalent genre of the new decade, most often because veterans began to reminisce. But the exigencies of the war also challenged traditional gender roles, just as Congressional debates on the Fifteenth Amendment to extend suffrage challenged the traditional exclusion of women from full citizenship. In popular magazines and on Capitol Hill, the field of American opportunity suddenly stretched across gender lines, even after the Fifteenth Amendment established suffrage solely for black men and thus split the women's movement between those who insisted on votes for women and those who continued to lobby for ex-slaves. The failure of women to gain firmer rhetorical ground and fuller rights as citizens coincided with the end of Congressional Reconstruction and the beginning of Redemptive governments in the South, for in the final debates on Constitutional reform the earlier "national household" or "family of states" to which women might rhetorically have belonged were demoted in favor of the "fellow-citizens" that Congress proved willing to enfranchise. Although built on loyalties closer to home when enlistments were crucial, a newly paramount national citizenship in the postwar years was thus recast as individual rather than communal, deracinated rather than local, and masculine rather than feminine. Reproducing the ties that bind finally transformed families into the binds that tied "fellow-citizens" down in the corporate era to come.

The purpose of this volume is to examine that transformation from the settled to the dynamic in the stories that Americans told about the Civil War at the very moment that the nation's social order and legal apparatus were undergoing reconstitution. During the fighting, when homes and families were most likely to be fractured and Old Homestead scenarios were most likely to collapse, the evident preoccupation with continuity recalled the Revolutionary vision of the founding fathers, just as the generic preference for a "new homestead" made Romances most adaptable to the issues of Reconstruction, and the selectivity of Adventures helped to put readers on the road to Redemptive white governments in the Democratic South.

But while the narrative resistance to invasion subsided after 1865, Old Homestead stories actually continued to appear in reduced numbers and altered circumstances throughout the decade of Reconstruction and beyond, whereas Romances began to disappear after 1870. In fact, the apparent anxiety about safeguarding a Revolutionary inheritance was given its most lasting nineteenth-century expression in 1892, when Francis Bellamy wrote the pledge of allegiance for schoolchildren to recite nationwide, while the flag was raised to celebrate the discovery of America. Published in *The Youth's Companion*, which had organized and promoted the Columbus Day festivities, the pledge of allegiance aimed to revive a patriotism that had eroded after the war ended and big business took its place. Staff writer Bellamy later confessed that he began with "allegiance" (as he put it, "the great word of the Civil War period"), dismissed "liberty, equality, fraternity" as too utopian, and settled on "liberty and justice" as the American ideals held in trust ("That's all any one nation can handle"). Bellamy's tribute, what he would later call "a short formula of Americanism," may serve as the latter-day key to the Revolutionary vision that Old Homestead stories sought to restore, Romances sought to reconstruct, and Adventures sought to redeem.[6]

Separately and together, the terms *liberty* and *justice* also recur in the popular press between 1861 and 1876 on both sides of the Mason-Dixon line, and so they may rightly stand for what Southerners as well as Northerners thought they were defending. As contemporary magazines reveal, however, the two sections differed markedly on their interpretation of the terms and the founding statements they revered. Southerners like George Fitzhugh in "The Revolutions of 1776 and 1861 Contrasted" maintained in the *Southern Literary Messenger* (November and December 1863) that freedom and independence lay in resisting Northern fanaticism and emancipating the Southern states in a national "divorce," with the Constitution as their surest ally. Northerners like the Reverend C. E. Lord in "The Constitution and Slavery" denied such charges in the *Continental Monthly* (June 1862) on the ground that the "natural rights" proclaimed in the Declaration of Independence could not be repudiated in the Constitution, which was "to preserve the fruits of the Revolution" through a strong central government. Fitzhugh and other eventual secessionists scorned the "bombastic absurdities" of the Declaration, but for Lord and the Northerners he represented the Declaration was the "great charter of civil and religious freedom." When Northern forces prevailed in 1865, therefore, it was with enthusiasm that Republicans in Congress spoke of writing the Declaration of Independence into the Constitution through the amendment process. Only in the Fifteenth Amendment debates did they acknowledge that "liberty and justice" might not be intended for women, Indians, the gypsies, or the immigrant Chinese, at which point the familiar domestic rhetoric of "insurrection in the household of David" that Lord had confidently employed underwent a metamorphosis.

The subsequent rhetorical tension between the models of household and fellowship in Congressional debates on suffrage exemplifies the continuing American problem of creating a coherent national culture out of diverse American pasts, which Werner Sollors has traced as a tension between descent and consent as governing principles. Translating a generational structure into a political model, Sollors sees descent as suggesting the pull of blood, heritage, and the past, while consent implies the pull of law, free agency, and the future. The genius of American democracy, as he describes it, is to embrace that tension by making "family" relations voluntary; anxiety over America's "errand" can then be resolved by choosing the founding fathers as the progenitors of a new "American" generation destined to fulfill the Revolutionary vision. The regularity with which domestic rhetoric was invoked in popular wartime magazines suggests the same transformative purpose: to enlist family roles in a drama of initiation that would enable postbellum America to realize its Revolutionary promise.[7]

But the countervailing model of "fellow-citizens" curtailed the effectiveness of the "household" by crimping its expansive gesture beyond local family alliances, not for the first time. As Linda Kerber has observed, the eighteenth-century figure of the "Republican Mother" was likewise employed to expand domestic authority into the public life, producing what Kerber sees as "an ideology of citizenship that merged the domestic domain of the preindustrial woman with the new public ideology of individual responsibility and civic virtue." In the nineteenth century, however, the "individual" tended to separate from the "civic" as the concept of gendered spheres was advanced. As a result, Kerber points out, enterprise drifted away from virtue, a split that separated "politics and intellect" from "domesticity and nurture" as Republican Mothers lost rhetorical ground.[8]

In their place, the related nineteenth-century concept of *household* prevailed in the popular press. Derived from kinship alliances and thus from the ancient pull of blood, the household was also open to social extension well beyond the modern nuclear family; in popular antebellum novels, family structure was expanded to include "servants" from Northern kitchens and Southern plantations, as well as bachelor cousins and spinster aunts in residence. With the outbreak of civil war, domestic models were further appropriated outside the home in descriptions of schoolrooms, hospitals, prisons, army camps, and company patrols. In 1863, for example, Winslow Homer painted two Federal soldiers in camp, a scene he entitled *Home, Sweet Home*. Cordial to such simulacra, the domestic model renewed Revolutionary authority by coding soldiers as fathers, lovers, or even friends, so long as they were defined by affective relations that tied them to the kitchens and parlors where women ruled. In the halls of Congress, however, the domestic bid on newly expanded citizenship fatefully miscarried.[9]

The pages that follow are thus a study of the rites of citizenship at that moment in the nineteenth century when the nation and its Constitution were being redefined, a process that citizens were called upon to approve through enlistment and ratification. Fundamental in guiding their endeavor was the role of popular narratives in domesticating the demands of national citizenship, North and South, which was forged both by the war and by the Reconstruction amendments to the Constitution. Sometimes sustaining and sometimes complicating the model of household in Constitutional reform, the stories circulating in the contemporary press also favored a rhetoric of home and family, which proved readier to embody the threat and opportunity of the Civil War than the Edenic vision of an antebellum elite.

Given the postwar Congressional challenge to its political currency, however, domestic rhetoric may be seen throughout the 1860s and 1870s as less insular and unqualified than the early success of *Godey's Lady's Book* once made its operations appear. In their occasional return to the slave auction block and their frequent dismay at bushwhackers in the backwoods, the Old Homestead stories in Chapter One reveal that Stowe's domestic priorities continued to be enlisted in the campaign against slavery, even in sundering what Karen Sanchez-Eppler has called the "bodily bonds" that perniciously tied black servants to white households. Likewise, the regenerative offices of the Romances considered in Chapter Two were regularly engaged in a nationalist cause; but their failed resolutions in the late 1860s indicate that the South was cast as "subverting the cult of domesticity" with the same vigor that Gertrude Reif Hughes has recognized in the poetry of Emily Dickinson. Challenged as well by the competing masculine claim to the open road, which the Adventures taken up in Chapter Three unfold, the cultural potency of the home was only sporadically bolstered by heroines who faced vigilantes or ran the blockade and thus promoted a "separate but superior" alternative, to borrow Joanne Dobson's term. Most publicly, however, the rhetoric of home and family was also employed by those in Congress who, unlike women writers or the antebellum press at large, had no immediate investment in its millennial promise or its local bids for women's status. In the following pages, domestic rhetoric therefore emerges as the discursive vehicle for registering the lacerated status of Revolutionary compromises and the persistent resuscitation of Revolutionary ideals.[10]

Looking ahead to Joel Chandler Harris and the Uncle Remus tales he began to publish after 1876, this volume concludes by examining the impact of wartime service on the household model that *Uncle Tom's Cabin* first consolidated, a model that with no less consequence would inspire the public resurrection of plantation life in the best-sellers of the 1880s and 1890s. At the outset of his career after the American Centennial, Harris was more committed to the Southern domestic relations that frame his tales than he would be in later years, and yet less likely to dilute the rambunctious characters Uncle Remus presents. His early work for the *Atlanta Constitution* thus provides both a chance to eavesdrop on the tenor of "New South" narratives and something analogous to the original intent of cultural reconstruction in the 1870s. As Constitutional scholars have acknowledged, the effort to discover the intentions of an earlier era is often befuddled by the opacity of the written word and driven by the conservative impulse to limit judicial activism, especially in the continuing quarrel over public symbols. But as Paul Brest has pointed out, the initial construction of a Constitutional amendment may be understood through immersion in the social moment that produced it, although the imperatives of that moment have since receded.[11] Certainly the purposes of Harris in the South, Congressional representatives in the North, and Civil War stories across the country were as robustly conservative as the domestic rhetoric they employed. In negotiating a fully national commitment to liberty and justice, however, the makers of law and literature in the wake of Fort Sumter's fall were also poised for a new birth of freedom, which their rhetorical maneuvers before a popular audience would do much to define, then and thereafter.

CHAPTER ONE

Domestic Narrative
and National Stability

By the mid-1850s, domestic rhetoric in the popular press had established the "homestead" as a set of predictable roles imaged as domestic
space and as the stage for national drama. With the fall of Fort Sumter,
however, the nation was no longer stable and even the premises of
home and family were no longer safe, in practice or in prose. True, by
the fall of 1863 the threat of Confederate troops was receding north
of the Potomac: Lee had retreated from Gettysburg's ridges and hills,
Grant had opened the Mississippi by taking Vicksburg, and the black
soldiers of the Fifty-fourth Massachusetts had stormed Fort Wagner
within shooting distance of Charleston. But for the Murray women
in one contemporary story of thanksgiving, military victories were no
guarantee of family security. When their brother was reported dead on
the battlefield, Miss Minty and Miss Molly thought that pumpkin and
mincemeat pies should be forgotten, along with their annual festivities.
Spinster sisters, they went to the meetinghouse and cried at the minister's sermon. Their servant Mehitable stayed home to cook, as was
her place, though she was no less fond of the young lieutenant. As the
head of the household, it was Mrs. Murray who insisted on the pies
and dinner after mourning clothes were made and the meetinghouse

attended. Rigorously Scotch Puritan, she did not break down until she had to say grace.

"Thanksgiving" was the only fiction about the Civil War that *Godey's Lady's Book* published between 1861 and 1876. Appearing in October 1863, S.G.B.'s story thus provides an unusual opportunity to discover what had become commonplace in domestic literature a decade after *Uncle Tom's Cabin* and more than two years after the Civil War began. Determined to avoid political controversy, *Godey's* tapped instead into a vein of civilian stories oriented to the "kitchen war" that the magazine's readers would be most likely to share. In "Thanksgiving" as elsewhere, the domestic conventions that structured such Old Homestead narratives guaranteed that no significant change would impede local or national inheritance, however variously Revolutionary liberty and justice were defined from one region to another. Yet by 1863 such promises were taxed even in popular stories by enlistment and the midwar draft, death and battlefield suffering, and the intruding presence of the war effort in the North as well as in the South and West. Though "the house divided" remained little more in contemporary narratives than Lincoln's biblical figure of speech, the war's demands threatened national stability and along with it the homes and family support upon which patriotism relied.[1]

The Old Homestead narratives published during the Civil War and Reconstruction more often asserted a house invaded, by the death of a young lieutenant or the sacrifice of the family's security as well as by enemy troops. Even when the collapse of the Confederacy ended the mounting strain on families north and south of the Mason-Dixon line, the Old Homestead promise of restoration remained in doubt. Not only had more than six hundred thousand soldiers died, but the reinvigorated demand for a constitutional amendment abolishing slavery sought to cancel forever a return to "the Constitution as it is, the Union as it was." In the Congresssional debates on the Thirteenth Amendment, which would guarantee personal liberty by changing the "supreme law" that gave the nation its identity and citizenship its force, the rhetoric of home and family would also come into play. But the Old Homestead stories published during and after the war suggest that the new national government empowered by such legislative action was hardly acknowledged in the local households to which magazine fare gave a voice.

So too the "contrabands" whose emancipation was secured by constitutional amendment did not move readily to new roles anywhere but in Congressional oratory; in the domestic stories Americans told in print, freedmen did not escape the parameters of antebellum plantation fiction or slave narratives any more speedily than they did the racial bias that characterized American life. Yet where ex-slaves did eventually assume greater dimension when stories of the war were told, they demonstrated that a house invaded could in turn become a house liberated, producing substantial choices with which reconstruction of an American nation and an American literature could begin.

Of the 321 Civil War stories in these magazines, about 41 center on the home and another 75 mix Old Homestead elements in some combination with other story types, more often the Romances that signaled transferred allegiances than the Adventures that left home and inheritance behind. That brings the total number of family stories worth considering to some 116, just over a third of the whole. As many as 93 of these appeared during the 1860s, 56 during the Civil War years alone, which suggests that the appeal of restorative domestic values was most often called upon when domestic precincts and national stability were most vulnerable, before the Thirteenth Amendment in 1865 moved the country decisively beyond the antebellum status quo. Still, just over 60 percent of the wartime stories and approximately one-quarter of the 116 narratives of the home appeared in *Harper's Weekly* before 1866, after which Civil War coverage throughout the newsmagazine virtually disappeared. Setting aside this single journal shifts the tally in all others significantly. Instead of declining, the total number of Old Homestead stories actually increased after the war, from 26 by war's end to 35 by the end of the decade and another 23 by the Centennial. Although more people read *Harper's Weekly* than any comparable magazine, the continuing appeal of restorative themes in journals like the *Lakeside Monthly* and *Lippincott's* suggests a competing anxiety about the terms on which a new national identity would be established, once the Constitution of Revolutionary days was amended.

Foremost among the domestic values that midcentury magazines promoted was continuity from one household or generation to the next, a preoccupation that was generally built into family narratives by way of a cast that ran to at least two generations, notably absent from stories of other types. Furthermore, as exercises in containment, Old Homestead stories usually began and generally remained indoors, whether in a cottage or a ballroom, a prison or a hospital ward, a tent or a lighthouse tower. They were also set in the South as often as in the North, regardless of where the stories were published; occasionally the West and the border areas figured as well. These variations on a formula were particularly apparent in *Harper's Weekly*, which was first to circulate Old Homestead stories in 1861 and least likely to complicate the communal emphasis of the genre. Promoting those "blessed" sacrifices "for Freedom's sake" noted in "Love's Sacrifice and Its Recompense" (5 March 1864), *Harper's Weekly* set the rhetorical pattern of enlisting home and family in the nation's cause, so that the claims of kinship came to define rather than to defy the increasing claims of citizenship and national service.

For Southerners and Northerners alike in narratives of the war, patriotism began at home. So did secession. As David M. Potter has persuasively argued, the Union sentiment that Southerners revolted against was not an "exclusive allegiance"; it was built upon a hierarchy of anterior loyalties based on family ties.[2] For Northerners, nationalism grew out of these familiar loyalties; with the election of "Father Abraham" in 1860, the sectional interests of the North were sure to dominate in the territories to the west and thus in the future of political debate. Southerners, however, saw their national prestige crumbling and their sectional interests failing to find votes in Congress or approval in the Northern press. Between national allegiance and states' rights, they had to choose.

As a result, there is reason to anticipate that the rhetoric of home and family was employed differently in Northern and Southern magazines, especially in registering the narrative threat to domestic continuity. Certainly contributors to the *Southern Literary Messenger* were quick in poems and essays to invoke the American Revolution and to call upon "Freedom's son," which rhymes with "Washington" in

G.B.J.'s reveille for "Men of the South!" (May 1861). Similarly, "The Philosophy of Secession" (September/October 1862) first looks back to the framers of the Constitution and their *"Representative Confederate Republic,"* an alliance among sovereign states now lapsing from the founders' vision into the "anarchy and despotism" that would later antagonize the *Land We Love* and the *Southern Magazine* after the war. Echoing the familial terms on which the Civil War would repeat the American Revolution for Confederates, even Boston's *Continental Monthly* in "The Constitution as it is—the Union as it Was" (October 1862) inveighed editorially against the "parricidal rebellion" that the South had launched, a charge that had previously been leveled against the patriots of 1776. Fighting for "Home, freedom, children, wife" as William Gilmore Simms put it in "Sons of the South, Arise" (*Southern Literary Messenger*, February and March 1862), the Confederacy had every reason to figure in Southern stories as demanding independence with the same zeal that led the founding fathers to Yorktown.[3]

Yet the recognized threats to homesteads in eleven Southern narratives published during and after the Civil War were remarkably similar to the threats that filled stories told in the North. In spite of the rhetoric of "freedom" and "despotism" that magazines themselves perpetuated, the same fears concerning military service and casualties in battle afflicted most American homesteads and most magazine characters even before the Murray women took stock in 1863: one of the eight enlistment stories appeared in the South, five of the twenty stories about death on and off the battlefield were carried by Southern magazines, and two of the forty-six stories of wartime disruption were Southern, as were three of the twenty stories that led to a family reunion. Not at all stories of rebellious "sons" or founding "fathers" overturning the tyranny of Northern oppressors, these Southern family narratives confirmed instead the same "life-currents flowing between each soldier and his home" that C. A. Hopkinson apostrophized in the *Atlantic Monthly*'s "Quicksands" (June 1866).

Southern narratives varied mainly in chronicling the strain on both homes and domestic discourse as the war drew to a close; for example, after General Sherman ordered Northern troops to ravage Georgia

("Destroy! destroy! Leave not a chimney for a crow to rest upon"), the *Land We Love*'s "Only Son of His Mother" (June 1868) duly headnoted his command. When pressed into defensive service, however, domestic discourse showed itself to be surprisingly resilient against the odds and remarkably adept at fixing civil allegiances. Mothers and sisters who saw the regiment march away gauged their patriotism by their sacrifice; both grew when battlefield casualties or fixed bayonets threatened the domestic premises that Old Homestead narratives ordinarily secured. In fact, the greater the odds against family survival in these stories, the greater their insistence on family roles, as characters who endured came to be defined by what they had lost.

Most unreflexive in appropriating domestic conventions were the enlistment stories that appeared early in *Harper's Weekly*, after Lincoln issued his call for seventy-five thousand volunteers in April 1861. Many other stories would translate personal sacrifice into patriotic duty for mothers and fiancées, but in these the call to arms embodies the war and the responsibilities beyond the home that the war uniformly imposed. Like Federal soldier-boys from Vermont and New York, George William Bagby's captain of the Rifle Grays in "My Uncle Flatback's Plantation" (*Southern Literary Messenger*, October 1863) volunteers as a matter of course, much as Uncle Flatback's uncle did in the American Revolution. In what might be called "We Are Coming" stories, the gauge of family cohesion was national enlistment, so that young men proved themselves to be good sons and young women worthy sisters by their dedication to the war effort.[4]

It is true that by 1863, when the practice of paying substitutes had increased the burden on poorer Northern families even before the summer's draft, hard-pressed wives and mothers like Mrs. Thurston in "Drafted!" (*Harper's Weekly*, 8 August 1863) bitterly complained about the privilege of the rich. But as Mrs. Thurston's story progresses, her family's contribution to the national cause garners immediate rewards: the rich man uses his money to relieve the needs of the poor, duty emerges as commendable enough to ease the class friction between them, and national service is translated into the means for achieving domestic stability. So naturally did the rhetoric of the home come to the aid of the country that enlisting in the army appeared to further both local and national ends.

In other stories, where the war simply complicated civilian lives, keeping the faith on the homefront also proved relatively easy, and domestic roles were often augmented by forays outside the home. Characterization was most likely to fluctuate when the war inspired comic misadventure; with wartime loss scaled down, fathers could also work for the Secret Service, household slaves could also storm the occasional chicken coop, and cousins could also hightail it home ahead of Federal scouts pursuing spies. When clashes were more ominous, characters were more homebound, both in their movements and in their delineation: a mother and daughter visiting New York during the draft riots of 1863 hide with their kin, and Southern families in border country bar their doors against marauders. As the war intensified in the stories Americans told, domestic roles became more exacting, domestic space more prominent, and domestic security more nearly a measure of national stability North and South.

Once the war was over, however, even Southern magazines looked beyond Manassas and Spotsylvania, and by 1869 and into the 1870s their stories of the war's progress at home favored recovery, marriage, and a second chance. This trend was most pronounced in reunion stories, especially when missing sons and lovers turned up on Thanksgiving or Christmas Eve. Most of these stories of the more fortunate appeared late in the war or well into Reconstruction, though *Harper's Weekly* anticipated the possibility of a second chance as early as 1862. By 1868, even the belligerent *Land We Love* was ready to return the "Only Son of His Mother" from an apparent grave. The subsequent recasting of domestic roles through marriage ("Post nubila, jubila!" or "After dark clouds, joy!") transforms the family's sorry removal from burning house to humble cabin. With the Southern soldier back "home" again, his fiancée displaces his mother as protagonist, an indication that narrative resistance to change had declined; in a further show of formal elasticity, the soldier's friend displaces the happy couple to offer his final blessing as narrator, another indication that the Old Homestead's grip on readers had subsided into Romance. Similarly, the demands of citizenship and kinship in "Only Son of His Mother" figuratively subside into a new union, signaled by the final "mist of floating white" that is both the nation's future and the Southern soldier's bride.

When the war did not ebb so gracefully, however, the expense of pledging allegiance to the country began to be tallied in more pronounced domestic rituals and a greater demand for domestic stability in popular magazines. North and South, women in Old Homestead narratives knit socks, cut shirts, nursed their own, nursed strangers, wrote letters, and kept their vows. In Southern magazines, however, such domestic rites were more sorely tried. Women were forced to hide their belongings from prying bayonets, driven from their homes by Northern troops, refused admittance to dying sons in Federal prisons, and faced with the deaths of so many sons and daughters and husbands and lovers that they often collapsed themselves. In fact, their roles as wives or mothers define their lives together with their narrative function: they reveal few personal idiosyncrasies and no evident need to supplement their activity at home with the additional role of hospital nurse, village seamstress, or local schoolteacher.

A case in point is "Road-Side Stories," an anonymous account also published in the postwar *Land We Love* (August 1866). As the narrative progresses, an old Southern woman sees her husband die, then her son-in-law; then her son enlists only to return starving and half-witted, their cottage burns, her daughter dies, and she is forced to sell water to Southern soldiers so she and her son can eat, until the well runs dry. The woman does survive and finds reassurance in the arms of an acquaintance in a railway station and the forgiveness of a soldier who still remembers the water he had to purchase. As in stories told by Northern narrators, sympathy and human kindness prevail. But losses impose upon this Southern home where family and household gods were meant to be safe; by the same token, the role of wife and mother apparently defines the few options available to the old woman and establishes the only ground on which the soldier and the reader can forgive her. Like the mothers who see their houses catch fire or their sons die in prison, the heroine of "Road-Side Stories" amounts to no more than the sum of her losses, which are cast in the domestic terms that make loss both intimate and profound.

There were other reasons why family allegiances appeared more pronounced in Old Homestead stories published in the South. Very few writers, for instance, referred to slavery and thus to the somewhat more extended relationships that Northern stories set on Southern soil tended to promote. In the *Southern Literary Messenger* or the *Land We Love*, a mother became a mistress only when she talked to the peripheral "servant." Southern family stories also tended to bridge generations from the perspective of aging parents, where stories in the Northern press focused instead on the younger generation, younger parents, their children, or even protagonists unrelated to the family. Of the four uncomplicated Old Homestead stories that appeared in Southern magazines before 1876, just one ignores parental authority, and then only to favor the brother and sister left alive to carry on. The place of an older order in Southern stories is marked even in bona fide Romances, while in Northern literature mothers and fathers and aunts and uncles usually failed to appear in the dramatis personae when marriage was the issue. Their presence in stories told in the South suggests how tenaciously some Americans held on to the settled past and the diminishing glory of the originally sovereign states.

The active role of an older generation in Civil War narratives also reveals the terms on which Southerners invoked the American Revolution. One available strategy was to repeat the older drama of filial independence and parental control by casting Southerners as founding fathers and leaving Northerners to echo the Crown's rebuke. But in the plantation tradition that had been evolving in Southern fiction since the abolitionist attacks of the 1830s, masters were cast as paternalistic and consequently as founding "fathers" who never died. There was then little room in the fictive plantation household to lead colonial revolt, a role that could not rightly fall to masters or tolerably fall to slaves. Instead of sponsoring rebellion, Southern stories valued inheritance and respected age, adroitly joining Revolutionary ideals in the process to the Old Homestead predilection for maintaining the estate.

Indeed, the preoccupation with aging relatives in Southern households indicates how much of an older social order was commonly associated in popular magazines with the South and now apparently in jeopardy. When Southerners seceded from the Union in 1861, they were represented as supporting state loyalties closer to home. When Federal troops prevailed in 1865, both Southerners and Northerners read in political defeat the power beyond the home that had forced those loyalties to collapse.[5]

The pull of local allegiances throughout the United States in the 1860s and 1870s can be gauged from the appearance of domestic stories in popular magazines. The "old homestead" they celebrate was almost never radically emblematic, almost never a sign of the national "household" that would emerge when the Union survived the war. Instead, Old Homestead stories bespoke the local households that were, until the 1860s, only loosely connected in the popular press to any national enterprise. Reactionary in design, these narratives supported a thoroughly local notion of citizenship as well as a sense that military service and national responsibility interrupted ordinary lives. Even for the duration, Old Homestead stories promised, the war's demands would not uproot families or keep soldiers from going home again. By 1870, however, the South was in the midst of reconstructing and the Constitution had been revised three times over. The "house invaded" was already undergoing repair.

The very few instances of divided families in popular war stories predictably split a single generation along fraternal lines. When political allegiances were at odds from one generation to the next, they most often turned Old Homestead stories into Romances, thus inviting gender distinctions and substituting the question of whether the potential marriage would take place for the question of whether the established household would survive. Of the 119 stories that center on domestic precincts, only five portrayed the home as the original American union and alienated brothers as dividing the household along sectional lines. All five stories appeared in Northern magazines and four took place in the disputed territory of Kentucky, Maryland, or Tennessee. Of these, three still tended to deflect the tensions that the politically volatile setting itself encouraged: "On the Kentucky Border" (*Harper's Weekly*, 1 February 1862) resolves into a joint defense of the home against unruly Tennessee soldiers, while "The Two Generals" (*Harper's Weekly*, 2 January 1864) and William Douglas O'Connor's "The Carpenter" (*Putnam's*, n.s., January 1868) end with reconciliation and marriage vows on Christmas Eve. Harriet E. Prescott's "Ray" (*Atlantic Monthly*, January 1864) acknowledges more passion, more friction, and more principle in the contest for "freedom" and for the Southern woman both brothers love; but the story ends with a temperate marriage to a Northern girl and the promise of recovery for the boy who kills his adored Southern brother on the battlefield.

In these border stories, fraternal strife seems more a regional misfortune than a national paradigm, a tendency to marginalize the "divided" household that is repeated in other stories: for example, Kate P. Kereven's "Dr. Aar" (*Lippincott's*, November 1868) alludes to a family at odds and then dismisses the subordinate storyline with little detail. While the deadly skirmishing in border territory recurred as a popular subject, it most often took the form of beleaguered Unionist households and thus confirmed that the gravest threat to Old Homesteads was seen as coming locally from without.

The final story of internecine warfare, Louise E. Chollet's "Tom Lodowne" (*Harper's Monthly*, May 1866), takes a more familiar turn in anticipating the national popularity of the divided kinsmen theme by several decades. But Chollet's narrative resembles an allegory and even in this form remains inconclusive on the central issue of the emancipated slaves. In the house jointly inherited by Jack and Dix, Chollet's characters fall out over the representative slave Tom Lodowne, especially after Uncle Abel arrives on the scene. Dix hits his mother, the boys fight, Jack wins Tom's freedom, and the house is reunited by the boys' mother, who tells the story. Titularly about the freedman, the story is curiously named for the single character who never says a word and, for that matter, has no postwar role. The story is interesting for precisely that reason: while other contemporary narratives raised the issue of slavery (it is, for example, the divisive issue in Prescott's "Ray"), they generally steered away from the formal development of black characters. Whether the national house was divided or invaded, destroyed or reunited, the issue of slavery could be made central in a narrative without making the role of slaves a formal reality and without imagining what the emancipated slaves would do. "Tom Lodowne" ends instead with the restoration of the house that the boys' father and the Constitution built ("painting and cleaning will soon set the old house to rights"), an indication that the Revolution was closer to home for magazine readers than was Reconstruction.

When Chollet's story appeared in 1866, however, there had already been a structural addition to "the old house" that the framed Constitution she describes nowhere credits. In January 1865, the House of Representatives passed the constitutional amendment to abolish slavery, which the Senate had approved the previous spring. By December it was ratified, since the Thirteenth Amendment had become one of the foundations of President Johnson's Reconstruction policy. As the first in a series of postwar Congressional reforms, the Thirteenth Amendment set in motion a legislative process that would permanently alter the relation of state and national governments, a process in which the rhetoric of home and family played a revealing part. Because of the difficulty in discerning what lawmakers originally intended in the mid-1860s, Chollet's story is again significant: from title to final query ("'What is to be done with Tom Lodowne?'"), the state of the Union was formally linked to the fate of the slaves, just as national citizenship and abolition came to be linked in Congress. Similarly, the Constitution and paternal "will" are uppermost, though "our old homestead" as Chollet describes it is not the site of border feud, plantation control, or independent household. Instead, "Tom Lodowne" represents the Revolutionary legacy as a single national family whose future depends on the uncertain status of freedmen. While discursive patterns arising from nature, scripture, the machinery of general government, or the body politic also came into play when the Senate took up the amendment, the use of domestic discourse in postwar Congressional debate signaled that a national "family" had likewise been imagined by some in Washington and that there was as yet little place in it for ex-slaves.

Charles Sumner of Massachusetts revealed the extent to which domestic virtues had already been harnessed in the abolitionist campaign when he took the Senate floor on 9 February 1864, after Lincoln had pointed out that the Emancipation Proclamation could be legally sustained only while the war lasted. On his desk Sumner displayed petitions signed by one hundred thousand men and women who supported a constitutional amendment to secure freedom for Southern slaves. When he rose to speak, he summoned up a domestic rhetoric unhampered by class distinctions and transformed it into a vigorous militarism; the petitions, he said, were "from the families of the educated and uneducated, rich and poor, of every profession, business, and calling in life, representing every sentiment, thought, hope, passion, activity, intelligence which inspires, strengthens, and adorns our social system. Here they are, a mighty army, one hundred thousand strong, without arms or banners, the advance guard of a yet larger army."[6] In 1864, his purported domestic phalanx stopped short of triumph; notwithstanding his appeal, Sumner's proposed amendment failed to convince fellow senators that social equality should be promoted, as the Declaration of Independence might have implied. But a reformulated amendment based on the narrower precedent of the Northwest Ordinance was approved by the Senate in April, only to be defeated at first in the House.[7]

"The sacred right of family," as Sumner put it in April, invited for some and prohibited for others a marked federal intervention on the slave's behalf. In the view of Sumner and many Republicans, slave families deserved legislative protection.[8] But even after ratification, the Thirteenth Amendment was accused by Indiana's senator Thomas Hendricks of having "broke asunder" the "private relation" that bound slave to master. Other Democrats saw Congress further intruding upon the domestic relations of parent and child, husband and wife, guardian and ward, which provided the model for the peculiar institution and the ground upon which social relations in the South were constructed.[9]

James M. Ashley of Ohio, who called for reconsideration of the joint resolution in the House, went a step further and tied the question of freedom for the slaves specifically to the issue of a renewed national authority. Defending the proposed amendment as fit to be put before the states, he found support for reforming the Constitution in the document itself and insisted that states can adopt whatever Constitutional adjustment three-fourths of them vote to approve. "If they cannot," he declared, "then is the clause of the Constitution just quoted a dead letter; the States sovereign, the Government a confederation, and the United States not a nation." [10] In spite of Democratic demurrals about a "consolidated nation," the language of the Congressional debate on the Thirteenth Amendment demonstrates that already for many lawmakers the Union constituted a family as much as families constituted the Union. Union soldiers from Kentucky were seen by Senator Powell of that state as "true sons of a proud mother," Congressman Orth of Indiana spoke of readmitting " 'wayward sisters' to the family circle," and even the unreconstructed Senator Saulsbury of Delaware intoned against the "unnatural war" that pitted "brother against brother." [11] Alert to Lincoln's rhetoric as well as to his policy, Sumner also invoked the Republic as "a house divided against itself," though in his Annual Message to Congress in December 1864 Lincoln was more concerned for the widows and orphans the war had created than any representation of national coherence.[12]

In none of these national constructs did the ex-slave figure; on the contrary, the Senate discussion of the Freedmen's Bureau Bill in 1866 reveals that many who approved the passage of the Thirteenth Amendment the year before simply voted slaves out of the master's family rather than into a national household. Said Cowan of Pennsylvania: "That amendment, everybody knows and nobody dare deny, was simply made to liberate the negro slave from his master. That is all there is of it. Will the chairman of the Committee of the Judiciary or anybody else undertake to say that that was to prevent the involuntary servitude of my child to me, of my apprentice to me, or the *quasi* servitude which the wife to some extent owes to her husband? Certainly not." [13] Demonstrably uneasy about governmental control of domestic relations, many senators and congressmen alike distinguished between *liberty* and *freedom*, refused to include suffrage in the amendment's proposed civil rights, and counted on the greater privileges allowed freedmen in court to resolve the "Negro Question." Although Homer Plessy would not challenge the habit of separating blacks and whites in America for more than twenty-five years, a "separate but equal" America for freedmen was already being articulated in the debates that many observers thought would set blacks free.

In 1865, the most ardent abolitionists thought securing emancipation by guaranteeing liberty would be victory enough for silent "Tom Lodownes" and all that sacrificial "Uncle Toms" ever dreamed. William Lloyd Garrison, for instance, greeted the ratification of the Thirteenth Amendment as the end of the abolitionist campaign begun in the *Liberator* in 1831. Recording the December proclamation that William Seward made as Secretary of State, Garrison wrote: "With our own hands we have put in type this unspeakably cheering and important official announcement that, at last, the old 'covenant with death' is annulled, and the 'agreement with hell' no longer stands." A week before the final number of the magazine appeared, Garrison exulted that millions of slaves had been granted "deliverance from the house of bondage," a metaphor linking domestic language with the biblical imperatives that had distinguished the *Liberator*'s moral stance from its early days. In the next column, S.M., Jr., called for protecting the freedmen with "the whole power of American law"; but his declaration failed once again to establish a national metaphor when the available figure of the house multiplied instead into the "homes and land" that further legislation should secure. Rejoicing in its farewells, the *Liberator* thus embraced the Freedmen's Bureau and the Freedmen's Commission while proposing a free society that Jefferson's yeoman farmers might have approved.

Less partisan than the abolitionist press, literary magazines were both less and more far-seeing in their response to Constitutional reform, and thus they provided varying political contexts in which Civil War stories were read. Concerning civil rights for ex-slaves, *Godey's* said nothing; in the America that its "fair readers" surveyed, the freedmen were allotted no more space than the war in which they had been emancipated. Other magazines were more forthcoming, however, especially the *Continental Monthly* in Boston and the *Southern Magazine* in Baltimore. As early as 1864, after the joint resolution to abolish slavery had been proposed in Congress and voted down, Henry Everett Russell tied abolition to national citizenship when he defended "The Constitutional Amendment" (*Continental Monthly*, September 1864) as ensuring "the nation's authority" and buttressing the Constitution, which he saw as "the basis of a *nation*, and not the compact of a *confederation*." Portraying the Union as "the asylum and hope of liberty," Russell insisted on a national identity greater than the sum of its parts, a position underlined by his preference throughout the essay for nouns in the singular; he writes, for example, that "a republic is a country where the whole people is the public, and the state the affair of the whole people." More than a single household, the American people make up for Russell a single body, "the bleeding body of the nation, whose poor, dumb mouths, if they had voice would cry out to Heaven against the system which has moved this foul treason against those liberties and laws." He would write upon the nation's "forefront" the words of Daniel Webster: "Liberty *and* Union, now and forever, one and inseparable." Welcoming "all the people of every state," Russell and the *Continental Monthly* saw the Thirteenth Amendment binding the slaves and the states to an American empire, which Washington had directed the "infant republic" to become.

At the other extreme was Judge William Archer Cocke's protest over the violent misuse of the Constitution in an essay entitled " 'The Federalist' and the U.S. Constitution" (*Southern Magazine*, January 1871). Grieved by the present state of Constitutional affairs, Cocke reviewed the jurisprudential foundation laid in *The Federalist* during the years after the Revolution and discovered that much had gone wrong, though the South was not at fault. Veering toward the despotism that Madison and Henry initially feared, the sectional interests of the North and West rather than the secession of the Southern states had destroyed the Union, which Cocke represents in a domestic metaphor as derived from the contributions of all the states; he refers to "that Union our fathers built upon the broad, strong, deep-laid foundation of the Constitutions of the State and Federal Governments." Here Cocke favors plural subjects and compound nouns, a verbal sign of the cooperative nature of an American republicanism that he saw disintegrating. With particular interest in the Fourteenth and Fifteenth Amendments, he warns of the danger to come, again with reference to domestic constructions: "it is only a question of time whether the building will crumble by piecemeal, or make by a sudden crash one simultaneous ruin." Aside from the "happy compromises" of the Constitutional Convention, Cocke does not mention slavery or emancipation, but weighs "a Union kept together by force" against "a Union of equal rights." He finally protests the amendments as illegal because the ratification process was imposed. With no hope of repair, Cocke assigns the "Federalist" Union to a flood of corruption, less because the center would not hold than because its constituent supports had only temporarily been lashed into place.

Substantiating Russell's sturdy empire or Cocke's crumbling foundation were the national constructs that other magazines proffered, yet only in the North was national identity linked to the slavery debate. Disdaining rehabilitation in the *Atlantic Monthly*, C. C. Hazewell envisioned a singular Union in 1864, but one that was man-made. Describing an American nation of free men unindebted to European powers in 1860, Hazewell speaks in "Democracy and the Secession War" (October 1864) of "that mowing-machine, the American sword" (505) and thereby links the biblical righteousness of the abolitionists to an image of technological might.

By contrast, Southern magazines maintained that the patient child of Southern independence was beyond help. In the aftermath of defeat, the *Land We Love* diagnosed the ailing Confederacy as mistreated by Northern "parents." Apologizing for a printer who substituted "starving" for "stoning" in an essay on domestic punishment under Mosaic law, the magazine's monthly "Editorial" (August 1866) explained: "Now our printer had heard so much of 'starving the rebellion to death' by the parental government, that when the case of the rebellious child came up, his fingers naturally set the type for 'starving' as the natural punishment" (303). Countering Northern claims for a vigorously national program, Southern magazines emphasized the difficulty of reorganizing the political "family."

Although Northern magazines provided more full-fledged support for eradicating slavery in other essays and Southern magazines insisted on the case for states' rights with greater frequency elsewhere, it is these reflexive metaphors for the state of the Union that reveal how ill-defined was the "United States" in 1865 and how undeveloped was the central authority that an amended Constitution would soon require. Like those in Congress who employed domestic rhetoric either to support or to eliminate legislative action, popular magazines described a Union still growing either up to or away from a cohesive nation.

Yet the Thirteenth Amendment appeared to do little immediately for freedmen beyond severing them legally from plantation households. In 1866, the ex-slaves were widely perceived as free to make their own way, especially since sympathetic whites who spoke out in popular magazines provided no other alternative. But popular stories did occasionally offer their own response to the "Negro Question" if only because the black characters who sometimes assumed greater play had to have something to do. Establishing a context for such free agents was not easy; not only were "Tom Lodownes" harder to develop in midcentury American culture than "Uncle Toms," but domestic assumptions were at their most restrictive when black characters were associated with the "cabins" of the past. In stories with less communal emphasis, slaves and freedmen could move into their own romances and adventures since these scenarios allowed greater flexibility to all characters for self-definition. But Old Homestead stories relied upon family orientation, and black characters who threw off their bonds generally risked appearing disloyal to those they served or inessential to the domestic principles that readers had learned to expect. Witness Stowe's George Harris, whose escape from slavery is fully sanctioned only when he is joined by the wife and child he left behind; Uncle Tom never sheds his responsibility for holding the (white) family together, while Tom Lodowne's only discernible identity comes from the national family in which he remains a bone of contention. But other writers fashioned what Stowe and Chollet had not: alternative roles for black characters to play and, more important, an alternative language for them to speak.

A very few, such as Miss S. C. Blackwell in "Fugitives at the West" (*Continental Monthly*, May 1862) and D. R. Castleton in "The St.

Leons" (*Harper's Monthly*, August 1866), picked up where the slave narrative tradition left off, without sounding the earlier autobiographical note. Their solution to the problem of domestic loyalty was to establish separate but equal slave families whose white households were seen to be secondary. As in Stowe's best-selling novel, the horrors of slavery appeared most keen when they disrupted family life in the quarters; the recurring event in Blackwell's narrative is that the slave couple flees, in Castleton's that the slave family is sold apart. In both stories, those who escape are mulatto, just as George and Eliza Harris were in *Uncle Tom's Cabin*.

Blackwell and Castleton were left, however, with the same problem in domestic fiction that confronted Stowe: although the genre celebrated staying put, the desirable norm for escaping slaves was flight. They could never go "home" again while they followed the North Star. Consequently, Stowe's fugitives disappear from much of her novel and finally from North America. Blackwell's fugitives are subordinated to secondary roles in favor of the white Ohio heroine who has to learn abolitionist principles from the minister's daughter. Castleton opts to focus on the stranded slave wife and children for whom the quadroon courier returns with cash in hand. Both magazine stories are therefore Old Homestead rather than Adventure or Romance tales, either because their white characters orient the reader toward domestic concerns or because the slave families must escape together for even a minimal "household" to remain intact. While they are unevenly developed as characters, these liberated slaves do speak Standard English or a colloquial patois ("You ole slaveholder, you, you jist go back to ole Virginny; you niver git my daughter agin!") whereas other blacks are confined to a stunted dialect. They also pointedly solve the problem of Southern class hierarchy, which ordinarily provided little economic chance or narrative occupation for ex-slaves. Therese, Leon, and Sallie all go north skilled enough to earn their own livings as cook, business courier, and seamstress.

But the slave narrative tradition was not widely employed in popular magazines during or after the Civil War, even in the remaining nineteen Old Homestead stories whose black characters stepped out of their peripheral "servant" roles. About a dozen of these were stories in which Adventure and/or Romance scenarios made some appearance, structurally freeing characters of Old Homestead ties. Even allowing for greater narrative movement, eight of the nineteen stories augmented black roles without challenging the premise that emancipation meant nothing to loyal slaves, whose primary concern was to serve the white households of which they had forcibly been made a part. In the other eleven stories, however, alternative developments emerged to show how malleable were the "natural" ties of kin and household and how purposefully imposed was the effort to ground citizenship in their recognizable domain. Nowhere is the shadow of social construction more apparent than in the contrast between the eight stories in which slaves happily serve their masters and the eleven stories in which they claim other roles.

Several of the "happy darkey" stories, for instance, supposedly come from the slaves themselves, which makes them fully or partially "slave narratives" of a different sort.[14] Here the principal slave function is to maintain white families; at his most successful, an "Old Uncle Hampshire" could almost bring back the "old times," as the resurgent plantation tradition was to do in Joel Chandler Harris's first "Uncle Remus" tale as early as 1877. Freedom for these slaves is portrayed as exile and free labor as punishment. In the absence of Southern masters during the war, they could occasionally assume the role of protector, especially if the threat to the home came from Southern bushwhackers. But slaves thereby reinforced the stability of the Southern plantation family and the advantages of "high-toned" society, a function only partially undercut if their white families were Unionists in the South. On the battlefield, loyal slaves even died voluntarily to secure the safety of white masters. So strong was the "private relation" between master and slave represented to be that black anger, when it surfaced, could be channeled in these narratives to bring about the Christian forgiveness and "family" reconciliation that Old Homestead conventions encouraged.

While their legal positions improved after the Emancipation Proclamation, with a noticeable increase in their stature as characters, these contrabands and freedmen generally continued to be defined by their family status; many retained their slave names once free, like Uncle Mem in "Dr. Aar" (*Lippincott's*, November 1868) and Uncle Tip in "Tippoo Saib" (*Harper's Weekly*, 2 April 1864). Their speech patterns were also distinctive, as were those of other characters short of a story's inner circle. The more unmistakably slaves were bound to their white households, the more frequently "ob" and "dem" came out in their talk. Unreconstructed blacks thus remained "innocent" children at home, an assurance that injustice had not educated them or freedom loosened their family affections.

Countering such assurances of contented service were the less facile maneuvers of stories in which black "family" roles were undercut. Eleven war narratives attempted to denaturalize the pull of blood and loyalty, by revealing that plantation households could breed violence instead of social stability and could disavow the claims of "kin" if the blood were black.[15] To be sure, several of these stories acknowledge that white masters had fled, and virtually all are set in the South though they were published in Northern magazines. Restrictive domestic ties for slaves were therefore offset by the presence of Federal troops and, in any case, the struggle was distant from Northern readers and social prejudices. Still, by running away, enlisting, or abetting Northern officers, slaves were seen to break with older loyalties and to complicate Old Homestead plots by declaring their independence from the conventions that constituted their hitherto fractional roles.

At its most tenuous, their liberation as characters took the form of a contest between personal freedom and family ties, a contest that pitted antislavery principles against generic conventions. In Old Homestead stories, the outcome was never certain. An escaping slave named Milly who chooses to save herself by abandoning her son in Helen W. Pierson's "Chip" (*Harper's Monthly*, July 1865) is captured by Southern soldiers during a battle and eventually forfeits her life, not for running away but for running away from her child. For Pierson, "child-forsaking" amounted to "God-forsaking," even though the "noble end" of Northern union was finally implicated in the "vile means" of the war. Both black freedom and Washington's authority were thereby indicted, though hapless Milly noticeably escapes becoming anybody's "aunt." Polly Pharaoh, the title character in Lizzie W. Champney's story (*Harper's Monthly*, July 1876), goes a step further to counteract her assigned name as more tractable characters did not. Reversing the reminder of Egyptian bondage, Polly helps a Northern officer escape Southern bushwhackers in rural Arkansas. Had Polly been white, the story might well have turned into a romance of North-South reunion; since Polly is instead a slave scarred by a household accident when a child, she sends the Yankee scout on his way to safety before rescuing the pink sunbonnet she wears in her father's cabin. Though slaves could thus escape white masters in Old Homestead stories, they could not readily escape the substitute generic deference to black families. Nor could they propel the action beyond the homes with which these narratives begin if they were to stay alive as characters long enough to be free.

Indeed, in the host of Old Homestead stories that appeared during the Civil War and Reconstruction, only one clear strategy emerged for securing black freedom without severing domestic ties. Fugitive slaves could gain glory the old-fashioned way: they could enlist. Volunteering for Federal service, they eluded the genre's prejudice against change by joining the national "family" that fought for the Union, especially if they paid with blood. As in Congressional debate, household responsibilities were thereby shaped into national roles in a drama that effectively transformed the house invaded into the house liberated, once escaped slaves moved out of peripheral standing and into narrative focus. The problem was to escape in the first place as Louisa May Alcott revealed in "The Brothers" (*Atlantic Monthly*, November 1863), a story worth examining since the burden of transforming the "national household" splits the narrative in half.

The first section of Alcott's story begins with the failure of domestic sanctity to keep the slave family together: upon the death of a kind master, his son sends the slave mother to labor in a rice swamp, forces himself on the slave wife, and whips her husband before selling him further south. Not only does plantation life provoke such violence, but it is also seen as part of the son's inheritance: the slave husband and the white master's son are half-brothers. By chance, years later, they are taken from a Virginia battlefield to the same Washington hospital, one a contraband intent on murder and the other a wounded captain near death. In what might have been a climactic scene, the contraband Robert reasserts the privacy and close quarters of their Southern home by shutting the hospital window and locking the door to their room. He also throws out Captain Ned's medicine. Across racial lines in "The Brothers," shared blood revokes the "natural" claims of kin and the generic claims of domestic fiction to engender disruption, threat, and collapse, no reassuring prospect for a nation with four million slaves or an Old Homestead narrative with a black protagonist.

Fortunately for the paradigm, a white hospital nurse intercedes to stop the fratricide by reminding Robert of his wife, whose name has "the power to arrest" and to return the story to its restorative promise. As Miss Dane notes, Lucy's name relieves "Slavery's black shadow" and shifts the reader's attention from the white family that fails Robert to the black family in which he placed his hope. The nurse's active presence on the scene also shifts the Old Homestead scenario impor tantly: the Southern family drawn together by blood and hate is saved through government-sponsored intervention. As a confirmed abolitionist, Miss Dane underlines the political implications of her advice: the black family can itself be enlisted to serve government-sponsored ends. As a nurse in wartime service, Miss Dane also furthers the story's success in enlarging domestic space to include the public hospital, a move that shifts the genre's focus slightly from restoration to recuperation. Recognizing the nurse's power to redefine *home* and *family*, Robert in turn repudiates his master's last name and substitutes hers, thereby reinforcing the public function of family and identity in wartime narratives.

Yet even thus far in "The Brothers," conventional Old Homestead assumptions are made precarious by the effort to incorporate slaves. In the first place, the family bonds traditionally asserted through patronymic and physique are shaken; not only does Robert despise his name, his brother has always despised Robert's face ("He always hated me, I looked so like old Marster: he don't—only the light skin an' hair").

Just as Federal intervention provides the slave with a new name, so the war provides the slave with a new face through the "ghastly wound" to cheek and forehead that mars the "comeliness" he inherited. Partially for that reason, however, Miss Dane initially finds it difficult to become his "friend" and reverts to the role of "mistress," another sign of the difficulty with which prevailing Old Homestead strategies were revised when contrabands moved into key roles.

Adding to the narrative load is the character of Robert Dane, whose customary silence lends him stature as a contraband but costs him an energetic voice of his own when his story is told. Ordinarily, the interior spaces of the conventional Old Homestead narrative ought to have eased his reticence, since he could have spoken in the Federal hospital to Miss Dane and in the cabin earlier to Lucy. But in Alcott's story, such spaces are oppressive: tending Captain Ned leads the nurse herself to feel "a prisoner," just as pleading with his brother back home leads Robert to a near-fatal whipping. As Miss Dane points out, Robert is "no saintly 'Uncle Tom,'" and the domestic spaces that secure white mothers against bushwhackers and Federal troops offer such black characters no protection against a master's lust or their own rage. The antidote to festering hatred in "The Brothers" is to move out, a narrative tactic that generally forces runaway slaves beyond the domestic space that Old Homestead stories require. Alcott does not escape that problem, which brings the action thus far to a close. Nor does she revise the genre's distinctive bias in favor of those who can afford homes of their own; even in a public hospital, the middle-class nurse takes charge where the impoverished patient hesitates, so that "The Brothers" initially demonstrates what white women accomplish and what black men do not.

If Robert's story had concluded with his departure from the hospital, the house invaded would at least have been put to rights, the generic promise of continuity and safety would have been back in place, and the prevailing Federal authority would have kept ex-slaves quiet in the Southern families they despised. With Captain Ned on the mend, Robert could be another Milly who did not drop her baby, another Polly who agreeably hid her face. But Robert enlists in the Fifty-fourth Massachusetts, the black regiment under the command of Robert Gould Shaw. Instead of going home again he assaults Fort Wagner, effectively replacing Miss Dane as the narrative's prime mover and winning on the battlefield a place in the national household. Again he meets Captain Ned at close quarters and again he is spared the crime of fratricide; though the circumstances of battle would have condoned a renewed attack, Captain Ned stabs him first and is killed in turn by the regiment's black drummer boy. Delivered to the hospital ship in Hilton Head harbor, Robert dies in the care of the reassigned Miss Dane, who bears witness to the "wife and home, eternal liberty and God" he finds on his deathbed. In his place he leaves his friend the drummer boy, who takes over as retrospective narrator for the events that happen offstage and who remains alive to enjoy a fully reconstructed vision of liberty for all.

Though Robert dies like Stowe's protagonist at the hands of his white master, Alcott insists on several adjustments in the example he sets. First, he does not submit like a good Christian but charges like a good soldier; he cares nothing for his master's salvation and everything for the national promise of freedom. As Robert's wounded comrades declare from their hospital pallets, "If our people's free, we can afford to die." The possible ambiguity of "our people" suggests a further move away from household roles allotted by race, since the troops seem to be fighting simultaneously for the liberation of the slaves and the stability of the Union.

It then matters little that the assault on Fort Wagner failed; in Alcott's story, neither battlefield success nor Christian redemption compares with the important shift in public opinion when the bravery of black troops is reported. As Miss Dane observes, "Through the cannon-smoke of that black night the manhood of the colored race shines before many eyes that would not see, rings in many ears that would not hear, wins many hearts that would not hitherto believe." Miss Dane herself finally ceases to be a "mistress" in Hilton Head harbor when she extends a phrase like "our boys" to include the wounded of the Fifty-fourth, a brief but suggestive reformulation of the national family.

Her presence is a reminder that the final action again takes place in a hospital, rather than at the white plantation where Uncle Tom dies. The hospital scene is thus both domestic and national, not figuratively but literally. Most important, since the decisive battlefield action takes place offstage, the narrative replaces the first section's climactic action with the second section's climactic memory, recorded in the irrepressible voice of the black drummer boy ("I never thought of anything but the damn' Rebs, that scalp, slash, an' cut our ears off, when they git us. I was bound to let daylight into one of 'em at least, an' I did"). In "The Brothers," black soldiers thus claim their place both in the events that enter national memory and in the stories that magazine readers were told. The national family that emerges from Alcott's story, the new nation conceived in liberty that would emerge from the Civil War, is thereafter indebted to what white women witness and what black men do for themselves.

Though Alcott's story is unusual among narratives of home and family, it suggests the extent to which redefining the nation after the Civil War depended upon redefining the roles that freedmen would play and reconceiving the function of the domestic rhetoric employed in Congress and literary magazines. Ordinarily conservative, the Old Homestead promises of continuity, safety, and restoration were more in keeping with the ideals of the Revolution than the radical projects of Reconstruction; in some ways, such promises were more adaptable to the cause of the antebellum plantation than to that of a national rebirth of freedom. Tributes to the "old folks," which kept the Revolution alive during the Civil War, established the house as a figure resisting narrative development and thus maintained a family model that served the white middle-class imagination. Augmenting the cast did not necessarily posit a new national story, even when Congress passed the Thirteenth Amendment and permanently put an end to slavery. But the amendment's enforcement clause did replace state sovereignty with Federal prerogative at least on paper, just as "The Brothers" replaced a plantation house invaded with a national hospital liberated and thereby gave the "old homestead" a Reconstructive future as well as a Revolutionary past.

Of course, so long as Old Homestead stories avoided the divisive issue of race, their houses could still be returned to a suspended order, as S.G.B. demonstrated to *Godey's* readers by returning Lieutenant Murray to his mother on Thanksgiving Day. Replacing grief with joy, the Murray women then fill the empty seat at the table with their "recovered treasure," a visible return on the Old Homestead promise of maintaining the status quo and a sudden reprieve from the casualty report that similarly troubled Homer's woman. Yet even in a New England cottage, wartime breakdown could lead to a measure of change. Mrs. Murray is able to declare a mother's love at last, and the sisters take "more friendly liberties" at home than they had before. Their reward for patriotic service is thus greater latitude in defining their relations, which acknowledges the impact of the war at home without changing the constitution of the local cum national household.

More acute would be the changes for freedmen, whose house invaded proved to be simultaneously the figure of shared blood and of spilled blood. The closer popular stories came to the further substitution of battlefield for plantation home in "The Brothers," the more difficult it was to invoke the generic promise of restoration or to engage anew in the fiction of domestic security. Once the adventure of enlistment became a narrative mainstay, the bonds of blood and the claims of household were seriously taxed, by the mobility of regiments as well as by their massed assaults. To keep other Roberts and Captain Neds at arm's length, writers like Mark Twain turned instead to the arresting power of the feminine and the story that Alcott's Lucy might have told. In doing so, they inevitably lent credence to a view of black matriarchs that could prove as politically damaging for Lucys who survived as domestic rhetoric generally proved in the pending fight for woman's suffrage. Even in the narrative economy of Twain's apology to his black cook, promoting a mother's perspective could mean reducing a son's achievement, a transaction that was to have far-reaching consequences for the way in which the project of national reconstruction would be understood.

Mark Twain, "A True Story,
Repeated Word for Word as I Heard It"

(*Atlantic Monthly*, November 1874)

IT WAS SUMMERTIME, and twilight. We were sitting on the porch of the farm-house, on the summit of the hill, and "Aunt Rachel" was sitting respectfully below our level, on the steps,—for she was our servant, and colored. She was of mighty frame and stature; she was sixty years old, but her eye was undimmed and her strength unabated. She was a cheerful, hearty soul, and it was no more trouble for her to laugh than it is for a bird to sing. She was under fire, now, as usual when the day was done. That is to say, she was being chaffed without mercy, and was enjoying it. She would let off peal after peal of laughter, and then sit with her face in her hands and shake with throes of enjoyment which she could no longer get breath enough to express. At such a moment as this a thought occurred to me, and I said:—

"Aunt Rachel, how is it that you've lived sixty years and never had any trouble?"

She stopped quaking. She paused, and there was a moment of silence. She turned her face over her shoulder toward me, and said, without even a smile in her voice:—

"Misto C——, is you in 'arnest?"

"Why, I thought—that is, I meant—why, you *can't* have had any trouble. I've never heard you sigh, and never seen your eye when there wasn't a laugh in it."

She faced fairly around, now, and was full of earnestness.

"Has I had any trouble? Misto C——, I's gwyne to tell you, den I leave it to you. I was bawn down 'mongst de slaves; I knows all 'bout slavery, 'case I ben one of 'em my own se'f. Well, sah, my ole man— dat's my husban'—he was lovin' an' kind to me, jist as kind as you is to yo' own wife. An' we had chil'en—seven chil'en—an' we loved dem chil'en jist de same as you loves yo' chil'en. Dey was black, but de Lord can't make no chil'en so black but what dey mother loves 'em an' wouldn't give 'em up, no, not for anything dat's in dis whole world.

"Well, sah, I was raised in old Fo'ginny, but my mother she was raised in Maryland; an' my *souls!* she was turrible when she'd git started! My *lan'!* but she'd make de fur fly! When she'd git into dem tantrums, she always had one word dat she said. She'd straighten herse'f up an' put her fists in her hips an' say, 'I want you to understan' dat I wa'n't bawn in de mash to be fool' by trash! I's one o' de ole Blue Hen's Chickens, *I* is!' 'Ca'se, you see, dat's what folks dat's bawn in Maryland calls deyselves, an' dey's proud of it. Well, dat was her word. I don't ever forgit it, beca'se she said it so much, an' beca'se she said it one day when my little Henry tore his wris' awful, an' mos' busted his head, right up at de top of his forehead, an' de niggers didn't fly aroun' fas' enough to 'tend to him. An' when dey talk' back at her, she up an' she says, 'Look-a-heah!' she says, 'I want you niggers to understan' dat I wa'n't bawn in de mash to be fool' by trash! I's one o' de ole Blue Hen's Chickens, *I* is!' an' den she clar' dat kitchen an' bandage' up de chile herse'f. So I says dat word, too, when I's riled

"Well, bymeby my ole mistis say she's broke, an' she got to sell all de niggers on de place. An' when I heah dat dey gwyne to sell us all off at oction in Richmon', oh de good gracious! I know what dat mean!"

Aunt Rachel had gradually risen, while she warmed to her subject, and now she towered above us, black against the stars.

"Dey put chains on us an' put us on a stan' as high as dis po'ch,—twenty foot high,—an' all de people stood aroun', crowds an' crowds. An' dey'd come up dah an' look at us all roun', an' squeeze our arm, an' make us git up an' walk, an' den say, 'Dis one too ole,' or 'Dis one lame,' or 'Dis one don't 'mount to much.' An' dey sole my ole man, an' took him away, an' dey begin to sell my chil'en an' take *dem* away, an' I begin to cry; an' de man say, 'Shet up yo' dam blubberin',' an' hit me on de mouf wid his han'. An' when de las' one was gone but my little Henry, I grab' *him* clost up to my breas' so, an' I ris up an' says, 'You shan't take him away,' I says; 'I'll kill de man dat tetches him!' I says. But my little Henry whisper an' say, 'I gwyne to run away, an' den I work an' buy yo' freedom.' Oh, bless de chile, he always so good! But dey got him—dey got him, de men did; but I took and tear de clo'es mos' off of 'em, an' beat 'em over de head wid my chain; an' *dey* give it to *me*, too, but I didn't mine dat.

"Well, dah was my ole man gone, an' all my chil'en, all my seven chil'en—an' six of 'em I hain't set eyes on ag'in to dis day, an' dat's twenty-two year ago las' Easter. De man dat bought me b'long' in New-bern, an' he took me dah. Well, bymeby de years roll on an' de waw come. My marster he was a Confedrit colonel, an' I was his family's cook. So when de Unions took dat town, dey all run away an' lef' me all by myse'f wid de other niggers in dat mons'us big house. So de big Union officers move in dah, an' dey ask me would I cook for *dem*. 'Lord bless you,' says I, 'dat's what I's *for*.'

"Dey wa'n't no small-fry officers, mine you, dey was de biggest dey *is;* an' de way dey made dem sojers mosey roun'! De Gen'l he tole me to boss dat kitchen; an' he say, 'If anybody come meddlin' wid you, you jist make 'em walk chalk; don't you be afeard,' he say; 'you's 'mong frens, now.'

"Well, I thinks to myse'f, if my little Henry ever got a chance to run away, he'd make to de Norf, o' course. So one day I comes in dah whah de big officers was, in de parlor, an' I drops a kurtchy, so, an' I up an' tole 'em 'bout my Henry, dey a-listenin' to my troubles jist de same as if I was white folks; an' I says, 'What I come for is beca'se if he got away and got up Norf whah you gemmen comes from, you might 'a' seen him, maybe, an' could tell me so as I could fine him ag'in; he was very little, an' he had a sk-yar on his lef' wris', an' at de top of his fore-head.' Den dey look mournful, an' de Gen'l say, 'How long sense you los' him?' an' I say, 'Thirteen year.' Den de Gen'l say, 'He wouldn't be little no mo', now—he's a man!'

"I never thought o' dat befo'! He was only dat little feller to *me*, yit. I never thought 'bout him growin' up an' bein' big. But I see it den. None o' de gemmen had run acrost him, so dey couldn't do nothin' for me. But all dat time, do' *I* didn't know it, my Henry *was* run off to de Norf, years an' years, an' he was a barber, too, an' worked for hisse'f. An' bymeby, when de waw come, he ups an' he says, 'I's done barberin',' he says; 'I's gwyne to fine my ole mammy, less'n she's dead.' So he sole out

an' went to whah dey was recruitin', an' hired hisse'f out to de colonel
for his servant; an' den he went all froo de battles everywhah, huntin'
for his ole mammy; yes indeedy, he'd hire to fust one officer an' den
another, tell he'd ransacked de whole Souf; but you see *I* didn't know
nuffin 'bout *dis*. How was *I* gwyne to know it?

"Well, one night we had a big sojer ball; de sojers dah at Newbern
was always havin' balls an' carryin' on. Dey had 'em in my kitchen,
heaps o' times, 'ca'se it was so big. Mine you, I was *down* on sich doin's;
beca'se my place was wid de officers, an' it rasp' me to have dem common sojers cavortin' roun' my kitchen like dat. But I alway' stood aroun'
an' kep' things straight, I did; an' sometimes dey'd git my dander up,
an' den I'd make 'em clar dat kitchen, mine I *tell* you!

"Well, one night—it was a Friday night—dey comes a whole plattoon
f'm a *nigger* ridgment dat was on guard at de house,—de house was
head-quarters, you know,—an' den I was jist a-*bilin'*! Mad? I was jist
a-*boomin'*! I swelled aroun', an' swelled aroun'; I jist was a-itchin' for
'em to do somefin for to start me. *An'* dey was a-waltzin' an a-dancin'!
my! but dey was havin' a time! an' I jist a-swellin' an' a-swellin' up!
Pooty soon, 'long comes sich a spruce young nigger a-sailin' down de
room wid a yaller wench roun' de wais'; an' roun' an' roun' an' roun'
dey went, enough to make a body drunk to look at 'em; an' when dey
got abreas' o' me, dey went to kin' o' balancin' aroun', fust on one leg
an' den on t'other, an' smilin' at my big red turban, an' makin' fun, an'
I ups an' says, "*Git* along wid you!—rubbage!' De young man's face
kin' o' changed, all of a sudden, for 'bout a second, but den he went to
smilin' ag'in, same as he was befo'. Well, 'bout dis time, in comes some
niggers dat played music an' b'long' to de ban', an' dey *never* could git
along widout puttin' on airs. An' de very fust air dey put on dat night, I
lit into 'em! Dey laughed, an' dat made me wuss. De res' o' de niggers
got to laughin', an' den my soul *alive* but I was hot! My eye was jist
a-blazin'! I jist straightened myself up, so,—jist as I is now, plum to
de ceilin', mos',—an' I digs my fists into my hips, an' I says, 'Look-
a-heah!' I says, 'I want you niggers to understan' dat I wa'n't bawn in
de mash to be fool' by trash! I's one o' de ole Blue Hen's Chickens, *I*
is!' an' den I see dat young man stan' a-starin' an' stiff, lookin' kin' o'

up at de ceilin' like he fo'got somefin, an' couldn't 'member it no mo'. Well, I jist march' on dem niggers,—so, lookin' like a gen'l,—an' dey jist cave' away befo' me an' out at de do'. An' as dis young man was a-goin' out, I heah him say to another nigger, 'Jim,' he says, 'you go 'long an' tell de cap'n I be on han' 'bout eight o'clock in de mawnin'; dey's somefin on my mine,' he says; 'I don't sleep no mo' dis night. You go 'long,' he says, 'an' leave me by my own se'f.'

"Dis was 'bout one o'clock in de mawnin'. Well, 'bout seven, I was up an' on han', gittin' de officers' breakfast. I was a-stoopin' down by de stove,—jist so, same as if yo' foot was de stove,—an' I'd opened de stove do wid my right han',—so, pushin' it back, jist as I pushes yo' foot,—an' I'd jist got de pan o' hot biscuits in my han' an' was 'bout to raise up, when I see a black face come aroun' under mine, an' de eyes a-lookin' up into mine, jist as I's a-lookin' up clost under yo' face now; an' I jist stopped *right dah*, an' never budged! jist gazed, an' gazed, so; an' de pan begin to tremble, an' all of a sudden I *knowed*! De pan drop' on de flo' an' I grab his lef' han' an' shove back his sleeve,—jist so, as I's doin' to you,—an' den I goes for his forehead an' push de hair back, so, an' 'Boy!' I says, 'if you an't my Henry, what is you doin' wid dis welt on yo' wris' an' dat sk-yar on yo' forehead? De Lord God ob heaven be praise', I got my own ag'in!'

"Oh, no, Misto C——, *I* hain't had no trouble. An' no *joy!*"

"One o' de ole Blue Hen's Chickens"

WHEN WILLIAM DEAN HOWELLS accepted "A True Story" for publication in the *Atlantic Monthly*, he took Mark Twain by surprise. Although Twain was set on breaking into the respectable circles that subscribed to the magazine, he had submitted several previous efforts without success. He sent "A True Story" hesitantly; it was, as he wrote to Howells, "rather out of my line." Purporting to be a faithful transcription of an account he heard from an ex-slave, the story carried little of Twain's signature humor. But Howells accepted it enthusiastically, paid Twain top dollar, and made the tale of separation and reunion Twain's first submission to appear in the pages of the *Atlantic Monthly*.[16]

As Twain's subtitle affirms, the details of his narrative were not of his making. During the summer of 1874, when he was staying with his family at Quarry Farm, Twain heard the account from Mary Ann Cord, a freed slave who had been born in Maryland and sold in Virginia to a North Carolina master. When the war ended, she came north to Elmira with her son Henry. In 1874 she was about seventy-six, looked sixty, and appeared carefree. But she still remembered the sale of her husband and children in 1852 and her rediscovery of Henry during the Civil War, a story her family has kept alive to this day.[17] Twain would later make her his model for "Aunty Phyllis" in the "Refuge of the Derelicts," as Arthur Pettit has shown, and many of the superstitions for which Jim is remembered in *Huckleberry Finn* Twain gathered from "Auntie" Cord. In the summer of 1874, however, he was still an outspoken Republican, fresh from his stint as the owner of the *Buffalo Express*, and as ready to reform Northern prejudices against the blacks as to condemn the "domestic institution" in the South.[18]

In Twain's hands, the slave narrative tradition gained currency in mainstream American culture and, specifically, in the literary magazines that middle-class Americans most often read. The similarities between the story he published and the story Auntie Cord passed down indicate that Twain was a willing amanuensis to his cook. But he nonetheless made several modifications in putting Auntie Cord's account in writing: he changed his heroine's name, changed the order in which events are told, and added the frame in which the porch steps and "Misto C——" appear. While these shifts cumulatively demonstrate both the liberating and restrictive energies of the Old Homestead genre when applied to ex-slaves, Twain also gave Aunt Rachel a language that such characters had never previously claimed, and indeed that Twain himself would never duplicate at such uninterrupted length for the rest of his career.

"A True Story" thus demonstrates that slaves could fill Old Homestead roles without redefining the genre or invoking their plantation status. Their eventual reunions still depended on remaining steadfast, since wisdom seemed to lie in staying put. At the same time, the slave narrative could be recast along domestic lines, a reorientation that allowed the antebellum genre in the hands of Reconstruction whites to challenge racial stereotypes without questioning the class barometers fundamental to the plantation tradition. Encouraging a slave matriarchy that would later skew perceptions of the black community, as the Moynihan Report has most recently revealed, "A True Story" was built around a conventional maternal role that was at once enobling and coercive, but open to reconstruction.[19]

The particular revisions that Twain made bear closer attention. By changing the slave's name from "Cord" to "Rachel," Twain brought to mind the biblical mother who lamented the loss of her family. The specific reference is to Jeremiah 31:15–17, in which Rachel weeps for her exiled children, while God promises that they will be returned.[20] With her sister Leah, Rachel has traditionally been recognized as the "mother" of the tribes of Israel, whose very name (*Is-ra-el*, or the men of the Rachel tribe) pays homage to her. Certainly Jeremiah's reference acknowledges the family imprint on historical events, the extent to which history itself was once the chronicle of family and then tribal affairs. The domestic imprimatur is reinforced when the passage is read as anticipating Herod's New Testament slaughter of the innocents in Bethlehem, or more broadly as representing Yahweh's weeping for fallen humankind, an interpretation richly suggestive of slave family separations in the antebellum South, the mounting casualties of the Civil War, and the nation "under God" that Lincoln apostrophized at Gettysburg.

As a "Rachel" on the auction block, Auntie Cord is seen to cry out against Henry's exile; just as Rachel was mother to Israel as well as to Joseph and Benjamin, so Aunt Rachel's lament may echo beyond slave cabins to signal the plight of Americans at war. Similarly, hope lies for Aunt Rachel as it did for her namesake in the return of what was lost, ultimately the coming of the son who promises to deliver her from bondage. Her story thereby promotes the Old Homestead guarantee of a return, but with an important difference where black families were concerned. In Twain's story, the events of the war and its aftermath set slaves free. Serving the Northern officers in Newbern and Misto C——up north, Aunt Rachel is " 'mong frens"; her son Henry has meanwhile joined a colored regiment, the surest promise of eventual citizenship for blacks that the Civil War allowed. The "old homestead" that their reunion affirms thus comes about on very different ground from the insolvent plantation on which they were sold.

The biblical reference to a mother's trials is also bolstered by Twain's reorganization of events. Favoring a chronological presentation, Twain brings Auntie Cord's account that "traveled both ways" closer to the "wayfarer" progress that Frances Smith Foster sees as typical of slave narratives, with New Testament "joy" as the anticipated climax of a journey through the wilderness.[21] Though it is impossible to say where Auntie Cord began her account, the "middle" to which Twain referred appears to be Newbern, where she lived before coming to New York and where the climactic reunion eventually takes place. By delaying the removal to North Carolina, Twain foregrounds the family's rupture and Henry's promise, just the moment of loss and comfort that Jeremiah underlines in Rachel's lamentation.

Besides emphasizing the traditional scene on the auction block, Twain's rearrangement also brings the narrative in line with the structural counterpoint that Harriet Beecher Stowe established in *Uncle Tom's Cabin*: from Virginia, Aunt Rachel moves further south into slavery while her son Henry escapes to freedom in the north, just as Uncle Tom was sold into the Deep South while George and Eliza Harris crossed the Ohio into the North. Unlike Uncle Tom, however, Aunt Rachel is not whipped to death; with the wartime advent of Northern troops, Aunt Rachel is released from the Southern owners of the "mons'us big house" who run off, and delivered into the arms of her own son in more than enough time to make the most of her freedom. Praising "de Lord God ob heaven" for the return of Henry, Aunt Rachel sings the wayfarer's song of joy in the Promised Land, a New Testament hymn of jubilation that contrasts with her memory of the family lost on Easter some twenty-two years before.

Twain's retelling of the story finally allows him to add the event of storytelling proper, the porch on which "Misto C———" hears the account from the steps below. Arguably, the rube employer who misreads the laughter of his cook takes his cue as a character from the rube Easterners who came to grief at the hands of Twain's Western "bumpkins," narrators who upset a snobbish cultural hierarchy by pulling the rug out from under their naive visitors.[22] But Aunt Rachel does not upset her listeners as Twain's Western tricksters did; instead, she stands her own ground "black against the stars." Recognizably ironic as is Twain's opening reference to their positions (" 'Aunt Rachel' was sitting respectfully below our level, on the steps—for she was our servant, and colored"), his purpose is also less iconoclastic than reconstructive. In his hands, the slave narrative does not emphasize freedom as characters move out or loyalty as they stay put, but respect for their personal stature as they literally move up from the lowly positions assigned them by prejudice to stand on their own two feet. After his narrative recognition of Aunt Rachel's emerging status, Misto C——— virtually disappears until Aunt Rachel herself names him in her concluding exclamation.

Certainly, the principal characters of "A True Story" represent a considerable advance over the minstrel darkies of Twain's earlier fiction, even as recently as *The Gilded Age* in 1873. During the summer of 1874, Twain was also at work on *Tom Sawyer* and thus already concluding his Western adventures and on his creative way back to Hannibal and the antebellum South. Essential to that rediscovered territory was his representation of Southern slaves, who had not fared well in the pitch and tumble of the Western humor Twain helped to popularize.[23] But from the "stretchers" he had already told, he had learned a striking lesson about constructing characters: who they were was how they talked. In composing "A True Story," Twain was exceedingly careful to find Aunt Rachel's voice, as he explained to Howells.[24] Out of his exercise in talking her language he was to craft *Huckleberry Finn*'s Jim and *Pudd'nhead Wilson*'s Roxy in the decades to come.

More immediately, "A True Story" served as the capstone for the Civil War narratives that Howells accepted and the *Atlantic Monthly* circulated in the years after Fort Sumter fell. Of the 116 stories that encouraged a return to the home, 16 appeared in the magazine; often combining with both other genres, they are among the most structurally complex, thematically daring, and formally innovative of all the stories Americans read in the 1860s and 1870s. They are also among the most politically forceful, though a comparison between Twain's story and Alcott's "The Brothers" reveals how temperate the Boston journal had become in the 1870s. Whereas ruined black families inspired revenge in 1863, they were almost gratuitously restored some ten years later, when slavery had offically been abolished and the magazine could modulate its abolitionist creed. From its inception, however, the *Atlantic Monthly* had known what to do with Tom Lodownes, as Mark Twain discovered before finding his way into the magazine's pages.

In crafting "A True Story" Twain also drew upon both the strengths of the Old Homestead genre and its unexpected resources. Whether Auntie Cord is identified with the black family she loses or the white families she serves, her household role defines her character in Twain's story. To Misto C—— and the masters before him, she is a cook; to Henry and her own kin, she is mother and daughter both in a pattern of domestic inheritance endorsed by her refrain. Because slaves functioned in two families, Aunt Rachel has somewhat more latitude in her manners than white matrons in country cottages, but she is no more likely to move beyond domestic responsibilities than Chollet's Stella or S.G.B.'s Mrs. Murray. Except when her home is denied her on the auction block, she never gets farther from the kitchen than the front steps, though "her" kitchen changes locale more than once. She is thus both as permanent in her devotions as Old Homestead verities required and as powerless to maintain her home as slave narratives insisted, and as white women regularly found themselves in stories about the war.[25] For Aunt Rachel, however, the war itself is not intrusive but restorative, one sure sign that for white authors and their audiences the Civil War was undergoing reevaluation by 1874 and coming to be seen as empowering rather than endangering an alternative vision of home.

The same reevaluative concern marks Twain's handling of the Old Homestead's generic resistance to change once slaves moved into domestic roles of their own. On the surface, a commitment to the steadfast persists. Not only does Aunt Rachel stay put in the kitchen, but she eventually knows her son Henry again because of the "sk-yars" he still bears. He, in turn, knows his mother by her unchanging refrain, which also structures the story into a series of returns to the same ornery incantation. Even Aunt Rachel's tribute to Maryland effectively suspends change over time: the Blue Hen's chickens never grow up, any more than citizens outgrow the mother state to which they are born. Instead, both birthright and its invocation are passed from one generation to the next, from mother to daughter, as though citizenship were an ever-renewing family affair.

At the same time, the circumstances in which the refrain is heard vary significantly: from the slave kitchen where Henry busts his head, to the officers' kitchen where he arrives in uniform, to the farm steps where the old black cook repeats her mother's legacy. In addition, once the "unions" take Newbern, all "Confedrit" claims on the status quo are cashiered: the whites run off and it is the slaves who come into the "mons'us big house." Where Chollet's Stella maintains her home and S.G.B.'s Mrs. Murray keeps Mehitable busy with pies, Aunt Rachel supplants white authority. The general himself urges her to "boss dat kitchen" by making meddlers "walk chalk," a white line to toe rather than the more familiar black line in the dirt. Ultimately, only a revolution in social affairs that sends Confederate colonels packing and bans the auction block could bring Henry round again to Aunt Rachel and thus restore the "old homestead" that slave mothers otherwise feared losing forever.

Yet very little of the cataclysmic changes that brought slaves their liberty appears in "A True Story." The Federal soldiers arrive without incident, Henry enlists offstage, the black regiment waltzes in the officers' kitchen unheckled. Change registers in Twain's story largely through Henry, who is sold as a slave boy and returns as a free man. But the narrative belongs to his mother, who does not celebrate her freedom so much as her recovery: "I got my own ag'in!" she declares at last. Other stories in the *Atlantic Monthly* pursued the adventures that Henry must have had; Harriet E. Prescott's "Down the River" (October 1865) and Mrs. Launt Thompson's "Story of a Contraband" (June

1875) detail slave stories of escape, while in Rebecca Harding Davis's "John Lamar" (April 1862) and Louisa May Alcott's "The Brothers" (November 1863) other Henrys moved at will to violate Old Homestead sanctities and draw blood.

By contrast, Twain gives Henry's story to his mother to tell and thereby substitutes Old Homestead constancy for the Adventurer's search, as Auntie Cord may well have done before him. Both the search and the auction invigorate Twain's narrative, however: the search carries readers out of the kitchen through a deft shift in narrative perspective, and the auction provides the language and occasion for Southern injustice to bring about domestic collapse. The possible stolidity of home-centered action is thereby offset when slave families come into focus by the audacity of slaves in escaping and by their vulnerability to sale, neither of which challenged the free labor ethic of white audiences in the North.

Imagining the uncertainty of slave homes in "A True Story" also suggests how gender driven the slave narrative tended to be as a genre. In the account that Twain provides, opting for freedom and moving out are cast as masculine, opting for service and staying put are cast as feminine. Where male slave narrators risked everything for freedom, as Jean Fagan Yellin has observed, female slave narrators held out for freedom and a home.[26] Without requiring the large canvas of *Uncle Tom's Cabin* or *Incidents in the Life of a Slave Girl*, "A True Story" demonstrates in its considerably more limited scope the preeminence of domestic responsibilities even for slave women, at least as they were articulated in Northern magazines whose writers and readers were weaned on domestic fare.[27] In "A True Story," both Auntie Cord and Henry also work: she as a cook, he as a barber. Both therefore ensure their success in the world of Northern industry to which they emigrate and to which Twain's narrative was directed.

While such nineteenth-century domestic strategies have come to haunt black women and their communities in Moynihan's America, the welfare state and the institutionalized poverty of female heads of household were unimaginable during the years after the Civil War. Rather than inviting suspicion, Twain's purpose in "A True Story" was to promote respect for a common humanity with emancipated slaves and thus to undercut the racial stereotypes that continued to circulate in the Northern press. In the story's opening scene, the laughing darkey on the porch steps calls upon Misto C—— to recognize the "trouble" she's seen; ironically or not, she points out that slave husbands loved their wives just like white men, and slave mothers likewise loved their children. "De Lord can't make no chil'en so black but what dey mother loves 'em an' wouldn't give 'em up, no, not for anything dat's in dis whole world," declares Aunt Rachel. Her claims on her children assume a formal correlate: she is clearly better prepared to tell her story than Misto C——, whom she squeezes out of the narrative's catbird seat early on.

That Auntie Cord could not likewise tell her own story in 1874 is unfortunate, especially since the account that Twain provides nowhere suggests the "discourse of distrust" that Robert B. Stepto sees as endemic to the stories that black narrators address to white audiences.[28] Still, the story's attention to reconstructive strategies is in place: not only is Misto C—— trounced, but Aunt Rachel's language replaces the tamer talk of her employer. His opening description of how she was "chaffed without mercy" pales beside her claim that she "wa'n't bawn in de mash to be fool' by trash!" Her refrain is itself geared to correct misperception ("I want you niggers to understan' dat I wa'n't bawn in de mash . . ."), just as her final words remind Misto C—— of his initial mistake. In its language, narrative strategy, and structural design, "A True Story" makes reevaluating character the central concern of black storytelling, a robustly formal strategy for proposing reconstruction as a substantive theme in this Old Homestead narrative.

It is somewhat surprising, then, that the class biases that bolstered the plantation tradition at the expense of antebellum slaves remain in place. Aunt Rachel's opening appeal to a common humanity is offset by her later insistence that she did not cook for "small-fry officers" or welcome "dem common sojers" in her kitchen. What she cannot abide about the band members when they arrive is that "dey *never* could git along widout puttin' on airs." Then as throughout the story, the refrain she summons up confirms her social position and that of her family as above the "trash," which appears to include almost all other blacks in sight. Even Henry finally sneaks under her stove door, his eyes "a-lookin' up" into hers. While it is impossible to know what Auntie Cord brought to her story and how differently she might have told it to her family at home, it is certainly true that in the narrative the *Atlantic Monthly* circulated in the 1870s the trappings of social rank define Aunt Rachel's position as noticeably as they did the plantation world she gladly leaves behind. Whether her standing was invoked to curb "trash," to substantiate Auntie Cord's anger after the auction, or to fuel the radical program to which the magazine's writers and readers lent their considerable support, the appeal to social authority is unmistakable. Its effect was to establish Reconstruction on the basis of social standing and inherited authority, another way in which family structure left its mark on the volatile events that Civil War stories chart.

CHAPTER TWO

The Romance of Union
as National Metaphor

THE NATIONAL HOUSEHOLD that "A True Story" represents was ample enough to place Aunt Rachel and Misto C—— on the same porch steps as Reconstruction neared its close. But when Twain sent his manuscript to the *Atlantic Monthly* in 1874, the Constitutional underpinnings of paramount national citizenship, which the Thirteenth Amendment had helped to secure, were already beginning to wobble. The year before, the Supreme Court had upheld a lower court decision against Myra Bradwell, who had originally brought suit in Illinois because the state refused to admit her to the bar. Appealing a judgment based on divine sanction for "different spheres of action" belonging to men and women, Mrs. Bradwell relied upon the new Fourteenth Amendment, which guaranteed federal protection of individual liberties against state usurpation.[1] Increasingly cited as landmark civil rights legislation and invoked to this day more often than any other addition to the Constitution, the Fourteenth Amendment from its inception sparked debate on the vigor of the states within traditional Federalism as they met with the authority of the General Government nationwide. At the heart of the Constitutional crisis in the 1860s and 1870s were the terms on which the national household would come together after the Civil War.

As Congressional debate on the Fourteenth Amendment was to reveal, however, the manner in which domestic rhetoric would be deployed shifted precipitously during the two years that elapsed between the amendment's passage in 1866 and its eventual ratification in 1868. What began on Capitol Hill as a cooperative gesture toward erring children was transformed by the resistance of Southern legislatures into a struggle for conquest that would humble the Southern "bride." Given the mounting language of gender relations rather than the generational relations that had recently characterized the "national family," it is significant that Myra Bradwell sought in her brief to cancel the claims of husband and family by representing herself to the State of Illinois as a *feme sole,* a bid that would prove equally unsuccessful in Springfield and in Washington. On both occasions, the court's decision turned first on the fact that she was married and then on the fact that she was female, thus bound by God and nature for the domestic sphere. On either score, the family paradigm that even a *feme sole* could not seem to escape after 1868 signaled less a movement toward rehabilitating Revolutionary guarantees than a summons to submit to the rule of traditions, statutes, and men.

That the "old homestead" would never be quite the same was clear even in literary magazines, where Old Homestead stories began to fluctuate after Appomattox. On hand, however, was the comparative vitality of the Romance, a genre that by definition made way for a new "union" to emerge. Less fixed to a specific place than Old Homestead stories, Romances were also more receptive to change, which allowed for the "new homestead" that marriage would establish, sometimes on a national scale. In their fashion, Romances nonetheless served domestic ends by positing change as both necessary and desirable. Declaring love made characters more malleable than did kinship ties, more likely to preempt loyalties that were always already in place, and thus more susceptible to the pull of national citizenship where their parents had privileged states' rights. Instead of confirming Revolutionary inheritance, Romances helped transfer Reconstructive allegiance at the altar of civil responsibilities.

The political function of such stories is most apparent in Eliza-

beth Haven Appleton's "What Five Years Will Do" (*Atlantic Monthly,*
November 1868), a representative story that is couched as a series of letters punctuated by comments from a Northern governess who accepts
"the comparative claims of the general and the State governments."
At the story's opening in Virginia during the summer of 1860, Miss
Gardiner's gentlemanly employer can already see that he will have to
stand by "his people" and go with the Confederacy, a common refrain
throughout the seceding states. But by "his people" Colonel Ridgeley
initially means those in the slave quarters; in volunteering for active
duty he stands ready to protect his home and the larger plantation
family for which he feels responsible. Events like the desertion of the
slaves shift his allegiances, however, and thus shift what the phrase "his
people" signifies. When the story draws to a close in Paris during the
months after Lee's surrender, his daughter sees "his people" as "his
State . . . his friends . . . the people he was so proud of belonging to."
Bridging the gap between personal and political affiliations, Colonel
Ridgeley himself observes to the Northern major that his daughter
will marry: "I am not the only Southerner who thought he was doing
his duty in standing by his State. Not for slavery, —you know what
my feeling has always been there, —but because we really believed
that our first duty was to our State, —to go with her, right or wrong."
Continuing to develop before the story's final paragraph, the Southern
emphasis of "our best men" itself lapses into a national recognition of
"our country's claims," as the Southern daughter prepares to become
the Northern bride.

Romances were adept at reassigning loyalties. Where Old Homestead stories favored parental decision, Romances favored youthful
choice. Where Old Homestead stories favored the stable household
that Colonel Ridgeley inherited, Romances favored the relocation that
Ida's marriage would require. Geared toward moving on rather than
staying put, Romances were also more narratively dynamic: instead of
the figure of the house invaded, they established the sequence of "girl
meets boy, chooses lover over decoy." In fact, Romances inherently
based personal identity on choice twice over: once in embracing the
lover, and then later in rejecting the decoy. So, too, a second chance was

often the predictable result of love's missteps, if only to keep the plot moving along. Throughout the 1860s, and particularly when South-ern states were gradually readmitted to the Union, Romances weighed love over duty, free choice over inherited loyalty, in characteristic ways that made the genre peculiarly instructive in the contest for political authority, the more so when love matches failed.

Out of some 321 stories of the war, about 98 moved toward marriage during the fighting and its aftermath; another 88 combined romance with stories of other types, more often Old Homestead stories that simi-larly buttressed home and family. Marriage thus figured in well over half of the narratives about the war: some 186 stories, or 58 percent of the total, as compared with 116 Old Homestead stories, though some stories figure on both counts. These numbers were distributed unevenly over the period between 1861 and 1876, which at first suggests a steady decline: 115 appeared during the war, 46 between the end of the war and the end of the decade, and 25 by the Centennial year. But setting aside the barrage of stories from *Harper's Weekly* reveals that produc-tion remained fairly constant in other magazines throughout the war and the period of Constitutional reform: 42 romances of some sort appeared before 1865 and 42 more before 1870, by which time most of the seceding states were represented in Congress once again and Romances began to drop off.

During that time, however, the narrative offices of regeneration were not always enlisted following Appleton's cross-sectional example, nor was a national metaphor always their aim. Before 1870 only 28 stories saw another Southern girl like Ida Ridgeley fall for another Major Thayer from the North, many times in *Harper's Weekly*. Some 17 addi-tional stories inverted gender assignments so that a "Miss Thayer" loved her "Mr. Ridgeley," often with more complex and disastrous results when sectional politics ran afoul of gender prerogatives. Yet against these competing bids to draw North and South together were some 141 romances in which Thayers sought Thayers and Ridgeleys sought Ridgeleys, with the sectional edge going decidedly to the North-ern characters and the more numerous Northern magazines and read-ers who preferred them. Girls from Massachusetts chose boys from the

Bay State, girls from Virginia chose boys from the Old Dominion. Elastic as Romances proved to be while the terms of "restoration" were contested, more than two stories out of every three attended to local affairs rather than to national reunion, another sign that national citizenship was as new to popular audiences as it was to the representatives they sent to Congress.

From the early days of organizing regiments, in short, the boy next door was most likely to come into narrative focus, sometimes so much so that the formula shifted to "boy meets girl." Whoever carried the action, the course of true love had been laid out often enough that the Civil War sometimes served as backdrop for a narrative engine running, under its own steam, into problems common to the genre: unacknowledged love or love unreturned, a coy mistress or a rival's jealousy. Still, lovers in the North occasionally faced problems that arose only with the war: Wall Street trading in Fred B. Perkins's "Thomas Elliot's Speculations" (*Harper's Monthly*, February 1863), buying substitutes in "Buying a Recruit" (*Harper's Weekly*, 12 November 1864), false casualty reports in Harriet E. Prescott's "Mrs. Buswell's Christmas" (*Harper's Weekly*, 31 December 1864), and political chicanery in Fitz Hugh Ludlow's "A Reformed Ring Man" (*Harper's Monthly*, August 1867).

Southern stories likewise acknowledged the war's imposition on ordinary happiness, though not so much in the deals lovers struck as in the strikes they were dealt: the suspended communications after battle in J.F.S.'s "An Amor-Cable Agreement" (*Southern Literary Messenger*, April 1862), the failing Southern fortunes in Maude Evelyn William's "The Young Priest" (*Lippincott's*, December 1868), and the damage caused by a speculator in "Road-Side Stories, II–III" (*Land We Love*, December 1866 and January 1867) or Union troops in Caroline Marsdale's "The Refugees" (*Southern Magazine*, September 1873). By war's end, even readers of *Harper's Monthly* could hear the bell tolling for Southerners in John Hay's "Shelby Cabell" (October 1866), when a onetime diplomat from the South who is disenchanted with "ouah cause" and disappointed in love jumps from the Arc de Triomphe. Imagining that final moment as his personal success in suicide, Cabell earlier explains what he would achieve: "The adoring world would have gathered up the scattered relics of the real man, while the Ideal Image would still have stood on high, defying the storms of heaven and history" (602). Though his remedy was extreme and his story appeared in the Northern press, Shelby Cabell spoke for other Southerners in 1866 who had little left to lose but their lives and none of the sustaining affection that other lovers enjoyed in print, especially in the North.

More often, however, the promises of the genre were tested by the same wartime demands that invaded family homes: enlistment and battlefield action, which could lead to death or, worse, prison. But where the call for volunteers registered in Old Homestead narratives as a crisis, wartime service frequently emerged in Romances as an opportunity, an occasion for characters and writers to break new ground. A bold example is "Colonel Charley's Wife" (*Harper's Weekly*, 8 October 1864), in which a young girl from New York enlists and serves for two years as "Mark Wilson" before marrying her colonel and becoming "Mother Jane" to his troops. In the interim, when most of the story takes place, Mosby's guerrillas pin down a party of bluejackets reconnoitering near the Potomac in 1863, and it is "Mark Wilson" who volunteers for a hazardous run out of the cut and along the gully back to camp. Only when she is badly wounded and the hospital surgeon compassionately moves her to a private house is her identity revealed. The "bully gal" never makes lieutenant, as she was promised in the cut; even bona fide adventure stories never allowed female characters to fight publicly during the Civil War. Instead she weds her enterprising captain; but Romance conventions did permit an altar made of regimental drums and a bower decked with flags. Her "new homestead" turns out to be a house in Alexandria that becomes a soldiers' hotel, a decided improvement over the outhouse in which her "she-devil" of a stepmother had locked her before she enlisted. In the story's closing scene, her son has become the pet of the regiment and Sergeant Blake is telling her story to new recruits, indications that "Mother Jane" is bringing new life to the regiment she originally served.

While the narrative latitude marking Jane's character was unusual and therefore an unlikely alternative for other heroines stuck at home, the capacity of the Romance to turn a character's loss into a narrative's gain is demonstrated when a character like Ella Morton in Izilda's "A True and Simple Tale of '61" (*Southern Monthly*, December 1861) becomes a nurse after her lover dies at Manassas, or Mary Ostrander in William W. Sikes's "One of My Scholars" (*Harper's Monthly*, October 1865) is adopted by her lover's mother after he dies imprisoned at Andersonville. In both instances, as in "Colonel Charley's Wife," the story's denouement is extended long enough to give the protagonist a new destination, the narrative a further sequence to chart, and the genre a more formal claim to regenerative status. Rarely do romantic leads return to the homes they left; Jane Hemmings prefers a soldiers' home to an outhouse and Ida Ridgeley elects an apartment in Paris in lieu of a scarred Virginia manor. Elsewhere, if protagonists and their intended spouses survived the war, they began anew; if the war proved too expensive, they devoted themselves to the cause. Either way the Romance typically valued love and duty rather than blood, how sweethearts acted rather than who kinfolk were.

The genre thereby allows for the social changes that Reconstruction provoked: unlike their parents, lovers were uniformly too young to be limited by what they had inherited and too protean to be defined by what they had lost. None of the problems that routinely waylaid young lovers in local romances were by themselves insurmountable: wills could be broken, slaveowners escaped, class differences bridged, false rumors dismissed, romantic illusions set aside, and border territory crossed. Even death, which signified the end of Old Homestead stability, could spell the beginning of Romance opportunity, since many protagonists refused to fold their tents and go home. As Ella Morton observes to her dying volunteer, "Instead of giving way to my grief, I will renounce it as you did happiness and ease, and henceforth devote myself to the care of those that were your brothers" (282). Defining her new "family" by civil ties, Ella reveals that the Romance's essential transformation—from daughter to bride, from old homestead to new, from "I" to "we"—could absorb the civil responsibilities that a newly emerging nation imposed, whether Federal or Confederate. In their role as citizens, concludes Izilda in the *Southern Monthly*, women had their own mission to be brave, from which they would "reap the reward of having done all for their country and the great cause of constitutional liberty that they could" (282). Refusing her father's wish that she return to Tennessee, Ella remains in Richmond to tend the wounded, much as Northern sweethearts from Massachusetts and Connecticut would remain at hospitals in Washington, D.C.

In fact, in those Romances that took their cue from recognized wartime roles for women rather than from a preemptive narrative design for reunification, many Northern and Southern lovers responded to the Civil War in remarkably similar ways. Because soldiers generally went away to war, in the South as well as in the North, the women who cared for them voiced the same encouragement to enlist and the same fear that their men would never return. Because they were generally exchanging one household for another, sweethearts anywhere might deal with fathers who advised and mothers who meddled. Because they pinned their hopes on sentiment, lovers were routinely vulnerable to enticing rivals and misguided passion. For these historical, familial, and generic reasons, sweethearts often came where their love lay scheming, to paraphrase Stephen Foster's lyric, with little regard for sectional friction.

So common were the patterns of local affairs, from magazine to magazine and region to region, that the same story was carried by both the Northern and Southern press in 1863. Only modest changes were necessary in a narrative about a girl who gives away her gold piece to a scarred stranger whom her father refuses to help, though neither knows that the dusty soldier has saved their boy from death and will eventually marry the pretty daughter. In "A Gift by the Way-side" (*Harper's Weekly*, 26 September 1863), the girl is a "little wild-flower of the hills," her brother fights in a skirmish along the Potomac, and the lovers eventually marry "among the fine folks down in Boston" (619). In "Sybil Miller; or the Wounded Soldier" (*Southern Illustrated News*, 7 November 1863), the girl is a "little wild flower of the valley," her brother fights at Gettysburg, and the lovers eventually marry "among the fine folks down in Richmond" (142). But from the old farmhouse where Sybil gives away her coin to the little music room where she sees it again, the stories are otherwise identical, even to the "delicate type of beauty" that simultaneously "belongs as much to the 'frozen North' as its pine forests and cliffs of eternal snow" and "belongs peculiarly to the Sunny South." Ever adaptable, local romances made the war familiar because their problems were so widely shared, their settings so recognizable, and their structure so amenable to the regional details that transformed the new demands of citizenship into the old sweet song of love.

Yet overarching such local concerns were the romances designed to reunite the country through a new national union. Fewer in number, they still increased during the war as did local romances, generally for the same reason: *Harper's Weekly* was both early and energetic in circulating such paradigms of national regeneration. Between 1861 and 1865, 32 of the 115 romances that appeared reached across the Mason-Dixon line, as compared with 13 out of 46 romances between 1866 and 1870, and only 4 out of 25 thereafter. In other words, slightly more or less than a quarter of all Romances aligned courtship rituals with sectional politics. Where romances on the whole were published fairly consistently in the middle years of the war, those that oriented the genre to national issues more than doubled after 1862 to fully 42 percent of the total in 1864. Again, where romances on the whole declined after 1865 and then increased markedly during 1868 and 1869, the enthusiasm for moving beyond local affections crested somewhat later: national romances represented 29 percent of the total in 1870 and 50 percent in 1869. Popular romances thus emerged as national metaphors when Northern ascendancy was most pronounced: after Lee was turned back at Gettysburg and after Congressional Reconstruction was most rigorously in place.

More formally adroit, these were romances in which the generic promise of compassion, improvement, and regeneration was tested even as the cast of characters was assembled. While local affairs tended to identify the problems that Northern lovers shared with their Southern counterparts, national romances used gender distinctions to articulate sectional differences that the lovers were meant to resolve in marriage. So in Appleton's "What Five Years Will Do," Horace Thayer represents the Army of the Potomac and the General Government, rough country stock and Northern social mobility; Ida Ridgeley supports Lee's Army of Northern Virginia and state government, country manors and select Southern society, all on her father's behalf. The social cum sectional contrast was widely employed: in "How Miss Avoyelles Kept Her Promise" (*Harper's Weekly*, 9 July 1864), New Yorker Garry King is a poor, would-be cotton factor and Grace Avoyelles a rich Louisiana heiress whose uncle manages miles and miles of her cotton fields. In John W. De Forest's "Rum Creeturs is Women" (*Harper's Monthly*, March 1867), Frederick Huntington stands for Yale, the provost-marshall's office, and Northern civil order, while Fannie Pendleton embodies Virginia, a failing plantation, and Southern guerrilla warfare. In each story, the lovers marry, generally at war's end; in each story, sectional tensions are resolved when she favors love over duty so that he can remain loyal to the Union. "With the masculine creature," explains De Forest, "love is an episode, and is not worthy of being related with that richness of detail which it deserves when the sufferer is that of the other sex whose inner life is epitomized in the word Affections" (486). Since Fannie Pendleton's "Affections" are undivided—her father has died, much like Ida Ridgeley's mother and both Avoyelles parents—her loyalty can be given wholly to the marriage and family that provide a more portable home and a way to begin anew. Out of difference, which the Romance can code as gender roles, submission is made "graceful" and the North, the General Government, business, and law are seen in these stories to prevail at home when the Army of the Potomac succeeds in the field.

The girl could even win the boy across the way if he were Southern and she Northern, though such cases of apparent political muscle in the arms of women were rare. More likely was the balked paradigm of "Love and Duty" (*Harper's Weekly*, 23 November 1861), a story in which Northern nurse and Southern officer both die when a converted church comes under Confederate fire. Still, the romance might work if the Southern lover had already emigrated to the North before Fort Sumter fell, as in Ella Rodman's "My Mission" (*Continental Monthly*, December 1863); if the Southern lover were wounded and, under the

Northern nurse's care, ready to give his parole for the duration, as in "Becky Vane's Valentine" (*Harper's Weekly*, 20 February 1864); if the Southern lover were so smitten with the heroine's principles that he fought for the Union, as in "A Southerner's Courtship" (*Harper's Weekly*, 23 July 1864); or if the Southern lover recognized his slave's humanity, as in Helen W. Pierson's "In Bonds" (*Harper's Monthly*, September 1864). Successful or not, such romances appeared infrequently, however; after 1864, they vanished altogether, but for a brief resurgence in 1869–70. Scanty in Northern magazines and absent in the Southern press, these inverted national romances between a "principled" North and a "manly" South reveal how keenly gender assumptions bore on the sectional differences that the genre sought to reconcile.

How fully the same gender assumptions contributed to sectional debate in Congressional rhetoric varied remarkably as the war drew to a close and Reconstruction policy emerged. In 1864 and 1865, when emancipation was uppermost in discussions of Constitutional reform, gender distinctions figured most often in the guise of sibling rivalry ("wayward sisters") or parental largesse ("the domestic relations of parent and child"), if they figured at all. But when the discussion later shifted to the terms on which Congress would seat returning representatives from the South, the rhetoric of family stability began to give way, especially once it became clear that Southern states tallying five-fifths of each freedman were poised to elect Democratic officials to Congress and the Electoral College in even greater numbers than they had been apportioned before the war. When the Thirty-ninth Congress convened in December 1865, the same month in which the Thirteenth Amendment offically ended slavery, Republican John A. Bingham in the House proposed a further Constitutional change, an amendment that was to become the keystone of Congressional Reconstruction and the foundation of constitutional law for at least a century. Like Colonel Ridgeley on the Pont Neuf relinquishing state sovereignty with his daughter Ida, Southern politicians were thought ready to accept the "truer wisdom" of a common country and a future in the nation's capital that ratification would secure.

The Fourteenth Amendment first took shape in the newly appointed

Joint Committee on Reconstruction, chaired by Thaddeus Stevens (Pa.)
of the House and William Pitt Fessenden (Maine) of the Senate. After
several drafts and preliminary House debate in February 1866, the
"Committee of Fifteen" returned the amendment for fuller discussion,
in the House on 8–10 May and in the Senate from 23 May to 8 June. As
Stevens noted in reporting the omnibus proposal in May, the amendment was to include five sections: Section 1 guaranteed equal protection of the laws, Section 2 reduced Congressional representation in
states that excluded voters from the polls, Section 3 prohibited Confederate officials from voting in national elections before 1870, Section 4
repudiated the rebel debt, and Section 5 allowed for Congressional enforcement as the Thirteenth Amendment had the year before. After the
Senate made two changes, adding a sentence on citizenship to Section 1
and weakening Section 3 to apply only to Confederate officials pledged
to uphold the Constitution before the war, the House finally passed the
amendment in revised form on 13 June 1866. Two years later, on 28 July
1868, Secretary of State Seward declared the Fourteenth Amendment
officially adopted, though only after the Reconstruction Acts voted by
Congress in 1867 had made ratification essential if Southern representatives were to be welcome in Washington.[2]

Because the Fourteenth Amendment was designed even in committee to secure the gains made by the Thirteenth Amendment and the
Civil Rights Act of 1866 and thus to establish the basis upon which
seceding states would return to the Union, the debate surrounding its
passage is a fair guide to the manner in which national citizenship
was at that time perceived. Most significant, given the contested legal
status of the seceding states, is the language in which both they and
the state of the Union were represented: the more dire the analogy,
the more pressing the need for Constitutional action. On that score,
Stevens set the terms for the discussion when he spoke of "a plan for rebuilding a shattered nation." As he put it, "In rebuilding, it is necessary
to clear away the rotten and defective portions of the old foundations,
and to sink deep and found the repaired edifice upon the firm foundation of eternal justice." Thereafter, debate in the House centered
on how much damage "the household" had sustained. Those who ar-

gued against the amendment, like Thayer of Pennsylvania, spoke of the "original landmarks of the Constitution" and the "military despotism" that centralization would bring. Those who favored Constitutional reform, like Schenck of Ohio, spoke of "the right to subdue" the seceding states and the need "to subject them to obedience." Thus, some insistently favored restoring the Constitution "unimpaired," while others sought a more coercive amendment that would fundamentally inhibit state jurisdiction as never before.[3]

The positions representatives took produced distinctly different maneuvers when domestic rhetoric was invoked. Granting the national "household" that Stevens posited and the Thirteenth Amendment helped to advance, the most remarkable exchange arose when the metaphor of a national family was introduced by General Schenck. Developing the theme of war as "conquest," he alluded to the "principle on which a father punishes his own child when he has misbehaved." Said Schenck: "In the domestic circle we shut the erring child up in a dark closet, or put him pouting in a corner, and keep him in disgrace away from the table, surrounded by the rest of the inmates of the family."[4] So, he claimed, the erring Southern states should be punished. To that, Smith of Kentucky responded that a just punishment did not require erring children to be exiled from home: "Now, I submit the question whether there was ever on the face of the earth a father who, though he chastised his child because of disobedience, refused that child, even after the chastisement, bread and clothing and a place in his house." How much more "unnatural" it was, said the Union Democrat, that "the great household of the nation" should refuse a place to those who wished to return. Reorienting Schenck's analogy, Smith invoked the wisdom of Solomon when he cast the Government of the United States as "our mother" and the Constitution and the Union as the child whom Northern and Southern harlots plotted to rend apart.[5] Not obedience to a stern father but mercy from a compassionate mother was key.

Underlying the analogy, whatever its form, was the ease with which a national "family" could be imagined in 1866, a bare year after the more hesitant maneuvers of Thirteenth Amendment debate brought home the question of race. Yet the ensuing roles within the recon-

structed family circle were still a matter of discussion. Responding to
Schenck's parent-child metaphor, Raymond of New York focused the
wariness about centralization when he questioned the disproportionate
assignment of power. "Well, sir," he observed, "this might answer if
the eight million people with whom we are dealing would consent to
be treated as children, and to regard us here in Congress as standing
in loco parentis toward them. . . . But they are not children. They are
men . . . fellow-citizens."[6] Finally, Stevens returned in his concluding remarks to the family terms on which the states would meet once
more. "Take them back as equal brothers?" he asked. With reference to
the Memphis riot in which belligerent whites had descended on black
neighborhoods just days before, Stevens charged: "Let not these friends
of secession sing to me their siren song of peace and good will until
they can stop my ears to the screams and groans of the dying victims
at Memphis."[7] With that the Fourteenth Amendment was brought to
a vote in the House and passed resoundingly.

In the Senate the same crisis in transition from the disrupted family
of the Revolution to the power politics of Reconstruction was apparent, once again with reference to the "national household" that was
quickly becoming a rhetorical commonplace. Fulminating against the
Committee of Fifteen as the "directory" and the "star chamber," Hendricks of Indiana attacked the Fourteenth Amendment as dangerous
remodeling: "The Constitution is to be changed; the foundations of the
Government are to be disturbed; some of the old oak timbers are to
be removed, and timber of recent growth is to be substituted. Upon
the foundations fixed by the fathers our institutions have rested firmly
and securely for three quarters of a century."[8] McDougall of California likewise invoked the country's "foundations" and "superstructure"
as he further elaborated a reconciliatory family metaphor. "Gentlemen
seek now what is called reconstruction," he observed. "There is no such
thing as reconstruction. There may be rehabilitation. We may take them
to our own house at home, those who wandered away, and again embrace them as brothers."[9] Reverence for the Revolutionary past rested
squarely, for such members, on leaving the country's domestic order
intact.

Upsetting the national family in 1866 was not so much a belligerent South as the ex-slaves whose political status was now uncertain. As
sponsor of the amendment for the ailing Fessenden, Howard of Michi-
gan spoke of the national future that freedmen would share and the
Fourteenth Amendment would help establish: "For weal or for woe, the
destiny of the colored race in this country is wrapped up with our own;
they are to remain in our midst, and here spend their years and here
bury their fathers and finally repose themselves." [10] Stewart of Nevada,
who was to advocate universal suffrage and universal amnesty in order
to get both freedmen and Southern states into the Union, elaborated
the domestic analogy: "The trying times which Mr. Lincoln thought
might come when the colored man could help 'to keep the jewel of liberty in the family of freedom' are upon us." [11] But the issue of civil rights
for ex-slaves opened the larger question of national citizenship for other
traditionally unenfranchised groups, at least for Cowan of Pennsylvania. Would citizenship be extended to the Chinese immigrants in
California? to the Gypsies in Pennsylvania? to the Indians across the
country? [12] The Fourteenth Amendment thus raised again the founding
issue of representation, with or without taxation. On these terms, what
President Johnson had called "rebuilding the shattered columns of the
Union," a more conservative reunion than Thaddeus Stevens proposed,
collided with the larger project of extending Revolutionary freedoms
to ex-slaves and of enlarging the citizenry that constituted the national
household.

When senators debating the Fourteenth Amendment employed a
family analogy to represent the unequal relations they foresaw, it was
not errant Southerners but traditionally excluded slaves who became
national "children." Challenging the amendment, Henderson of Mis-
souri insisted on the natural "inferiority" of slaves. "The father is the
patriarch and governor of the family, because of this inferiority. Until
the child is twenty-one years of age the father has the power of cor-
rection and enjoys the fruits of his labor." Citing Confederate vice-
president Alexander H. Stephens, he went on to claim that the "corner-
stone" of the government was the principle of inferiority, "that the
negro is not equal to the white man." [13]

When Yates of Illinois picked up the family analogy to different purpose, it became clear how ambiguous national "citizenship" was in 1866, how instrumental the role of freedmen would be in reconstructing the term, and how utterly the Revolutionary legacy of liberty and justice would be contested in the process. Looking back to the ratification of the Thirteenth Amendment at the beginning of the session, Yates observed: "I took the ground that the former slaves in every State of the United States, being made free by this amendment, occupied precisely the same position with any other part of the body politic, that a son of a colored man born in the State of Wisconsin under the broad aegis of this amendment to the Constitution, had the same rights that my son had." [14] Without finally resolving the confusing question of citizenship that extending rights to freed slaves had provoked, the Senate passed the Fourteenth Amendment by a narrower margin than the House on 8 June.

Subsequent House discussion of Senate changes was brief; before repassing the amendment, Stevens spoke of "patching up the worst portions of the ancient edifice, and leaving it, in many of its parts, to be swept through by the tempests, the frosts, and the storms of despotism." Philip Johnson of Pennsylvania asserted the need to address "reconstruction" rather than the "restoration" he preferred. "The great danger," he said, "is that the seceders may soon overwhelm the loyal men in Congress." [15] Fending off another invasion of the national household, Johnson voted with his colleagues to reconstitute the Union, to redefine national civil rights, and to reconstruct the South.

In the years since Congressional discussion and state ratification, the amendment's first section has emerged as by far the most significant guarantee of civil liberties since the Bill of Rights. Of principal note is the sentence originally drafted by Bingham in the Joint Committee on Reconstruction, with its attention to "privileges or immunities," "due process," and "equal protection of the laws." But in the spring of 1866, with the fall elections approaching, Congressional Republicans were far more concerned with suffrage in the South and Southern representation in Washington. Consequently, the amendment's second and third sections, designed to protect freedmen and to punish Confederate officeholders, occasioned more heated exchanges and a pronounced tendency to trade the Democratic figure of the merciful mother for the Republican figure of the lover bent on conquest.

In fact, the Congressional session that passed the Fourteenth Amendment likewise witnessed a shift in rhetoric that recalled earlier Constitutional debates and set the stage for disturbing rhetorical developments to come. While domestic paradigms continued to orient the debate in part, the move away from the figure of family solidarity revealed that the project of restoring the Union was slowly being recast. When the Thirty-ninth Congress had first convened in December 1865, President Johnson's report on the Southern states had noted that "sectional animosity is surely and rapidly merging itself into a spirit of nationality" which would further a "harmonious restoration of the relations of the States to the national Union." [16] But by July, after the Fourteenth Amendment had been passed and Tennessee had become the first Southern state to ratify it, the bill to restore that state to the Union was greeted with more sternness than harmony and a greater show of gendered clout than the president's reassurances had earlier inspired. Instead of family solidarity, the figure of female vulnerability recurred, as simple restoration gave way to more energetic repair.

The House passed the resolution to readmit Tennessee on 20 July, with a preamble acknowledging that the state had "shown, to the satisfaction of Congress, by a proper spirit of obedience in the body of her people, her return to due allegiance to the Government, laws, and authority of the United States." [17] The Senate voted down the preamble but carried the rhetoric of feminine submission into its discussion. Sherman of Ohio, for instance, observed that Tennessee had ratified the Fourteenth Amendment and that "she [had] complied with all the conditions you have imposed on her." [18] The import of his analogy to forced compliance can be measured against a similar observation about the growing tension between legislators and the president, who had also been forced to bow to Congressional authority. Instead of alluding to a willing bride, Sherman portrayed that rift as a fistfight deferred: "We have asserted the power; we have exercised the power; we have this day the power; and I will never surrender it; but I will not force it into his teeth and compel him to acquiesce in the assertion of the power . . . I will exercise it, but I would not thrust it into his teeth by a joint resolution." [19] Where Sherman might easily have employed the same figure for both exercises of Congressional prerogative, he cast the state of Tennessee as gracious and the president as standing firm.

Had the other Southern states moved as quickly to ratify the Four teenth Amendment, it is possible that the postwar "marriage" of North and South would have gone off without a hitch and the threat to John- son would not have resulted in an impeachment trial. Refusing to aban- don his efforts to restore the Union, however, the president from Ten- nessee encouraged Southern states to reject the proposed amendment and, one by one in the fall and winter of 1866, they did. By the fol- lowing spring, Congress was calling these states "rebellious" and their governments "bogus"; Southern Unionists were seen to be threatened by "barbarians" as civil turmoil in the South increased.

The result was the Reconstruction Acts of 1867, designed to curb a lawless and inchoate territory by dividing it into five military dis- tricts that Federal troops would patrol. In his speech "Regeneration before Reconstruction," Congressman George Washington Julian of Indiana caught the prevailing Congressional temper when he warned against too speedy a restoration. Arguing like many other Republicans that Southern states would rather lose apportioned representation than allow freed slaves to vote, a possibility that the amendment's second section permitted, he invoked the metaphor of a national "marriage" that was gaining troubled ground. Countenancing the sly maneuver to disenfranchise freed slaves, said Julian, would "pollute the very foun- tains of our national life by the unnatural marriage of the Constitution to the foul heresy of State rights." [20] In response, Congress moved to require new state constitutions guaranteeing impartial voting rights and to force Southern ratification of the Fourteenth Amendment. As Federal troops marched back into the South, Congress put the recon- structive wedding on hold without letting go of the shotgun that had brought the South to the altar.

With the advent of Black Codes and further civil disruption, the gen- dered rhetoric that greeted Tennessee's return to the Union in 1866 grew apace, as is evident in the Congressional debate on readmitting Arkansas almost two years later. The obedience that Tennessee had "properly" shown was still a prerequisite in the House but it had been contorted by the rancorous process of ratifying imposed state constitutions, a process that Congressional conservatives reviled. According to James Burnie Beck of Kentucky, the barbarians had won in Arkansas, where white men "like whipped spaniels on their bended knees lick[ed] the hand that scourged them."[21] Woodward of Pennsylvania, another Democrat, railed against the constitutions forced by "Federal bayonet"; as he put it, "If this be not the overturning of a sovereign State by Federal power and the forcing upon her a fundamental law not of her own choosing, the boys in school in this country will need to be taught the first principles of common sense."[22]

In the Senate, the discussion was, if anything, more vituperative and more geared to the language of sexual assault. Fowler of Tennessee, a Union Republican, attacked the bill establishing military governments as a "naked sword of power suspended by a fragile thread over the heads of these devoted States."[23] McCreery of Kentucky joined his Democratic colleagues in deriding the new Arkansas constitution. "It is neither the child nor the adopted child of Arkansas," he declared. "She spurns it from her presence and appeals to the Government and the world to save her character from the stigma of having given birth to such a monster." The residents of the state he portrayed as "prostrate and powerless" and the state itself as suffering the consequences of resisting the conqueror who required submission: "Chained to the chariot wheels of the victor, a captive and a slave, she swells his triumph, but speaks, moves, and breathes only by his permission."[24] More rapist than lover and more stranger than kin, the Senate passed the bill to readmit Arkansas on 1 June 1868, and then passed it again over the president's veto on 22 June.

Long gone was the Thanksgiving table that *Godey's* spread in 1863, or the "compliance" of Tennessee in 1866. By July 1868, when the Fourteenth Amendment was finally declared official, the "national household" created by the Thirteenth Amendment had disappeared. In its place, the need to safeguard the rights of freedmen and "nationalize" the South had recast the drama of Reconstruction as one of force and submission that only a fortunate few, like Ida Ridgeley, could escape in Paris.

The same fitful trajectory from cooperation to conquest can be traced in the contemporary journalistic response to Congressional intervention in the South. Not only the course of the Fourteenth Amendment through the ratification process but the editorial policy of various magazines and the shifting politics of seasoned observers revealed that there were alternatives to force in the North and growing fears of violation in the South. In "The Fruits of the War" (*Galaxy*, July 1867), for example, early Republican Horace Greeley diluted his antislavery policy into a surprisingly moderate stand on Reconstruction and a genuinely conciliatory rhetoric, as few had in Congress. Naturally Greeley insisted on the war's accomplishments: the preservation of the Union, the abolition of slavery, the end of future confrontation between North and South, and the collapse of state sovereignty. Rather than attack the South, however, he indicts the "dissatisfied croakers" of the North who were calling for Southern "gibbets" and "dangling carcasses." More subtly, he relies as the essay develops on a comprehensive "us," which initially appears to indicate a successful North ("State Sovereignty, as a practical assumption, will trouble us no more") but later subsides into a more generously national gesture. "Our former feuds," for instance, were not sectional and "our great civil war" has settled the slavery question forever. Where Greeley might have employed the same gendered logic that animated Congressional debates, he passes up the opportunities that fleetingly arise: the antebellum slave territory was indeed "more fertile, genial, and inviting," but more rhetorically potent were the "sacred marriage bond" that was denied to slaves and the claims for state sovereignty that "served as wadding to the cannon of Lee and Johnston, vanished in the smoke of Atlanta and Appomattox." Instead of applauding the Northern "empire" that the war had produced, Greeley offers a "warm hand" to the war's survivors and a cooperative effort at reconstruction. His concluding proposal to "rebuild the waste places of our common country" suggests the essentially conservative spirit with which many outside Congress still approached the reconstruction of the South.

In Southern magazines, such good grace was less apparent than an aggrieved sense that the foundations of Revolutionary America had been shattered. Consequently, R. L. Dabney sharpened the rhetorical struggle in "The Duty of the Hour" (*Land We Love*, December 1868), an address to the Eumenean and Philanthropic Societies of Davidson College in North Carolina that he delivered after the war had been lost, slavery abolished, and the Fourteenth Amendment ratified. For Dabney, the early metaphor of young men close to the South's maternal bosom exemplified the last, best hope that the legacy of "revolutionary sires" would be restored. But his family allusion wavers in the face of a new danger, that of "the fearful force of conquest and despotism," which in turn occasions the disturbing metaphor of a "nuptial scene" wrecked by a "brutal" use of power and a bride's forced submission. Dabney ties his metaphor specifically to the Confederacy when he speaks of the "gigantic foe" driven back at Manassas, the "violation of every belligerent right" thereafter, and the later "subjection" of the South. He warns his audience against "seduction" from honor, "ensnaring" oaths, and the "degradation" that their "conquerors" had imposed. To counter these, he returns to the family metaphor that he still sees embodying the South and the "glorious traditions" of freedom, now fatefully strained. "The death of a beloved child," as he puts it, "may determine its mother to bury its decaying body out of her sight: even to hide in the wintry earth that which, before, she cherished in her bosom. But its death will never make the true mother repudiate the relation of maternity to it, or deny its memory, or acquiesce in any slander upon its filial loveliness" (117). In fact, Dabney's concluding summons is not to the young gentlemen in his audience at all but to the women of the South, who rule in their homes "with the sceptre of affection" rather than the "domination" of conquerors.

That the American Republic was being redefined after the Civil War was commonly acknowledged, even by the conciliatory Greeley. That the Fourteenth Amendment was instrumental in that redefinition was the position Carl Schurz took in "The True Problem" (*Atlantic Monthly*, March 1867). As Schurz incisively observed, the proposed amendment would complete "the transformation of a community of masters and bondsmen into a community of citizens." The threat to such a "great social revolution," as Schurz saw it, did not arise from despotic national authority but from the Southern enthusiasm for "the old order of things" that Dabney in the *Land We Love* did his best to encourage. For Schurz, such devotion to the past spelled a commitment to slavery and an entrenched resistance to free labor as the only guarantee that "the fundamental principles of our system of government" would be extended to freedmen. Precisely because he advocated American democratic principles, Schurz looked for the very submission of the South that Dabney remonstrated against, that "obedience to recognized necessity" that could be "fulfilled in her social and political organization."

Pinpointing "the great transformation" he foresees, Schurz moves from recognizing the plural nature of the original American confederacy to championing the singular achievement of the forthcoming republic. Describing the citizens of such a republic, Schurz once again reaches for the family metaphor that Dabney used, with a wholly different result: "self-government" would indeed force the citizen "outside of the narrow circle of his domestic concerns" and into new civil duties. Recognizing that the "ascendency of Northern sentiment" derived its legitimacy from the Thirteenth Amendment, Schurz encourages the freedmen as "wards of the nation" to come of age, echoing Congressman Yates's concern for the sons of colored fathers and Congressman Stevens's plea on behalf of the black victims in Memphis. For each of them, the American family was constituted less by the "revolutionary forefathers" Dabney revered than by the reconstructive urgency to extend the promise of justice for all.

How the "great social revolution" would be secured in the South was nonetheless a pressing question in the months following the amendment's ratification, for the nature of political affairs in the Southern states would determine the success of the difficult postwar romance of union that popular narratives laid out. Nowhere is that clearer than in "Southern Reconstruction" (*Lippincott's*, February 1869), written by the Reverend Francis Mitchell Grace from the University of Tennessee at Knoxville. The family metaphor allowed Grace to propose two babes warring in a mother's womb, the Jacob of states' rights and the Esau of national sovereignty. He concludes, however, by describing the reconstructed country as "a natural union" in which "the energy and zeal of higher latitudes shall be joined with the grace and ease of Southern sentiment, where truth and power shall be subordinate to love." Once again generational continuity gives way to feminine submission in a union of "truth and power" in the North to "love" in the South.

The Reverend Grace finally praises "the more advanced intellect of the North" whose "dissatisfied croakers" Greeley had reproved, the "energy and zeal of higher latitudes" whose conquest Dabney had forsworn, and the "fostering hand of our great national government" which would deliver the capital and white labor whose enterprise Schurz had linked to the Fourteenth Amendment. Instead of a restored family, Grace proposes a reconstructed union, as the South he imagines takes at last the arm of her consort. "For weal or for woe, for better, for worse," he concludes, "we are to be henceforth one people," an unconscious echo of the language in which Howard first proposed the Fourteenth Amendment to a conservative Senate.

In the last years of the war decade, therefore, the romance of union had become a prevailing cultural figure for Reconstruction policy. The new national homestead could be won by love and compliance or by force and conquest, but the South would at length submit, even if she had to be chained to the chariot wheels of the triumphant North. Less evident in contemporary rhetoric were the imagined consequences of Southern resistance, for the freedmen that Northerners aimed to protect or the national union they were determined to enforce. For that reason, the Romances circulated by popular magazines are revelatory, not so much when love's course ran true as when love's labors were lost. Though in most Civil War love stories girl met boy and chose appropriately, a few strained the conventional promises of desirable change fatally, in ways that are as culturally significant as the choices of youth over money or experience over enthusiasm when they fared well. The few failed Romances suggest what could hinder the transfer of affections at the altar of national allegiance, what in the Revolutionary past could deflect a Reconstructive future.

Of the 186 Civil War Romances, about 25 collapsed on a national scale. They were published entirely by Northern magazines and generally appeared in clusters: 11 surfaced during 1863 and 1864, another 8 during 1869 and 1870. Since Romances of all descriptions were more numerous in these years, it is possible to read the appearance of these fractured narratives as statistically predictable and formally shrewd. But from the earlier years of Northern successes on the battlefield to the later years of Congressional Reconstruction, the failure quotient almost doubled, while the reasons for broken vows changed remarkably. In 1863 and 1864, when emancipation had been proclaimed, almost half of the failed Romances foundered because of the heroine's antislavery principles, which she refused to sacrifice for love. After the war, not a single such story appeared, despite Congressional preoccupation with the founding sin of slavery. Instead, the heroine's black blood, her willingness to cheat love in spying for her Southern homeland, or her unswerving loyalty to a degenerate South canceled all claims on the future. In each instance, the past proved difficult for would-be sweethearts to dismiss. Where wartime heroines forfeited love for duty, postwar heroines more often forfeited love for daddy, as their older and earlier affections failed to subside. Bound rhetorically to honor ties to the home, they could not renounce blood for choice, local loyalty for national allegiance, or the Old South for the New.

Exactly the reverse was true of the Northern heroines whose hearts were given to Southern lovers when the war began: they were seen as loyal to a principle rather than a place and thus allied with national aims by default. It was never their families who frustrated their choice; it was their commitment to liberty, which ought to have "unsexed" them and did not. Slavery was instead seen as the snake in their gardens, even when slaves were not welcome in their homes. As the protagonist of "A Wren's Song" (*Continental Monthly*, October 1864) observes at her lover's plantation, "What with my fear of snakes, and my dislike of the black servants, whom I thought either inefficient or impertinent, and my unconquerable liking for freedom, I was not so fascinated." Like Old Homestead stories, Romances could also founder in the antislavery cause without much formal recognition of black "servants." When the slave-bound home of the past ("the Sodom before the flood") dies with Laura's childhood love in "A Wren's Song," however, she is feminine enough to regret its disappearance ("there is nothing left of the old days") and yet Northern enough to move on. "I must now try to make myself a new life elsewhere," she finally decides, "and tomorrow I go forth, shaking off the dust that soils my garments." For other Northern heroines, too, the solid ground of affection became dust, the earth of a particular place "soiled" their principles, and they moved with "the promise of the rainbow" to a new national home distant from the "white cross" of the past.

In other failed Romances during and after the war, the past likewise figured as Southern, but it was more often female as well, with provocative results. Where Laura's status as heroine assures the virtue of liberty and a continuity with the Revolutionary underpinnings of justice for freedmen, the past that Southern heroines safeguard is tainted, deceptive, and crumbling, like the rotting edifice that radical Republicans wanted to renovate. The result is that choice, identity, and good faith are cast in doubt when the mulatto heroine of Maria Louise Pool's "Told by an Octoroon" (*Galaxy*, December 1870) tries to "outride" her "sad past" or the scintillating widow of "Trapped" (*Harper's Weekly*, 22 February 1862) betrays a foolish secretary with government secrets or the trusting Northern wife of a Southern veteran is murdered in W. C. Elam's "Murder Most Foul" (*Lippincott's*, November 1869) by his passionate Virginia cousin. In all three stories, a guilty past haunts the threshold of a new home, like the raving Virginia cousin who hangs herself in Elam's jail yard where the Southern veteran has been mistakenly executed. Arrayed in white, like the pale skin of Pool's mulatto or the deathly pallor of the "trapped" widow spy, the convulsing body of the jealous cousin on the scaffold complicates the issue of sectional guilt for *Lippincott's* readers and insinuates doubt about the justice of postwar retribution. Even Pool's grieving octoroon approves "the path love pointed out," which converts her slaveholding lover to the Northern cause and almost saves their happiness.

In these several stories, national romance succumbs to the sins of the past, one reason for the harsh rhetorical penalties that Congress sought to impose on a recalcitrant South. But the "gibbets" that Horace

Greeley feared and the "dangling carcasses" that he wanted to avoid impose upon Elam's otherwise reconstructive vision, his cross-sectional romance that initially seemed resourceful enough to rescue a blood-stained rebel from the "smoke and carnage and thunder" of Gettysburg. When the rebel hangs and his cousin hangs and his wife dies, there is nowhere for Elam's narrative to go, just as there is no articulate future for Pool's octoroon in the North or for the widow's victim in the Army of the Potomac. Forfeiting love, these protagonists forfeit their narrative capacity to choose, a disquieting signal that Reconstruction would proceed with a backward glance to broken promises even as "our country's claims" secured a debilitated Southern bride.

Yet the incisive accomplishment of the national Romances that failed in the late 1860s was to identify some retrogressive pull on heroines, one that readers would deem strong enough to thwart the genre's promised regeneration. For Pool's octoroon, the compromising agent was the black blood she inherited when her father and master seduced a slave. For the widowed spy of "Trapped," it was the mission she undertook for Confederate traitors. For Elam's doomed Northern wife, it was her husband's faith plighted already to family and section, later contorted into the mad Virginia cousin's spite. For Homer's Richmond mistress, it was the hidden tug of the fate of her slave, who actually appears closer to the open air of freedom than she does. In each case, love foundered on the shoals of past alliances, betrayed by those who had been loved before. Given the ideological offices of Civil War Romances, especially in transforming the old homestead of kin into the new homestead of country, it is revealing that John W. De Forest's postwar narratives occasionally refused the change of heart he foresaw when he began *Miss Ravenel's Conversion* in 1864 or even the convenient deaths of "Rum Creeturs is Women" in 1867. By 1868, when Southern intransigence could no longer be ignored, the heroine he imagined would be forced twice over to choose between a Northern future and a Southern past, a choice so fraught with domestic disaster and national import that it would again break the narrative in half.

John W. De Forest,
"Parole d'Honneur"

(*Harper's Monthly*, August and September 1868)

PART I

WHATEVER THE FIRST Monday of the month may be in other grand divisions of the earth, it is always "sale day" in South Carolina. On that day, with a wide-spread unanimity which has in it something of the sublime, as many auctioneers as there are court-houses in the State mount suitable elevations and shout "Going, going, gone!" over bottom-lands, uplands, wood-lands, houses, log-cabins, buggies, stock, and household articles past enumeration. It is unchallengeably the great day of the month; it is an institution, and lacks little of being a solemnity. There are South Carolinians who ride ten or fifteen miles to every monthly sale, and who would feel it to be something like Sabbath-breaking to fail in so doing, although mayhap they never bid off an article in their lives. Sale day is the occasion for meeting one's friends, hearing the gossip of the district, discussing the political news, learning market-prices, and making trades. By such as get drunk and fight it is also considered a proper time for those festivities.

After this introduction I need hardly say that there was a noticeable crowd in Brownville, South Carolina, on the first Monday of September, 1865. Quite a number of vehicles, wonderfully various in appearance, but mostly rough wagons or rougher carts or dilapidated buggies, with ragged little oxen or the sorriest of horses and mules, dotted Main Street throughout its visible length of over a quarter of a mile. Not more than two or three of these "conveyances" had leather tops; but some of the wagons were protected by rounded canvas roofs, usually rising to a peak fore and aft; and several of the buggies had white cotton umbrellas, six feet in diameter, standing in a socket fastened to the seat. The farmers' wives and daughters were in the shops trading, or sat patiently in the drizzling rain staring at the stir of the village. The sorry horses were munching their little bundles of corn-husk fodder, much put upon and plundered by the impudent cows and bushwhacking pigs of Brownville. Now and then a "lone woman," a widow of the "low down" class of whites, pipe in mouth perhaps, stalked through the mud with a long, mannish stride, bent on begging, or, in her own dialect, on "tryin' to git." Negroes were frequent, some busy and some lazy, and negro boys—these last "powerful lazy." The spires of four churches were in their proper places, and the Baptist Female College was where it should be. On the eminence across Reedy River rose the little stuccoed University, showing unnaturally magnificent through the enchantment of drizzle and distance.

Brownville boasted an old and a new court-house. With rare boldness the Commissioners of Public Buildings had placed the latter directly opposite the former, so that citizens might judge daily how much the village, the district, and the world had gained by the additional outlay. Hardly fourteen thousand dollars, one would say, unless speaking from a "legal tender" basis. The elder court-house was a jolly, plethoric, high-colored old gentleman of plain brick, his port-wine visage set off by a second-story portico of Doric fashion, as white as painted pine usually is after years of exposure. The lower floor was solidly vaulted, the tinned roof was steep and tight, and the building was likely to smile on the ruins of its successor. The new court-house was a stuccoed affair, with a fever-and-ague complexion, a tendency to castellation about the corners, and a broad perception of Gothic in the doorways and windows. It was meant for an airy structure, but it was also an aqueous one. The flat roof was a water privilege: it could outleak any other surface of its size. In short, superior bigness was the main brag of the new edifice over the old.

Around the court-houses, or rather between them, things were as they should be of a sale day. On the stone steps of the senior building Mr. Thompson Bulger, the auctioneer—a thin and seedy man, with a correspondingly emaciated and threadbare voice—was knocking down Hardin Boggs's farm for delinquent taxes. Around him were gathered fifty or sixty men, mostly in long-waisted frock-coats and narrow trowsers of gray homespun, tall and lengthy in limb, with faces even more thin and haggard than the Northern type of American. Here and there, on the outskirts of the group, were little knots of three and four, squatting on their heels in discussion or barter. Notwithstanding the drizzling rain there were not half a dozen umbrellas in the assemblage, nor did many persons take cover under the portico of the court-house. The general look of the people was hardy and fearless, with an occasional dash of devil-may-care pugnacity, although the mustache, that supposed emblem of fastness and fierceness, was less common than in a similar crowd of Northerners. The bidding was deliberate and considerate, and Hardin Boggs's estate went at a dollar an acre. However, Boggs himself admitted that it was "a mighty poo' track."

An interesting sale day this had been for Alexander M'Call—a handsomely built, tall, fair-complexioned, gray-eyed young man, who stood on the steps of the new court-house. Why it had been so we may learn from a dialogue between him and Harrison Few, the clerk of the District Court.

"Begun on the land, hey?" said Mr. Few, appearing in the doorway. "Well, Alec, how'd the furniture go off?"

"Oh, as well as broken-down things could be expected to go in a broken-down country," was the reply.

Harrison Few understood the half sigh of spiritual pain which accompanied these words. Although not far from six feet in the girth, red-faced, and nearly fifty years of age, he was a man of tender heart and delicate perceptions, who could imagine that it must be a hard trial for the family of old Colonel M'Call of Richland District to have its furniture publicly knocked down by the hammer of poverty. It had not been pleasant for him, the son of an overseer, and in a measure the architect of his own respectability, to see his horse, buggy, and harness go on last sale day to buy bacon and hominy for his family. Yet, accustomed as he was to these sacrifices of venerable and intimate belongings, he discovered a special hardship in this one. The M'Calls had been among the "highest toned" people of Richland District; the Colonel had owned two hundred head of "stock," and cultivated one thousand acres, besides holding twice as much more in "old-field" and wood-land; and it was quite painful to think of the widow of such a man being driven to sell her furniture for bread. Well, there was a great deal of trouble in the world, and that was a sort of consolation, though niggardly. He stepped out of the doorway, squinted at every corner of the lowering heaven, fired his tobacco juice at a hitching-post with comforting accuracy, and then stood there in the drizzling rain, as indifferent to it as the lean cows and saucy pigs. All this while he was thinking up some balm for his young friend.

"Well, Alec, the man who turned you off the track did as much by a crowd more," he said, for lack of better encouragement. "He sot in for a big stroke of mischief, and he done it."

"Confound him!" muttered Alec, sullenly, as he, too, stepped into the rain. "I don't care about myself, you understand," he resumed. "As deputy-sheriff here I am just as jolly as I ever was on the plantation. But I hate to see my mother and sisters pinched."

"Things have gone off well enough to give 'em a lift, I hope," answered Few, staring at the portico of the old court-house.

"Yes; I reckon so. Between what's left and what's sold we can lodge and feed two or three people. Do you know of any one who wants board?"

"Yes; that's just it. There's the post commandant, Cap'n Humphreys, was asking me this morning if I knew of a place. He's a right good fellow, Humphreys is, and it's sure pay," added Few, seeing that Alec scowled.

"I know; he's well enough," responded the young man, conscious that the elder was trying to persuade him to his own good. "I could put up with Yankees. I've fed them as prisoners, and been fed by them as a prisoner. The war is over, and I know it. But the women don't, Mr. Few."

"Yes, there 'tis; the women don't know it. I wish to God they did know it a little more'n they do. This scowling at Yankees an't a-going to help us, Mac. It'll keep out money and emigration. And there 'tis; we want money and emigration; them's just what we want."

He had been poking a chip into a puddle with his foot, and he now gave it a kick to launch it on its brief voyage. Alec, hands in pockets, was walking up and down in the thin red mud of the earthen sidewalk, with a gloomy frown under his slouched black hat.

"I say," resumed Few, with hesitation, "sha'n't I speak to Cap'n Humphreys about it?"

"No, thank you," answered Alec, still frowning.

"Well—no offense—I thought I'd name it to you."

Harrison Few had a profound respect for Alec M'Call, as being a descendant of high-toned gentlemen, although he was now only deputy-sheriff, with a curiously small income. He called him Alec and Mac, to be sure; but that was friendship—that was the Brownville way. He was himself called Hassy Few by half his acquaintance.

"All right; I am much obliged to you," said the young man. "But I know my mother and sisters wouldn't have a Yankee in the house. I can't blame them. Two brothers dead on the battle-field, you know, and our buildings all burnt, and the plantation turned into a common. Not so much as a fence-rail left, by Jove!"

"Yes, there 'tis; it's tough work forgiving. It's a big lift for the stoutest kind of a Christian," mused Few. After a minute he added, "Don't you mean to start the old place again some day?"

"Of course. But we can't do it till we can raise money to put up buildings. Hands won't sleep out of doors, you know. And they must have seed, too, and plows, and stock."

"Yes, there 'tis; hard to get a start. By George! it was as much as we could do to set in to work up here, where Sherman never come. Where he did come folks was broke up for a good while, of course."

"Where he did come he turned the country into old-field, as sure as you're born," answered Alec.

Like many another man Alec had two dialects—one for family life and choice society, and one for converse with out-of-door comrades; the former bearing the stamp of universal English, and the latter colored with provincialisms, and alive with inchoate metaphor. By-the-way, you must not infer from this local tang in his discourse that his manners were rustic. They were graceful, self-possessed, dignified, and not far from the ideal of lordly. He had never seen, to his knowledge, a better-born gentleman than himself; nor did he believe that there was any finer society in the world than that of his native district.

At this moment Mr. Few's eye was attracted by a female figure sitting in an open wagon on the opposite side of the street. Although a married man and corpulent, he had a keen eye for beauty in general, and never let a pretty woman pass without refreshing himself with a gaze.

"Who's that, Mac?" he asked, nodding his head in the direction of the wagon. "She's a right pretty gal, she is, and I don't think I ever saw her befo'. Wait till she turns her face this way again."

The object of curiosity was in rusty black, a common enough attire in South Carolina at that period; but there was that indescribable something in the outline and carriage by which youth proclaims itself to the eye. Yes, she was a stranger; the young man could tell by her back that she did not belong in the neighborhood; he had served writs all over the district without encountering that figure. And still it seemed to him that he had somewhere met it, and under pleasant circumstances. The young lady looked persistently at the auctioneer, and thus kept her face turned from the two gazers at the new court-house. The wagon in which she sat was an old, shackling affair, with newly added sides of rough boards and a seat which had evidently been transplanted from some defunct buggy. From the seat rose one of those huge white umbrellas already described. In the after-part of the wagon were a few articles of stone-ware, a trunk, and a little fodder.

The small bundles of corn husks and leaves had, of course, been brought for the benefit of the black mule who stood between the shafts; but one of those Brownville cows who lie in wait to plunder country cattle was already reaching out her neck and tongue for the crisp delicacy. Finding it a little beyond her reach, she rose on her hind-legs, planted her fore-feet in the vehicle, and seized a couple of bundles. Startled by the noise, the young lady turned, cut at the intruder with her whip, and seemed half inclined to give chase. It was indeed a serious matter; scarcely half a dinner remained for the mule. At the sight of that face Alec M'Call sprang across the street. The cow went off at a gallop, with her plunder dangling from her mouth; but our young deputy-sheriff was neither beaten by her agility nor daunted by the absurdity of the adventure; he kept up the pursuit until one bundle dropped after the other; then he brought both back to the wagon.

"Thank you, Sir," said the young lady, showing a beautiful set of teeth. "You have really done me a favor."

She was a brunette, with a clear, pale complexion, the blackest of eyes, and features of the statuesque type. She was extraordinarily handsome, and would have been as nearly a perfect beauty as is ever seen, only that there was a little too much breadth to her cheek-bones and a little too much strength in her lower jaw. But even with these defects, even with the determined, Helen Mar-ish air which they gave her, she was wonderfully handsome.

"I am happy to have obliged you," answered Alec, raising his hat and bowing in a style which would not have put his grandiose father to shame could he have seen it. Then the two looked at each other, each thinking, "I have seen you somewhere."

"You don't remember me," said Alec, the first to reach the point of recognition.

"Yes, I do," she answered. "You were in the hospital at Dalton."

"And you helped nurse me," he added, putting out his hand.

"But you have forgotten my name," she said, laughing again, with her hand in his. "It is Mollie Prater. Now you must tell me yours."

"Alec—" he began.

"M'Call," she interrupted; "Oh yes, Alec M'Call."

It was pleasant to him to hear his name repeated by those flexible rosy lips, and he continued to hold her hand until she gently withdrew it.

"And that was almost two years ago," she said; "and then we still had hopes, and now we are conquered."

"And ruined."

"Yes, and ruined. I never will forgive them," she continued, with an excitement which made her face less pleasing. "Other people may make peace, but I sha'n't. I am a Prater, and that is our way."

Alec's countenance became sterner than was its wont, but he made no spoken reply.

"You shouldn't have forgotten a nurse," she resumed, archly. "However, I am changed, I suppose," glancing at her rusty dress. "I was a school-girl then, and now I am a school-ma'am."

"And I am a deputy-sheriff," said he; "the deputy-sheriff of this district."

She burst into one of her quick, gay laughs. "Isn't it comical?" she said, "and horrible! What, sheriff here? Then we shall be neighbors. Don't you see my trunk? I have just come on to be schoolma'am in the Baptist Female College."

"Indeed!" exclaimed Alec, visibly gratified. "I wondered why you were here. I supposed you were going through to take the railroad for the low country. But is your father living in the district? I haven't heard of him."

"Of course you wouldn't hear of him in the district," she said, with a laugh which seemed slightly forced. "Georgia doesn't belong to your district."

"Well, you have had a long journey—for such a wagon as this."

"You mustn't laugh at my wagon, Sir; it is my best. Ah! there comes my driver; now I must go. You will call on me, I hope. I am going to live in the college, like a good, sedate, responsible schoolma'am."

"I thank you," said Alec. "I certainly shall come to see you. Good-morning."

With a slight suspicion that she wanted just at that moment to get rid of him, and with the glimpse of a reminiscence that he had seen that same old negro driver somewhere in the district, he made his bow and returned to the steps of the new court-house. But almost immediately these ideas were lost in thinking how handsome she was, and how pleasant it would be to see her frequently.

In a few days he found that to see Mollie Prater was very pleasant. He took his sisters to the college, and then Mollie called upon his mother.

"I wish I could board with you, Mrs. M'Call," said the young lady before many days of this acquaintanceship had elapsed. "It would be so much jollier than at the college!"

"I wish you could," sighed the impoverished lady. "We seem to get no boarders, and what we are to do soon I don't know. I beg your pardon, my dear. We are in such straits that I can't help thinking of making money."

"Can't we hunt up some boarders?" said Mollie. "I'll tell you what we'll do: Sophie and I will burn somebody's house, and make them go out to boarding."

"Yes, and Alec will arrest us," answered Sophie M'Call, a sweet-faced blonde of twenty. "Alec is perfectly awful on a sense of duty. You would arrest us and put us in jail, wouldn't you, Alec?"

"Ah! this is too sober a business to joke about," said the young man, with something like a groan. "I believe that women never do feel properly given over to poverty so long as they have a man in the house."

"Mamma does," responded Sophie. "She does take it to heart in a style that nobody can find any fault with."

Both Sophie M'Call and Mollie Prater were in calico dresses, cut and made by themselves. Neither of them had a silk; Sophie had a silk apron, and Mollie had an old bombazine; but that was all their finery.

"Yes, I do take it to heart," almost whimpered pale Mrs. M'Call, pressing one hand against the thin blonde hair, streaked with gray, which only partially hid her sunken temples. "If we don't have some boarders in another month we must come down to corn meal. Here we all are, living on Alec."

The son rose and paced the room rapidly. He was willing to bear his burden; but then he was not bearing it; he could not. His few hardly-earned, uncertain dollars a month would not support himself, his mother, Sophie, and his other sister Grace.

"Mother, we must give up this nonsense," he said, stopping short and facing her. "We must take in those Yankees. They were at Hassy Few again to-day for a boarding-place. The three will pay us sixty dollars a month, and the profit on that will keep us from starving. What do you say, mother?"

"I agree with you, Alec," answered Mrs. M'Call, while her two daughters simply whispered bitterly, "Yankees!"

Alec looked at Mollie Prater with a serious air which claimed her advice.

"Yes, I suppose you must do it," she said in answer. "You must try to live off the enemy; it is all there is left. Only I do hope you will keep on hating them. I can't bear that any Southerner should ever have any feeling for them but hatred."

"Mamma, if we do get a boarder, you must give me a handkerchief," put in Grace, a rosy, jolly girl of thirteen. "I haven't but two left, and they are right shabby."

"Don't be so absurd, Grace," replied Mrs. M'Call. "If you want a handkerchief, make one. There must be an old chemise somewhere."

"No, there isn't, ma. I cut up the last one for handkerchiefs the day we made Chloe a dress out of the red damask curtains."

"Well, *don't* pester me now," implored the heavy-laden mistress of the family. "Try to think of saving, instead of spending."

"But what will you do, Mollie?" asked Sophie. "You mustn't stop coming here, and you may meet these creatures."

"If I meet them I'll behave myself, and not throw plates at them. I'll remember that we can't afford to break the plates. Seriously, I will be civil."

"That is right," was Alec's cordial comment. "If we can't help our feelings, we can govern our manners. I surrendered with Joe Johnston, and that ended the war for me. I don't love Yankees, but I stand by my word. If I meet them, I will treat them well; and if I act with them, I'll do it like a gentleman. That is just where I stand."

"But you mustn't act with them," insisted Mollie.

"I may have to do it. Suppose the post commandant should call on me to aid him in some arrest?"

"Get around it," persisted the beautiful rebel, her eyes becoming almost defiant at the word "arrest."

"No, no," answered Alec, shaking his head. "I've sworn to be faithful in future to the United States. Word of honor! word of a gentleman!"

"Ah, that is going too far; I don't like that," she continued, warmly; then, suddenly quelling her excitement of manner, "Well, go and hunt your Yankees."

James Humphreys, captain of a company in a New England volunteer regiment, was a man of twenty-eight, no profession, moderate fortune, studious tastes, good breeding, and good breed. His two lieutenants, Jackson and Jones, had fought their way up from the ranks, and were farmers' boys who had attained their present social polish as clerks in country groceries. All three were tired of soldiering, tired of messing, and longed for the amenities of civil life, and especially for feminine society. Hence their persistent effort to obtain board in a respectable Brownville household.

Their first meal with the M'Calls was rather a grave and even solemn affair. The ladies, who had all cried that morning over "the lost cause," the ruined fortune, and the fallen sons of the family, sat down opposite the blue uniforms with an emotion which even Second Lieutenant Jones was able to guess of; and at the same time were, woman-like, anxious as to the proper serving of their table, and mortified over some of its napkin and crockery shortcomings. The two junior officers, always in awe of their captain, and stricken with bashfulness before the feminine M'Calls, ate with soldierly speed and in strenuous silence. Humphreys, fearful of hurting Southern sensibilities, trod charily and delicately in the conversation. The most noticeable circumstance of the occasion was, that all three guests glanced so often at Sophie M'Call as to put the girl's cheeks in a flame long before the close of the entertainment. The poor fellows had not sat down to table with a young lady before for years, and they could not help enjoying the consciousness of such a sweet propinquity with ravenousness, and, in short, were in a condition to fall in love on the smallest known provocation. It was evident enough that they had no desire to be Vandals in the eyes of Sophie M'Call.

"You have got a beau, Sophie," giggled Grace, as soon as they had left the room. "You have got three."

"Wasn't it perfectly outrageous?" answered Sophie. "How like idiots they did stare!"

But she cast a look at the one parlor mirror which remained in the family, and was not at heart so furious as she seemed. Her mother glanced at her and wondered whether she should have to keep nunnery as well as boarding-house. A Yankee for a son-in-law? Well, that could be borne; she had sunk very low in pride and pugnacity of late, had Mrs. Colonel M'Call; but he must prove himself a Yankee of character and property before he could have Sophie.

This trial, however, was not to be. A Saturday soon came on which Mollie Prater was caught at the M'Call house by a storm of rain, and had to stay to tea with the three Goths, or Vandals, whichever they might be. Captain Humphreys, an undersized man, with blue eyes and light complexion, was overwhelmed by the beauty of this tall, full-formed, dazzling brunette, and exerted himself with so much earnestness and cleverness to please her that the girl more than fulfilled her promise to behave herself. She talked with the barbarians, played whist, euchre, and muggins with them, and did not refuse the Captain's company when he sent for a buggy and offered to drive her home. From that evening the dominion and danger of Sophie M'Call were over.

"You have cut me out," she said. "It is right shabby of you, only I don't care."

"I suppose you don't. I suppose you care about it as little as I do. But, Sophie, I mean to make it a matter of some importance to *him*. I mean to make him propose, and refuse him."

"Oh!" said Sophie. She did not approve of the idea; she was kind-hearted, and had a high sense of honor; in short, she thought it was "rather mean in Mollie."

"It is a woman's only revenge," continued Mollie. "And I do hate these people—oh, I do! I do!"

As Sophie was still indisposed to either assent or object the dialogue dropped. But the flirtation which now opened between Captain Humphreys and Mollie Prater gave rise to complications which the young lady had not foreseen, and worried her more than she ever confessed to her confidante. The main trouble was that Alec M'Call became jealous of the Vandal, and as a consequence began to think himself seriously in love with Mollie. The human heart, at least when it is of the male gender, frequently works in this absurd fashion.

"I know it is nonsense," thought this young deputy-sheriff, glancing at his homespun suit in hopes that the beggarly spectacle might make him rational. "I know I can't support a wife. But confound the Captain!"

He had one advantage over his rival; he could call on the lady at the college, where she would not have dared receive a Yankee; and of this superiority he availed himself, driven by that "stirring of the blood" which benefits the race at the cost of so much trouble to the individual. Mollie was courted at one end of the village by Alec, and at the other by Captain Humphreys. The situation was pleasant, as any woman can imagine; but still it had its embarrassments, and demanded much serious reflection. What was she eventually to do with these two lovers? Should she refuse them both, or take—which? If Alec were able to work his plantation, or even if he had not his mother and sisters on his hands, she would have had no hesitations; but she knew as well as he that it would be pauperism for him to marry at present, or perhaps for years to come; and being a clear-headed puss, she was able to judge somewhat according to knowledge. At times the Captain was very attractive to her womanly ambition. He was a gentleman in his manners; he was well educated, even to the point of some fashionable accomplishments; and, what was decidedly telling, he was evidently deep in love with her. But the great point in his favor was that he could certainly support her. Ah, what a temptation that was to a young lady in a community that was "dead broke!" She thought of her father, struggling to feed his family on a hired plantation consisting mainly of "old-field," and she guessed shrewdly that, notwithstanding his service in the Confederate army, he would not reject a Yankee son-in-law who could lend him money. Yet, at times it was very pleasant to think of marrying Captain Humphreys and living stylishly in some Northern city. You could see this occasionally in her manner toward the Vandal.

"It seems to me that you have got over your hatred for Yankees," said Alec to her on one of the days when jealousy made life a burden to him.

"I don't know what you mean, Sir," she replied, tartly. Her indignation at this interference was all the greater because the remark had struck her in the midst of one of those fascinating reveries about Northern life. Alec made no reply, but looked exceedingly bitter, feeling that *la donna e mobile*. She saw his misery, guessed that it was for her sake, and softened toward him.

"See here, Alec," she said, gently, "do you think that a Southern lady should be uncivil to these people?"

"Oh, it's all right," he answered, rising and pacing the room, painfully conscious of his own feebleness and folly. "No, I don't think so. This non-intercourse idea is stuff. You mustn't mind me. I meant nothing. But it's horrible to be so poor," he continued, rushing on to show that he did mean something. "To be bankrupt and beggarly and a deputy-sheriff and have no home but a boarding-house kept by one's mother! I tell you, Miss Prater, that I sometimes wish I had been killed in the war. No outlook—no chance ahead—nothing but lifelong bankruptcy! I suppose you know that our plantation was mortgaged to its full value before the war, and that there isn't one probability in a thousand of redeeming it."

He felt now a little relieved; he had done, as he thought, what was honorable; he had let her know that he would marry her if he could, and that he could not. In reality he had, unconsciously to himself, made a powerful appeal to her heart. It was such an appeal as would be perilous to nine young ladies out of ten; and if he had proposed at that moment to Mollie Prater she would have taken him. An hour later, riding by himself on some errand of justice, this high-toned gentleman of twenty-three reflected that his conduct had not been altogether chivalrous, and felt much remorse of conscience over his selfish folly.

"I have no business to stand in the way of her luck," he thought. "She is a lucky girl to have such a fellow as Humphreys after her. He's a good fellow and a gentleman, if he is a Yankee; and he can support such a splendid girl in a style worthy of her; and I am a poor miserable dog, who can only offer a kennel. I have talked my last nonsense to her, word of honor! word of a gentleman!"

Strengthened in soul by these magical words, so much more of a spell in the South than in the North, he thereafter avoided Mollie as much as was consistent with civility, and in her presence bore himself like a mere acquaintance. It was a terrible thing to see the Captain sedulously advancing his courtship; but he endured it according to his ideal of a "chivalrous Southron," who was also a M'Call. What made the matter worse was that Humphreys did not suspect his state of mind, and frequently talked to him about Miss Prater.

"She is the most brilliant brunette that I ever saw," said the enamored Goth. "By Jove! I don't think there's another such pair of eyes in the

United States. And such a superbly moulded face! it's almost perfect Greek. Just a little too strongly marked about the cheek-bones and the lower jaw. But I like it all the better for that; it shows character, don't you think so?"

"Yes," admitted Alec, who had sometimes suspected that Miss Mollie possessed a trifle too much character.

"By-the-way, do you know any thing of her family?" inquired the Captain, not yet altogether deprived of forethought.

"I don't. Her father was colonel of a Georgia regiment, but I never saw him. I understand that he used to run a large plantation."

"They must have been nice people," persisted the infatuated soldier. "The young lady shows breeding. The fact is that it is almost impossible for such a perfectly formed woman to appear ill-bred."

"When are you going to take a trip with me into the mountains, Captain?" inquired Alec, unable to talk comfortably about Miss Prater.

"I really don't know when I can get away," answered Humphreys, who had been quite anxious for such an expedition a month previous.

Meantime Mollie had her talks about the Captain, not so much impelled thereto by the necessities of her heart as by the gossips of the village. "I hear that this commandant is playing the amiable to you, Miss Prater," said one of her married acquaintance. Mrs. De Gama Cobb, a refugee from Pensacola, was a dumpy, bullet-headed, dark-skinned person, with the blackest of eyes, a sheet of wavy black hair growing low on her forehead, and a downy black mustache. Her speech was rapid, her gestures ready and energetic, her whole style as unlike the Northern idea of what is American as is possible. Yet her family had been two hundred years on American soil. "You will excuse me for being so frank with you," she added, "but I hope there is nothing in the scandal."

"Of course not," replied Mollie, coloring with a desire to slap Mrs. De Gama Cobb for the interference, and especially for that word "scandal."

"Of course not," echoed the Floridiana, sarcastically. "Oh, that is an old history! All young ladies say of course not. But what I want to know is the truth. I don't care to hear commonplaces."

"Mrs. Cobb, what business is it of yours?" demanded Mollie, unable longer to keep her temper.

"It is my business, Miss Prater. You are a young lady all alone, without natural protectors at hand. Your father and mother are distant. I have taken an interest in you. I have received you. It *is* my business."

"Then, Mrs. Cobb, I wish that for once you would not mind your business. I can take care of myself. I am twenty-one years old, and even my father could not control me in this matter, and I certainly shall not let myself be controlled by others."

"But have you no regard for society—for the proprieties—for patriotism?" cried Mrs. Cobb, in a furious twitter, as if she were a very large and very angry canary-bird. "Marry a Yankee! A Southern girl marry a Yankee! The daughter of a Confederate colonel marry a Yankee! Oh, Miss Prater! you are not the person I took you up for!"

"If you have taken me up I wish you would let me down again," said Mollie. "And as for marrying a Yankee, who said that I was going to do it? Really, Mrs. Cobb, you—but I won't talk on the subject—good-morning, Madame."

"I don't comprehend how the principal of the college can put up with such things," was Madame's parting shot.

"I should like to see him interfere," answered Mollie, from her distance.

Mrs. De Gama Cobb's quarrels amounted to nothing. The little Spanish bantam had squabbled with nearly every lady in the village, and then had been immediately as friendly as before, but also as ready for another spurring match. Mollie had heretofore fought her in a joking humor; but this subject of the Yankee beau had become a sore one; and then, ladies have their cross days.

Not long after the above affair Captain Humphreys managed to have a private interview with his hostess.

"Mrs. M'Call—excuse me, Madame—something of importance to say to you," he stammered.

The lady looked at him anxiously, fearing that her table had given dissatisfaction, and that she might be about to lose her only boarders. Her affairs were already prospering meekly under their regular payments. Only that morning she had bought additional crockery at an auction, and would no longer be obliged to borrow dishes to supply her rare transients.

"It is through you, Madame," continued the officer, "that I have been happy enough to make the acquaintance of Miss Prater."

"Ah!" said Mrs. M'Call to herself, and went off on three trains of thought at once. One was that a Mrs. Humphreys would be another boarder; the second was, "I am glad of this, for it saves Alec;" the third was woman's sympathy with a love affair.

"For that reason," said the Captain, "and as she has no relations here, I feel bound to consider you her protector, and to say to you that I wish to make her my wife. I can give you proofs that, aside from my salary, I am able to support her; and—and—"

In short, the commandant of the post found it difficult to say all that he wanted; and Mrs. M'Call, pitying a lover, however much he might be a Yankee, came to his assistance.

"I understand you, Sir. But I can say so little! Really, I can not consider myself very much responsible for this young lady. I know little of her, except that she was kind to my son in hospital."

"And you will not object to my speaking to her?" demanded the Captain, who had a vague idea that every body south of Mason and Dixon's line might have a right to object to his marrying Miss Prater.

"No, I will not—I can not. How can I refuse, or consent? Really, Captain Humphreys, you must not make me responsible."

"Oh no, Madame! I did not think of such a thing. I only wished not to make you responsible—to warn you, or at least—but perhaps I have blundered. At all events, I am so obliged to you!"

He was a little confused in his statements, but Mrs. M'Call thought none the worse of him for that. She appreciated the delicacy of his intentions in warning her of what he proposed, and she closed the interview by saying, "Although I can do nothing for you, or against you, you have my kind wishes."

So the next time Mollie came to tea there was a mysterious vacuum formed around her and the Captain. Alec, ruthlessly informed of what was to take place, went off in dire misery to prowl in the outskirts of the village and curse his stars by the light of another's moon. Sophie and Grace got away to their bedroom and whispered in the cold about the solemnity that was transacting by the parlor fire. Mrs. M'Call put on her hat and shawl and ran across the garden to the Baptist prayer-meeting.

"Miss Prater," the Captain commenced, abruptly, "I wish that you knew me better."

There was a shake in his voice which told her what was coming, and she felt herself tremble a little.

"For then," he pursued, recovering his steadiness—"then you would be better able to judge of what I am about to say to you. I wish to make you my wife."

Never did a young lady think more seriously and energetically than did Mollie during the few seconds of silence which followed this declaration. For the last time—once for all—should it be? Should she accept him, be comfortable for life, be taken care of and supported, be well dressed and stylish, be the mistress of a home? Or should she seize this opportunity of wreaking the vengeance of her section and her family, and, indeed, of her own heart, on a Yankee?

"See here, Captain Humphreys," she said, pausing and facing the unhappy man, who was doomed to misery, whether accepted or rejected. "You are good enough for me; you are every bit good enough. If you were a Southerner, with half your advantages, I would marry you. But you are not. You are of a race that I hate. I hate your government and your uniform and your flag. I never told you so before, because I wanted to tell you at this moment. Don't speak, Sir. There is no moving me; I am a Prater—I tell you, I am a Prater. When we hate, we hate for life. Well, Sir, I refuse you. Now will you please to leave me alone? Good-by, Sir."

It was melodramatic, and irrational, and not nice; but it crushed the Captain, and he went.

PART II

MANY A BLOW fails of half its intended effect because it is given in a fury. If Miss Mollie Prater had struck with only a woman's ordinary strength at Captain Humphreys—if she had refused him on account

of his personal insufficiencies, and not, as it were, *en masse*, because
he was one of several millions of Yankees—she would have hurt him
far worse than she did. In fact, the words which she uttered against his
race, his government, and his uniform helped him. At times he was
able to think that he did not want to marry such a spit-fire of a rebel.
Not always, however; there were hours when he could not help brood-
ing over her conversion to loyalty and love; there were even hours when
he would have resumed that pious labor could he have found a chance.

"I can't come here to tea any more," said Mollie to the M'Calls. "If I
do you will lose your boarders. I have had it out with my Yankee, and I
have given him the devil."

"Why, Mollie!" exclaimed both the girls, aghast at the vigorous
phrase, while the mother started in visible disgust.

"Oh! there are times when nothing but swearing will express one's
feelings," pursued Mollie, unabashed. "You don't know how wild I am.
It is the only revenge that I have ever had on these people. And I fairly
jumped at it. Oh! I am a Southerner, and I take it Prater fashion."

Then she narrated, with some equatorial exaggeration, the scene of
the refusal, not even checking herself when Alec entered. When she left
the room to put on her hat Grace, to whose thirteen-year-old mind this
discomfiture of a Yankee was a dazzling triumph, and who in imagination was already spurning a Northern admirer of her own, broke out
with, "Oh, wasn't it splendid, ma!"

"Yes, splendid for Captain Humphreys," answered Mrs. M'Call. "It
will be easy for him to find a better woman and a truer lady than Mollie
Prater."

"Why, ma!" protested Grace; but her mother took no further notice
of her; the remark had been intended to influence Alec.

Alec, however, was under a spell. He had heard the condemnation
of Mollie as he passed out of the room, but he had not even minded it
so far as to reason upon it. How could he receive a prejudice against
the magnificent creature whose black eyes flashed into his so confidently as she met him in the hall, and who had just refused his rival?
He waited on her home in a state of elation, glad, flattered, feeling that
he owed her a debt, and willing to pay it on the spot, if only he could

have gone on paying it for life. He had known many finer women—
and there were far finer in the little circle of his own family—and he
was himself her moral and intellectual superior, yet she seemed to him
worshipful. How many delusions there are! This earth passed itself off
upon us for a long time as the centre of the universe. If we could see
things in their naked truth, we should lose our spirits and "go into a
decline."

Out of his admirable, absurd, dangerous hallucination Alec was
saved by an adventure which seemed to him very cruel. As he was
lounging with Hassy Few one morning in front of the new court-house,
Captain Humphreys, whose head-quarters were in the old court-house,
came across the street with an official envelope in his hand.

"Gentlemen," he said, "I wish to speak to you confidentially. I must
warn you that it is a matter which requires profound secrecy. Do you
know a man named Leroy Prater—Doctor Leroy Prater?"

He looked specially, and with evident anxiety, at Alec as he pronounced this name, so formidable to both.

"Leroy Prater? What? in this district?" inquired Hassy Few. "No, I
don't. Do you, Alec? You've hunted the ground all over."

"I never heard of such a person," returned the young fellow, after an
instant of anxious recollection.

The Captain drew a sigh of relief as he continued, "There is such a
man. He headed a band of outlaws in Western North Carolina during
the last months of the war, and for a short time after the peace. Did you
never hear of him?"

"Can't say as I ever did," rejoined Hassy. "Lord bless you, Cap'n! it
took both eyes to see the plundering that went on under our own noses.
We had Brown's raid here, and some of Wheeler's cavalry broke loose,
and the Old Harry knows what all. As for hearing any thing from outside? Why, there were no mails and no travel. Every man staid behind
his own tree, waiting for creation to bust and be done with it."

"And so you don't know any Praters in the district?" mused the
Captain.

"Oh yes! lots of Praters; more Praters than there's any call for. And
they are a mighty poor showing, the Brownville Praters. Praters won't

do. I've no use for 'em. I could justify myself in popping at most any of our Praters. They're a low-flung set. But Leroy Prater? Doctor Leroy Prater? Why, Leroy *is* a North Carolina name; there 'tis. I guess the paper may be right, Cap'n. Leroys is thicker than snakes in Henderson County, North Carolina. But where's the man roosting now? Does it say?"

"He is reported as living in what is called the Old Ponder Mejunkin place."

"Old Ponder Mejunkin place! You don't say! Why, Alec, has young Ponder played out?"

"Oh yes; gone to Texas. Don't you remember that he shot Wils Tony, and skedaddled?"

"Exactly; there 'tis. So he did shoot Wils. There's been so many of these jokes played in the last year or so that a fellow can't remember them all. Well, there 'tis. Ponder has traveled, and this other chap has got his hole. By George! he must have squatted like a turkey, to stay unbeknown as he has. Well, are you going to get after him, Cap'n? You'll want a guide. I never was at the Old Ponder Mejunkin place; but they say it's the queerest spot to go for in the district. I guess Mac can take you to it, though."

"I never was there," responded Alec. "But I know about where the cross-road turns off that leads to it."

"I shall be obliged to request you to accompany me, then," said Humphreys.

"Very good," observed Alec, after a moment of hesitation, of which the Captain guessed the cause. "How shall you go?"

"I shall take three men, mounted and armed with pistols. It is twenty-fives miles there. What time do you think we had best start? You know the ways of people hereabout better than I."

"We ought to leave by two o'clock. We must get within four or five miles of the place before it comes very dark, and then lie by till a little after midnight. We must be around the house at daybreak."

"That's so," said Few. "People are out before sun-up in the country, and such birds most especially. You ought to be harking at his do' befo' it's light enough for him to fire out of his windows. And my advice is,

Cap'n, not to wear any very shiny shoulder-straps," concluded Hassy, who was as well reconstructed as a man might be who could not take the iron-clad oath.

"Thank you," laughed the officer. "I shall take your advice. I have been as much shot at as I want. Well, Mr. M'Call, suppose we meet at two o'clock at Keith's mill, on the Henderson Road, a mile or so from the village. By-the-way, let me see you alone a moment, if you please."

The two stepped a little to one side, and the officer put his hand on the civilian's arm.

"You have never been on United States duty before?" he whispered. "Are you perfectly willing to do it to the best of your ability? Can you trust yourself with it?"

"Captain, I have been a rebel, and a good rebel. I am now a citizen, and a good citizen. I have taken an oath to execute the laws; and what is more, I give you my word—word of a gentleman!"

It was spoken with a slight exaltation of manner, which was natural in a young man, and especially in a young man of the South.

"Thank you, Mr. M'Call. I confide in you entirely. Well, at Keith's mill."

As Alec walked home to prepare for his journey, and inform his mother in private of his contemplated absence, he meditated on the faint possibility that this Leroy Prater might be the father of Mollie. No, it could not be; he had heard her speak of him proudly as Colonel John Prater; he had never heard her allude to him otherwise than as residing in Georgia. He found the young lady with his sister, for there were no lessons that day at the college.

"Good-morning," she said, gayly. "Is it holiday with you too? I don't believe you do any thing at that court-house but stand around the doorway."

"Do something naughty, and see how quick we would be after you," he answered. "Have you heard from home lately?"

"Yes; a letter last night; such an old letter! It seems as if it must have been written when I was a baby. I do wish this miserable government would hurry up and reconstruct us—at least the mails."

"I think the females need the most reconstructing," said Alec, pun-

ning out of a grave spirit. "How is your father doing with the plantation? Is he at home?"

"Yes. Nobody leaves Georgia who can live in it. That is just the
trouble now—to live in it."

She looked at him steadily as she said this; she always looked thus at
people who spoke of her father. Alec's eyes dropped under the glance,
fond as he was of gazing into hers; but he left the room contented, be-
lieving that he might safely arrest Doctor Leroy Prater. "By Jove! she's
the handsomest creature living," he thought. "Oh, for a chance to slave
for her and not starve her!"

At two, mounted on the sheriff's gray horse, he found the Captain, a
corporal, and three privates awaiting him at Keith's mill. The cavalcade
immediately set off at a moderate trot on the Henderson Road, the two
officials leading, and the soldiers following at a distance of some thirty
paces. For several minutes there was no conversation beyond casual
remarks about the weather, the landscape, etc. Humphreys and Alec
respected and liked each other, and their intercourse would long since
have been familiar, if not cordial, only that Mollie Prater had stood
between them. At first the Carolinian had been dumb with jealousy,
and then the Yankee. Although Humphreys had only seen Mollie at a
distance since his refusal, he could not help knowing, in one way or
another, that Alec frequently called on her; and he had begun to suspect that the young man was the true cause of his own discomfiture. Of
course he suspected this only at times and among other suppositions;
for a refused man has many whims, and changes his sore spot every
hour. Of course, too, he had no intention of quarreling with Alec about
the matter, for he was a gentleman at heart, and his disappointment
had not bereft him of his common-sense. And now a dreadful possibility half drove the rejection out of his mind; now he feared that he
had this girl's misery in his hand, rather than her happiness; and very
soon reticence became impossible.

"Mr. M'Call," he said, "but for one thing I should have sent a lieutenant on this business. I wanted to make sure that this person should
be arrested without receiving injury or insult. It has occurred to me that
he might be the—a relative of Miss Prater."

"Exactly, Captain," responded Alec, who had cringed at hearing the name, just as Humphreys had cringed in pronouncing it. "But I have looked into that—cautiously, you know. She tells me that her father is in Georgia. She has just received a letter from him."

"Oh, thank you!" said Humphreys, with a deep breath of relief, like the sigh of a wearied man who throws himself down to rest. Both now had sufficient food for meditation to give them silence for half a mile.

"This fellow must be caught," resumed the officer, "We must take him, dead or alive. He has been an atrocious villain. It is proper, I think, to state to you what he is charged with. It seems that he and his gang committed depredations on people of all parties, though chiefly on Union men. He is said to have killed four or five persons with his own hands. He burned a farmer's house, with seven persons in it, including two women and three children. When they tried to break out he and his gang fired on them. Not one escaped—not even the baby. It seems incredible."

"I dare say he may have done it," said Alec, coolly. "Such things were done. All through the mountain region, where people were divided against each other from house to house, the war was savage. I'll tell you what I saw myself. When we occupied East Tennessee the commandant of the post where I was stationed had an application for assistance from Champ Ferguson. You have heard of Champ; he was one of *our* blackguards. It seems that a Jack Johnson, who was the captain of a Tory gang, had got the better of Champ in a fight and was hunting him. Champ came to us, said his house was burned, his family in the swamps, and his gang broke up; but he could get them together again if we would lend him a company. I was a lieutenant of cavalry then, and the commandant sent me on the service with thirty men. Champ picked up his people under our cover, and we had a big skirmish with Johnson and whipped him. Well, after the battle one of my men told me that our bushwhackers were going to murder their prisoners. I rode over to their camp to stop it; I thought that my order would be sufficient. But d——d if the scoundrels didn't hoot at me; they were more than a hundred strong, and I had only twenty-three men left. Yes, Sir; they just defied me. And I saw Champ himself take the six prisoners, one after the other, tied as they were—take each man by the beard or the collar and run a knife into him standing—run it in two or three times till he dropped. And three of them were old acquaintances of his, and he talked to them and called them by their christen names as he stabbed them. By Jove, Sir! it's true," asseverated Alec, scowling and clenching his fist over the recollection.

"But those fellows were not so much for either party as they were for themselves and against every body else," he resumed, after a brief silence. "When we got into Eastern Kentucky we thought that we were in a Confederate country, and that it would be perfectly safe to run about. But we soon took notice that if an officer left camp without an escort he didn't come back. True as you are born, Sir, we had to throw out pickets and use patrols just the same as in East Tennessee. I tell you that all that Alleghany country was full of trifling [worthless] fellows who bushwhacked every body that couldn't bushwhack them."

"What did Ponder Mejunkin shoot his man for?" inquired Humphreys, after another silence.

"There was an unpleasantness between them," said Alec. "I never heard what. I suppose that whisky was at the bottom of it, as it generally is of fights. But he took a curious way of doing it. He asked Wils to load the pistol for him, and then shot him with it as soon as he handed it back. Didn't say a word; just pulled trigger. I think that perhaps his idea was this: if Wils wanted to shoot him he'd give him a chance; if not, he'd take a crack himself."

Alec's experience as a deputy-sheriff enabled him to speak of such tragedies with a calmness which he could not have acquired merely as a soldier, or a "chivalrous Southron." The Captain marveled at this monotoned description of an "unpleasantness," and said to himself, "We have different vices in New England."

"No pursuit?" he inquired.

"Oh yes; the settlement turned out and hunted Ponder; but there was no law. It was right away after the surrender, and society was just lying loose."

The party slackened its pace after leaving Brownville five miles behind, and had plenty of leisure to notice the face of the country. It was a rolling landscape, not more than half cleared, the original forest deciduous, the new growth pines, bottoms of rich blackish earth, uplands of pulverous gray, the numerous streaks of old-field either barren red or brown with weeds. The frosts had blackened the rare patches of cotton, and the "fodder pulling" had stripped the enormous corn-field to bare stalks. Still the land was so fairly fertile that Humphreys wondered anew at the slatternly farm-houses, and at the rusty log-cabins, chinked with mud and destitute of window-glass. Of course he moralized about slavery, its deteriorating influence upon agriculture, etc., etc.

An occasional cart, buggy, or equestrian, all like those to be seen in Brownville, met the party. People stared, but bowed civilly, and perhaps said "Good-evening," for in that land evening begins at noon. One farmer in homespun, with a very red face under his slouched hat, who appeared to be trying to drive both sides of a sapling, and had got fast locked, roared out, "Hullo! you going after Largent? Let me tell you you won't catch him with your stock. But if you do light on him, you'd better begin to shoot mighty sudden. He carries three revolvers, and that's half your fit-out."

"Nobody seems to suspect whom we are after," muttered the Captain.

"That's lucky," said Alec. "Such fellows generally have friends, or at least people who are scared of them, to give them warning."

"I have sent three parties after Largent without success," was Humphreys's next remark.

"I believe I could track him. And if I couldn't bring him in I could save him. Such cut-throats ought to be chased down by every decent citizen. They pretend to be hunting Tories and niggers, but what they really hurt is the South. They hurt its character," concluded Alec, superbly.

By sunset they were among spurs of the southern extension of the Alleghanies; rounded hills and ridges of monotonous outline, clothed thinly with stunted trees; gaps here and there showing the long blue bars of the parent range. Guided by Alec they left the road at the foot of a ridge, turned into a deep wooded hollow, and halted. It was the

23rd of December, and although the day had been pleasantly warm the night was frosty.

"We are far enough from the road to risk a fire," suggested Alec. "If people notice it they will take us for North Carolina wagoners or Tennessee pig-drivers camping out."

There was a supper off the contents of haversacks, and then a partially successful attempt at sleep. At two in the morning Alec proposed to move forward. "We are still four miles from the cross-road," he said, "and after that there must be a mile or more to the house. We must be there before he can see to draw a bead on us, or get warning to take to the swamp."

To diminish the clatter of hoofs they advanced at a walk. The darkness and the silence gave the impression of a world of utter solitude. After what seemed an hour, during which they had perhaps gone three miles, Alec halted, and said, "Do you see that black lump—blacker than any thing else—off to the right? That is a cabin. I think we had better have that fellow out, and take him along with us. I don't feel at all sure of my running after we leave the high-road for the swamp."

He gave a long, tenor halloo, and repeated it three or four times. A hurricane of dogs responded, rushing down upon the party, and baying savagely. Presently there was a sound as of a door opening, and a voice from the black mass answered the halloo.

"Come on; he won't shoot now," said Alec, and rode up to the house with the Captain. A smouldering fire within gave just light enough to show them a human figure standing partially behind the door-post, with a gun so held in the right hand that it could be readily brought to an aim.

"It's all square," said Alec. "This is the post commandant, and I am the deputy-sheriff."

"Oh! how are you, Mr. Mac?" was the reply. "Captain, your sarvent. I reckoned you mought be bushwhackers. Git down and come in. Wait till I git somethin' light."

He set down his gun, blew at the fire a moment, and returned with a blazing pine-torch. He was a small, spare man, with an uncombed shock of long, straw-colored hair, a complexion like freckled putty, a dozen deep wrinkles on a face that was still young, an obsequious grin, and a crouching carriage. Evidently he was something between a poor farmer and a "low down creetur."

"Captain, your sarvent," he repeated, humble, like all his class, to military power. "I'm powerful glad to see a Yankee at my house, I am. I was allays agin the war, and never owned no black uns. I was a Union man till I was forced in."

"We haven't come for *you*," said Alec, contemptuously, well knowing this stamp of loyalty. "You are all right, Mr.—what's your name?"

"Scalf—Johnny Scalf. Don't you 'member?"

"Well, Mr. Scalf, all we want of you is to take us to the Old Ponder Mejunkin place."

A new alarm pinched Mr. Scalf's putty features at this demand; but after one anxious spasm he settled into a totally blank expression, as if no power on earth could make him remember the locality of the Old Ponder Mejunkin place.

"Oh, we don't want you to point out any body," continued Alec. "Just show us the house; that's all. The Government wants to buy it for a nigger school-house, perhaps. Nobody can go for you because you show us the house, don't you see? Nothing unneighborly in that."

"Wa'al, no grct," admitted Mr. Scalf, but still hesitated, evidently in much trouble.

"Come, get up your chunk of a pony," persisted Alec. "I saw you on one at the court-house last week."

"Wa'al, all right," assented Mr. Scalf, dropping the idea of denying that he had a horse. "You git ahead a piece, and I'll come after, like I fell in with ye."

The party moved on slowly, and was presently overtaken by Mr. Scalf on his chunk of a pony. "How far is it to the swamp road?" demanded Alec.

"Better'n a mile, and then better'n a mile to the house," responded the guide. He was in a tremble with cold or terror, and his voice shook noticeably, although he spoke in a whisper.

"Is there a large family?" inquired the Captain. "More than one man?"

"Lord's sake! don't speak s'loud," implored Mr. Scalf; "folks lies out sometimes. Sometimes there's a large family, and sometimes not."

At the bottom of a black hollow the guide turned square to the right, and entered what was apparently a narrow lane fenced in on both sides from a dense forest. It was impossible to perceive more, or to see even this distinctly, but it was evident from the stumbling and sliding of the horses that the footing was uneven and miry. The party could only move in single file, and not a word was uttered. After what seemed an interminable walk they reached drier ground, where the road broadened and took a slope upward. Here the chunk of a pony halted until Humphreys and Alec came abreast of it.

"How far are we from the house now?" asked the latter, in a whisper.

" 'Bout a quarter of a mile. You can't miss it. Nary another round yere, and the road butts right agin it," stated Mr. Scalf, who was clearly very anxious to take the back track.

"Very good," said the Captain. "Well, Sir, you can go; we are much obliged to you. By-the-way, you had better not speak of this for a day or two."

Alec laughed low and muttered, "He *never* will speak of it; dogs couldn't tear it out of him."

Twenty rods further brought them out of the swampy forest, and they became conscious of a clearing and a dark mass upon a low ridge.

"Dismount," directed the Captain. "Corporal, you will remain with the horses. If any body comes up the road halt him and hold him; don't fire, if you can help it; just hold him. Simson, you will go to the rear of the house, Hogan to the right, and Speed to the left. Take a large circuit, and be still about it; but don't let any one pass. If you hear a whistle close in."

The men silently vanished in the obscurity, while Humphreys and Alec advanced straight toward the house. Six or eight yards from the dark mass they were halted by a rude stone-wall, evidently the inclosure of a front yard.

"Very lucky," muttered the officer. "We can lie behind this till daybreak, and summon him when he comes out."

They waited for a few minutes, shivering with cold and the anxiety of watching.

"Captain, this won't do," whispered Alec. "I beg pardon for advising; but this won't work in our favor. We shall get so numbed that we sha'n't be able to handle our shooting-irons; and besides, these fellows always look before they step out, and a blue coat is the easiest thing in the world to see. He may open on us and save one or two, or perhaps raise a crowd of his own. Take my word for it, Captain, we had much better close in."

"You know this kind of thing best," was the answer; and in another minute they were on the steps of the house. They could make out that there was a veranda, the flooring rotten and loose; and by passing their hands along the clap-boarding they discovered two doorways. "Do you watch the other," said Humphreys, and commenced tapping gently on the right-hand door. Presently a girlish voice called, "Who's there?" immediately after which there was a movement within, the door opened an inch or two, and the same voice repeated, "Who's there?"

"Is Doctor Prater at home?" Humphreys asked.

"Tell him no," said a whisper inside, and the voice at the crack echoed, "No."

At the same moment Alec gave a sharp whistle and burst in the other door with a plunge of his heavy shoulder. As Humphreys rushed into the room thus unceremoniously opened, he drew a match, and by its flicker saw a tall man, undressed, groping toward a corner in which stood a fowling-piece.

"Stand stock still," said Alec, with his revolver aimed, and the man halted. A candle which Humphreys immediately lighted where it stood on a pine table showed that Doctor Leroy Prater was as white as a ghost. While the three glared at each other in the first moment of surprise, a tall woman sprang out of the bed which the man had left, threw the coverlet around her, leaped out upon the veranda, and uttered a long, piercing cry, which Humphreys afterward described as "a rebel yell," and Alec as "a keen whoop—you could have heard it a mile."

"There's no time to lose, Captain," said the young man. "Doctor, get on your things in a d——d hurry."

The woman rushed in and glared at them, looking like a spectre with her pale face and white drapery. She had piercing gray eyes, a mass of long, loose black hair, imperious aquiline features, and a sort of savage queenliness of manner, heightened no doubt by her wild excitement. She could not have been much over forty, and she was still a superb face and figure.

"Madame, you had better quit that noise," said Alec. "It may do harm to your own crowd."

Her only reply was another swift rush and piercing yell.

"Let her shout," muttered the Captain. "She is crazy with the surprise."

"I wouldn't care for her whoop if it hadn't been answered," growled Alec.

"Answered?"

"Yes; from the right; more than half a mile off. Oh, they heard it as well as I. But it's no use, Doctor: keep on dressing."

The young fellow seemed to grow and swell with pugnacity; his nostrils dilated as if scenting battle with defiant satisfaction.

By the time the prisoner had dressed the soldiers were in, and two of them led him arm in arm toward the horses. Thus far neither husband nor wife had spoken a distinguishable word; they seemed to be able to comprehend and manage the situation without language; it was as if they were practiced actors in such scenes. But as the man passed through the broken gate of his front yard he said, in a bass voice, which now at least was steady enough, "What does this all mean?"

"Doctor Leroy Prater is our man," responded Alec.

"That is my name, certainly. But still I think there must be some mistake. I am a quiet farmer, conscious of no crime—except poverty."

The voice had a cultivated intonation, and the pronunciation was that of an educated man.

"Move on, if you please, Sir," said Humphreys. "It will all be explained to you by the proper authorities."

On reaching the horses they beheld, by the gray glimmer of dawn, another man, standing quiet under the aim of the corporal's revolver.

"This fellow came out of the swamp, and I halted him," explained the soldier.

"Keep him there," directed the Captain. "When we have got ahead a little you can let him go, and follow us."

The Doctor was mounted behind the stoutest trooper, his arms passed around the man's body, and his hands bound together.

"Ah!" exclaimed Alec, as they emerged from the swampy lane upon the high-road. "We are all right. But that cross-cut was a beautiful place to bushwhack us in."

Daylight showed them that their prisoner was a man of fifty, tall and powerfully built, dressed in well-worn homespun, slouched hat of seedy black, long and careless iron gray hair, haggard but massive aquiline features, stony-blue eyes, and an expression which was determined rather than brutal. He did not look like a desperado, but desperadoes seldom do look as they ought. Humphreys had a soldier's habit of not questioning prisoners, leaving that to superior authority; and as the Doctor chose to remain grimly silent, there was no conversation between captors and captive. The Scalf cabin was closed when they passed it, and there was no other house within miles of the Ponder Mejunkin place; and they were an hour on the road before they saw a human being. It was full "sun-up" when they were joined by an old farmer of the mountain type—a middle-sized, broad, thin, springy man, with a face full of wrinkles, and hardly a gray hair in his head—a man who seemed at once demure, resolute, conscientious, and merciless— a Cromwellian round-head, none the gentler for his birth in the "Dark Corner." Switching his lean, small horse alongside of Humphreys, who had fallen in rear of the cavalcade, he opened conversation in a slow, dour utterance, as hard as the grinding of a cart-wheel.

"Mornin', Colonel. Well—I'm right glad you've got that creetur. What ye goin' to do to him?"

"He is to be tried, I suppose."

"Tried! I was in hopes you was goin' to shute him," he answered, in his deliberate, cart-wheel fashion, meaning every word that he said. "What's the use of tryin' him, Colonel? I tell you he's guilty. That's Leroy Prater. He bushwhacked our people in Henderson County. He's one of the worst rebs on the face of the yeath. He's a heap worse, Colonel, nor rebs in general; why, he was turned out of *their* army for some low-downness. Thar ain't no sort of use in tryin' him. You'd better shute him right yere, and done with him. And, Colonel, I kin show ye a heap more that needs killin','" he concluded, with an air of solemn conviction.

"If he is such a bad fellow, why haven't you informed on him before?" said Humphreys, a little disgusted with this cantankerous counselor.

"Yes, and git myself burned out. Colonel, thar's a gang belongs to this man. You was powerful lucky to catch him without a fight. He's a nigh neighbor of mine, on'y three miles off, and I know what goes on at his place. Sometimes thar'll be eight or ten thar. Then next mornin' they're gone, and somebody misses stock. You was powerful lucky. He don't always stop at home. One night he's at home, and then he totes his blankets over the river. I'm a Union man, allays was one, Colonel; it's in our breed. My father fowt for his country in the old war, and I laid out in this, hunted by the rebs. I've showed your men through the lines. Colonel, jest believe *me;* you'd better shute him."

With this piece of Carlylean advice the old man departed.

The party had accomplished half their journey when a negro beckoned to Humphreys out of a field of young pines, and told him through the twelve-rail fence that Joly, the bushwhacker, had passed the night at his employer's house.

"D'no whar y'is now, boss," explained the freedman. "I gits up mighty yairly this mor'n, and gits out into the old field, 'cos he's a mighty onsafe man to be with. Then I seed you a comin', and I 'lowed you was sont to fotch him. Ef you'll take round that ar track 'long the piny woods you'll come out behind the house, and then you kin shute him mebbe. Don't miss him, boss; he's mighty quick at firin'. And don't say nothin' 'bout me."

The temptation was irresistible. Joly, Largent, and Texas Brown were the three most illustrious bushwhackers of Western South Carolina; and if the arrest of one of them could be added to that of Doctor Leroy Prater, the day would indeed be a glorious one. Humphreys directed Alec and one of the privates to remain with the prisoner while he should lead the three other men on a circuit to flank the farm-house. The doctor was dismounted and laid upon the ground by the road-side. The soldier reclined at a little distance, holding his horse by the bridle. Alec fastened his beast to a sapling, seated himself with his back against a deserted hovel, which had evidently been a smithy, and waited. The negro had disappeared.

Alec, as we may suppose, had already glanced many times at the prisoner to see if he could discover in him any possibility of relationship with Mollie Prater. He now studied him anew; no resemblance, thank God! Presently he noticed that the soldier's lids had fallen, and that his breathing was that of slumber. Then he became conscious that want of sleep, the chill of the night, the long ride, and the warmth of the morning sun were soothing his own nerves as with an opiate. He sought to keep himself awake by thinking of Mollie Prater; but although that subject was interesting it was also lulling. In his reverie he seemed to hear her speaking pleasantly, to feel that she was comforting him after his long journey, to know that his head was drooping against her shoulder. It was a dream, and she awoke him from it. Starting up with a suspicion that he had dozed, he saw her coming toward him with a stealthy and hurried step, her Greek face as white as if it were that of a statue. In the road stood two horses, one with a side-saddle, the other mounted by a boy. The soldier was still unconscious, and the prisoner slept beside him.

"You have arrested my father," the girl whispered, seizing Alec by the arm and glaring into his face. "Cut him loose."

People comprehend quickly under such pressure: the whole magnitude and cruelty of the situation burst upon Alec; he had awakened numb and half blind with fatigue, but he understood every thing.

"*I* will," she muttered, drawing a penknife from her pocket and attempting to pass him.

One of the terrible features of this conversation was, that it was carried on in a whisper.

"Wait! I can't!" he gasped, with a parched throat, seizing her dress.

She raised the knife as if to strike him with it, and then, because he did not flinch, she turned to pleading.

"Oh, Alec! Don't send him to die! *My* father, Alec!"

"But perhaps he is not guilty."

"He *is*. He has done what they say. But it was not wrong, Alec. Don't you dare to look it! They were Tories—and he killed them for the good cause—the lost cause. Oh, tomorrow is Christmas, and we were all to be there! Oh, what a Christmas you are making for me, Alec!"

"Oh my God!" he sobbed, but still held her fast. Suddenly she put her arms around his, leaned her whole weight upon him, and kissed his lips. "Alec, I refused the other for your sake. I will be every thing that you wish. Only let me save him. There, lie down and sleep. You can say that you were asleep."

She had pushed him gently to the ground, behind the corner of the ruined smithy, where he could not see her father. Now she stepped away from him with a swift tread, holding the open knife in her hand, and watching the sleeping soldier with an eye which betokened danger for him if there should be no salvation for the prisoner. Alec was in an agony; he remembered his "word of a gentleman—word of honor;" all his chivalrous, ecstatic, Quixotic education of honor rushed upon him and reproached him; all the M'Calls of the past seemed to cry to him, "Word of honor!" Accidentally his hand touched his pistol, and with the swiftness of instinct he drew the trigger, sending the bullet into the ground near his feet. The prisoner opened his eyes, and the soldier started up, muttering "Fall in!" Mollie Prater turned, rushed back upon Alec, lifted him to his feet, and dragged him several paces with a strength which was like that of a maniac or of a wild beast.

"Oh you hound!" she gasped. "Curse you! curse you! curse you!"

The next instant she was on her horse, waving a speechless farewell to her father and riding swiftly homeward, probably with some vain hope of rescue.

A minute later Humphreys returned from his unsuccessful search after Joly, and the journey toward Brownville was resumed.

"What is the matter with you?" asked the Captain, dropping in the rear to place himself alongside of Alec. "You are perfectly white."

The young fellow, turning in his saddle, gazed so sternly and fixedly toward the rear that Humphreys looked that way also, and saw two equestrian figures rising a hill not far distant.

"Upon my honor—that is like Miss Prater," stammered the officer, already suspicious of something horrible. "Did she pass here?"

Alec rode a few steps in silence, and then mumbled, "It is her father. She wanted me to let him loose."

"*Her* father!" exclaimed the post commandant, becoming as white as his companion. "Oh my God! I wish he could escape."

Not in self-excuse—not to be heard by this Yankee who had seemed to reproach him—merely to steady his own soul—Alec muttered, "Word of a gentleman."

With a quick remembrance of duty and a complete comprehension of the young man's enthusiasm of honor, Humphreys leaned sidewise, seized Alec's hand, and said, "Yes, it *was* the word of a gentleman."

"A Woman's Only Revenge"

UNLIKE MANY WHO told stories of the war in the popular press, John W. De Forest saw wartime action as an infantry officer and later government service as a brevet major in the Freedmen's Bureau during Reconstruction. In October 1866, when he took up the tasks of an assistant commissioner in Greenville, South Carolina was already on the road to becoming part of Military District Number Two. The state legislature refused in December to ratify the Fourteenth Amendment; the following March, the first of the Reconstruction Acts of 1867 went into effect. Sent to the northwestern part of the state, away from the large cotton and rice plantations of the South Carolina lowlands, De Forest saw few of the ex-slaves that the amendment was designed to assist but plenty of the bushwhacking gangs and local outrages that had prompted Congress to impose military order from Washington. For him, as for other Northern Republicans, the freedmen remained something of a cypher, often stereotyped and only part of the task of reconstructing the South.

More preponderant were the role of law and the advent of free labor, both of which inspired De Forest's official concern. The territory he served covered some three thousand square miles spread out over three counties, what he described in "A Report of Outrages" as "a vast region of hills and mountains, wild in its landscape, and hardly less wild in the character of many of its inhabitants, always noted for displays of individual pugnacity" (*Harper's Monthly*, December 1868). Joly and Largent, both ex-Confederates, preyed on Union loyalists and freedmen by preference, though they were not always particular; Texas Brown, said to have deserted from Wheeler's cavalry, put his gun out for hire and his hands on anything he could get. The small farmers and planters of the district protected and feared such desperadoes, one of many reasons why they were less inclined to work than De Forest thought proper. His job was to rescue what he called his "pashalic" for the North. "I never forgot," he wrote in "A Bureau Major's Business and Pleasures," "that my main duty should consist in educating the entire population around me to settle their difficulties by the civil law; in other words, I considered myself an instrument of reconstruction" (*Harper's Monthly*, November 1868). Only upon the basis of the law would Southerners come to prize their roles as citizens, in his view, even if Federal troops reinforced the class stratification that was as potent in the South Carolina hill country as in the Connecticut social circles from which De Forest came.[25]

In "Parole d'Honneur," the prospects for a national union are initially hopeful. The story's first section takes the form of a Romance, which means that transformation of the "feminine" South in the figure of Mollie Prater is seen as desirable and that the domestic assumptions promoting her marriage favor gender distinctions while masking class priorities. Once the well-bred Captain Humphreys has set his heart on Mollie, after all, Sophie M'Call is considered safe from the Yankees, although his less polished lieutenants presumably have hearts of their own. No matter, if the law of love could bring Yankee and rebel together, making a loyal wife out of a vengeful young lady. But the collapse of the cross-sectional romance forces the "high-toned" gentleman to choose between Southern homestead and the adventure of citizenship, between family and the "lost cause" on one side and itinerancy and the law on the other. For Mollie's refusal to marry thrusts the story out of domestic precincts and on the road to a different vision of the nation's future, modeled on the companionship of men and the ferocity of class war. When the Romance fails, Mollie Prater is effectively displaced as the avatar of the New South in favor of Alexander M'Call, the type of the new citizen.

The scope De Forest gives the Romance to portray the dynamics of Reconstruction is typical of his professional skill and of the conciliatory emphasis of *Harper's Monthly*. Reviewing the writer's major fiction a few years later, Clarence Gordon noted De Forest's "breadth, strength, and movement" and his attention to the "histories of average humanity" (*Atlantic Monthly*, November 1873). On just these terms, the magazine likewise excelled, publishing sixty Civil War stories before the Centennial was over and encouraging the rich development of the American short story as a form. The magazine's intentions were honorably self-serving: after the war, it was essential to lure back the Southern readers who had once made its subscription lists fat. "Parole d'Honneur" and further essays from the bureau major contributed to the magazine's interest in the progress of Reconstruction, though its prevailing commitment to free labor made *Harper's Monthly* less cordial to Southern apologists than to Southern Unionists like William M. Baker in "The Survival of the Fittest" (December 1874) and "Natural Selection" (January 1876) or to Southern visitors like Constance Fenimore Woolson in "The French Broad" (April 1875) and "Old Gardiston" (April 1876). Like De Forest, these writers were sympathetic to the desolation they discovered in the postwar South and often turned to the Romance, in forty-one of the magazine's fifty-nine stories, to deliver the region and the nation from the errors of the past.

Yoking the genre to Reconstructive purposes, De Forest parlayed the heroine's schematic need to choose between lover and decoy into a strategy of successive oppositions that structure the story's first section. Pursued by both Captain Humphreys and Alexander M'Call, Mollie finds herself courted by the Northern captain at home and by his Southern rival at school, which keeps her and the story moving from one end of the town to the other. Still domestic in its emphasis on the new home to come, Mollie's courtship establishes a keen narrative dynamic that differs substantially from the settled figure of the house invaded and the Old Homestead's resistance to change.

The Romance's greater liberty is revealed when Mrs. De Gama Cobb takes a hand in Mollie's affairs. In her shrill twitter, the refugee from Pensacola berates Mollie ("the daughter of a Confederate colonel!") for considering marriage to a Yankee and forsaking the claims of society, the proprieties, and patriotism, claims familiar to Mrs. Murray in "Thanksgiving." Mollie's retort demonstrates the comparative mobility of marriageable daughters when the narrative instead favors their affairs of the heart. "I am twenty-one years old," says Mollie, "and even my father could not control me in this matter, and I certainly shall not let myself be controlled by others." Resisting the possible interference of the seminary principal, too, she stands firmly for free choice, at least as far as her situation allows. When the quarrel between Mrs. De Gama Cobb and Mollie Prater is added to the romantic alternatives already in place, Mollie's insistence on free agency casts a cloud over the Captain and the home he offers, since genuine rebellion seems to lie beyond its confines.

But the story's opening scene works against the heroine's subsequent will, specifically by deploying a somewhat different set of oppositions that the Romance is meant to bridge generically through Mollie's correct matrimonial choice. In this first glimpse of Brownville, the city's two public buildings, the old courthouse and the new, are paramount. Around these cluster further oppositions that draw "Parole d'Honneur" closer to the gendered separation of spheres that Mollie's profession and her high spirits flout. The old courthouse is solid, where the new courthouse is simply big. On the stone steps of the old courthouse stands the auctioneer, who has just sold the furniture that the M'Call women will miss. On the steps across the way stands Alexander M'Call, who declares himself happy enough off the plantation where his mother and sisters are "pinched." Against what is old and homey and female, in other words, this scene posits what is new and footloose and male.

The contrast is furthered when Hassy Few's talk of folks "broke up" by Sherman encourages Alec to slip into his own "local tang," the dialect "colored with provincialisms and alive with inchoate metaphor" that serves these "out-of-door comrades" when they are away from the society that requires a more dignified language. At its most irregular, the out-of-door dialect belongs in this opening scene to the poor whites from whom Hassy Few is descended, while the "universal English" of society belongs to the gentry of whom Alexander M'Call is a self-conscious representative. What is old is thereby seen to be both dignified and high-toned, while the new appears rambunctious and low-down. When M'Call reflects on the losses that the women in his family will not forget ("Two brothers dead on the battle-field, you know, and our buildings all burnt, and the plantation turned into a common"), it is fully apparent that to the old and housebound and elite belongs the pull of memory, of retention, of death, and finally of the Old South. For Alec and Hassy Few on the steps of the new courthouse, the world belongs instead to money and emigration, to divestiture, to life with the Yankees, and to the New South that Congress was even then constructing.

Joining old to new, women to men, and memory to emigration is Mollie's promise of social regeneration through marriage, the generic promise of the Romance. Coming onto the narrative scene just as the terms of opposition are set, she shows evidence of performing her role deftly, since she arrives in an "old, shackling" wagon with new sides and seat, the feminine grace note of a white umbrella, and the baggage of a Prater on the move. Her personal capacities are also quickly established: she was previously at the hospital in Dalton, where she nursed the wounded M'Call. Like his sisters who can turn old chemises into handkerchiefs and damask curtains into dresses, Mollie seems able to rehabilitate the worn-out past, the distinctive role of the heroine in the cross-sectional romance of 1868.

Most suggestive is her own promise to be "civil" to the Yankees, by which she means that she will be polite. Combined with the roles of Alec and Captain Humphreys as officers of the law, however, her promise takes on the luster of national regeneration. De Forest himself was to recommend exactly that tack in "Chivalrous and Semi-Chivalrous Southrons" when he wrote: "The Republican party, while firmly maintaining the integrity of the country and the great results of the war in the advancement of human freedom, ought to labor zealously for the prosperity of the South, treat tenderly its wounded pride, forget the angry past, be patient with the perturbed present, and so create a true, heart-felt national unity" (*Harper's Monthly*, February 1869). When Mollie eventually weighs the heart, family, and section she has long known against the race, government, and uniform of Captain Humphreys, she is indeed poised to surrender poverty for comfort, the past for the future, and state sovereignty for national citizenship.

That she refuses the genre's promised transformation and ultimately breaches both good manners and the law testifies to the pull of Southern heritage for romantic heroines and to the perspicacity of the story's opening scene. The women apparently do not know the war is over, at least not the Praters. By reiterating her family name throughout this first section, Mollie underlines her unwillingness to change it in marrying; but in the domain of the Romance, even so independent a creature as Mollie Prater has few other options in seeking revenge for the invasion of the South. Since she cannot afford to marry Alexander M'Call, her operative choice is reduced to accepting the Yankee or forfeiting the right to choose, precisely the status of the Southern states when Congress proposed the Fourteenth Amendment for ratification. In "Parole d'Honneur," there is even a trace of the acquiescence chosen in 1866 by Tennessee: although reluctantly, the M'Call women have agreed to take in the Yankee boarders, Alec's mother has wished the captain well in his suit, and Mollie herself has occasionally been more unbending in her manner toward the "Vandal." Finally, however, the M'Calls are willing to bear in silence the dead brothers and dying plantation; Mollie is not. The graceless offer of reconstruction that Captain Humphreys extends ("I wish to make you my wife") she refuses outright, with the energy of Southern legislatures refusing to disenfranchise their ruling class.

It is no accident that attention shifts almost immediately to Mollie's father and through him to the problems of class that the twists of the romance have tended thus far to efface. The hierarchy that traditionally descended from Southern planters is skewed in "Parole d'Honneur" by De Forest's competing determination to educate both South Carolinians and the readers of *Harper's Monthly* in the work ethic, which prompts him to reach for improbable accommodations in limning his characters. It is unlikely, for instance, that the patrician Alexander M'Call would serve as a deputy sheriff in the Reconstruction South, a post more commonly reserved for the Hassy Fews. The complications of mingling Southern characters and Northern social imperatives similarly distort the role that the Praters are required to play. Whereas Mollie and her bushwhacking father would rightly belong to the "semi-chivalrous" class that managed crops on hired plantations as Doctor Prater does in Georgia, they are wonderfully well educated and yet remarkably mean, the embodiment of the "lost cause" that the "high-toned" M'Call has handsomely given up.

Thus dismantled and reconstructed, the class system of the South appears as fluid as the Northern social order that throws the moneyed Captain Humphreys together with lieutenants Jackson and Jones, the boys who have come up through the ranks in the army and up to the social polish of clerks in their New England towns. Much of this confusion is obscured by the initial focus on young love; the slippery Doctor Prater remains on the edge of town and of the romance, while the two lieutenants simply disappear from the cast. In their absence, De Forest can enlist the honor of the "chivalrous" M'Calls in the New South and quietly reward the Federal officers with the social standing they have long sought.

When the good offices of Mrs. M'Call prove insufficient and the suit of Captain Humphreys is crushed, however, these civil arrangements fall apart. With Mollie's revenge, the domestic principles that were to be sanctified anew in a national marriage likewise default; they are replaced by a male paradigm of companionship and the open road. In fact, mapping the territory of good citizenship becomes a military adventure: instead of tracing the courtship of the South from one end of town to the other, the narrative follows a Federal detail that rides out to hunt. Behind them the soldiers leave "rolling landscape" and "fertile" land for more uncharted territory, the mountain "spurs" and unseen "swamp" in which the class tensions among men become as unmanageable as the irregular terrain. The obsequious Johnny Scalf swears loyalty ("I was allays agin the war, and never owned no black uns") in the face of Alec's patrician contempt. The "Cromwellian" farmer on the road recommends that they "shute" Prater before he can terrorize those in the hills who helped the Yankees through the lines. The Negro informant beckons through the fence rails for the Yankees to go "fotch" Largent on the sly. For the rest of the story, everybody sneaks, a sign that national allegiance might well become yet another maneuver in a local struggle between those with full corn cribs and those without.

In fact, the principle of descent that Mollie invoked in refusing Captain Humphreys becomes in this substitute landscape a descent into barbarism that turns the cultivated Doctor Prater into an "atrocious villain" and Mollie into a man. The good doctor's crimes are churlish: burning a farmer's house with women and children inside, killing even the baby. The signs of character in Mollie's face now unsex her: the "breadth to her cheek-bones and strength in her lower jaw" foreshadow her descent into a man's second dialect ("I have had it out with my Yankee, and I have given him the devil"), and her increasing self-reliance makes her something of a "lone woman." Stymied in her effort to free her father, she first pulls a penknife and then rides off swearing on a horse. Instead of guaranteeing her the sanctity of a home, her loyalty to her father gives her the strength "of a maniac or of a wild beast," almost the "savage queenliness" with which Doctor Prater's wife (and Mollie's mother?) defies the Yankees who break into her house. Invading the Southern home in De Forest's story makes bushwhackers of cultivated men and beasts of their women.

They are fended off by Northern-sponsored patricians like Alec M'Call, who are joined by low-downers and Negroes when they see their chance. The real enemy, evidently, is the ex-Confederate who plunders, the bushwhacker whom local residents hide or betray. M'Call describes the true threat that worries De Forest, the "cut-throats" that "every decent citizen" should hunt down. "They pretend to be hunting Tories and niggers," says the deputy sheriff, "but what they really hurt is the South. They hurt its character." So Alec replaces Mollie as protagonist to portray what the South may become with Northern assistance, what the nation may become on his behalf.[26]

The adventure of citizenship that De Forest imagines in "Parole d'Honneur" is constructed on the littered ground of the house invaded, though the black inheritors like Auntie Cord are nowhere in sight. Instead, the M'Call family and fortune are destroyed by the war and the Prater family is under attack; in the story's final scene, Alec himself leans against a "deserted hovel" while guarding his prisoner. The central event of the story's second section is the invasion of the Old Ponder Mejunkin place, with Captain Humphreys stationed at one doorway and Alexander M'Call at the other. Compounding the disruption of home and family is the fact that the house they invade does not rightly belong to the Praters; it has passed from one Southern skedaddler to another. Home is therefore twice debilitated: first by transient and doubtful ownership, and then by direct assault. Only with domestic premises thus imperiled can the "word of honor, word of a gentleman" become law.

"Parole d'Honneur" is a Northern story set on Southern soil. Thematically, it endorses duty over love, order over degeneracy, and Northern supremacy over Southern resistance, regardless of the ideological complications it inspires. Formally, however, it subverts its own premises. The scenario for reconciliation is first undone by Mollie when she stands by the loyalties to section she was designed to represent. The second time around, she again refuses to desert one family for another. As a result, the genre miscarries as history compromises its customary direction. Without Mollie, Alec M'Call and Captain Humphreys have no foreseeable future, since they have no family to begin.

In fact, without Mollie they have no story. In the narrative De Forest sets up, she carries the action. She rides into the story on a wagon and out of it on a horse. Like the narrator of "Tom Lodowne," she is also structurally at the story's center, promising a new synthesis of settled past and dynamic future, but only by demolishing the romance that readers recognized and by forfeiting the regeneration she was meant to effect. Instead of transforming the rebel through marriage into the loyal wife, "Parole D'Honneur" ultimately transforms the rebel into a citizen on the basis of class. Democracy in the emerging nation was thereby joined to class privilege in ways that would cement the claims of redemptive Southern governments, ways that a reconstructing Congress had neither anticipated nor restrained.

CHAPTER THREE

The Adventure
of National Initiation

MOLLIE PRATER WAS NOT the only petitioner with much to gain and much to lose in the ramshackle years following the Civil War. For those women who had early joined political forces with the antislavery movement, "first the slave, then the woman!" had been the battle cry for years. Passage of the Fourteenth Amendment, however, had shaken their alliances profoundly. Not all citizens but the "male inhabitants" of the states were to be protected in the exercise of their rights. "Including the negro in the body politic" was uppermost, as Frederick Douglass pointed out in the *Atlantic Monthly* in 1867, and the Republican Party had no intention of jeopardizing two million voting freedmen in Southern constituencies. Outside the parameters of domestic tropes, national citizenship could be shaped by the rhetorical bond between men and the law they fashioned, as "Parole d'Honneur" amply demonstrated. Within months of the Fourteenth Amendment's ratification in 1868, the Fifteenth Amendment specifically extending voting rights had already been proposed. Intent on shoring up control and subjugating both Democrats and the unrepentant South, Republicans in Congress seized their opportunity for delivering viable political freedom to black Americans, North and South, before future elections eased them out of office.

In soliciting black loyalty and white approval for expanded Federal authority over suffrage, the Republican program in Congress and in the popular press was assisted by the growing popularity of Adventure stories, which traded old homesteads for wider spaces and delayed romance in favor of the open road. Enlisted in a nationalistic campaign, Adventure stories helped to reinvent the self, now to be defined by the state instead of the family. Home in Adventure stories was far away and sweethearts absent; in their place, generally, were the comforts of a makeshift shelter and the romance of stories that veterans had to tell. The more the war receded, the more such stories got told in the pages in popular magazines and the more the predilections of the genre came to delineate the distinctive new shape of national citizenship. Indeed, the problems that troubled "citizens" on the open road reveal the unacknowledged tensions in serving the General Government.

Particularly suggestive in this regard is "The Scout's Narration" (*Harper's Weekly*, 9 January 1864), an unsigned tale of midnight roads and scant moonlight among the Blue Ridge mountains in western Virginia. Cut loose in short order from his family when he enlists, from his regiment when he volunteers as a scout, and from the Federal lines when he receives his first assignment, Charlie Leighton makes for the rebel camp to discover how the enemy forces have been deployed to meet an imminent Federal attack. Clearly his mission is admirable if dangerous: Captain Leighton is handsome and intelligent, his dark curls a suggestion of the "natural love of excitement and restlessness of soul" that the story celebrates in the Union cause. Because he is deft at describing the threat to the lone scout ("every turn of the road may conceal a finger on a hair-trigger") that has already cost another scout his life, it is easy to applaud Leighton's zeal in racing down the deserted road, his bravado in impersonating a Southern orderly, and his wit in charging the rebel picket lines yelling "Tallahassee!" as the only possible countersign. But Leighton himself pulls up short when he must kill a guard in cold blood in order to eavesdrop on rebel battle plans. With the bowie knife buried in the soldier's midriff, the scout pauses over the "noble" face, the "beautifully shaped" hands and feet, the "mansion of a gallant, gentle soul." On the verge of discovering the information that will undoubtedly save Northern lives at dawn, he wonders: "Was it a fair fight? did I attack him justly?" For a moment, before he slips into the dead guard's overcoat and slouched hat, the "lion-hunter" with the "stealth of a panther" almost kneels, a protean citizen surprised by the tug of Christian remorse.

In the light that shines through the tent's canvas walls, Charlie Leighton is as good a Civil War hero as any the genre has to offer, since he embodies the Adventure story's promise of service, courage, and invention. Outside the tent's military conference and tended space, he is likewise outside the domestic sanctions that Old Homestead stories propose, a figure lit briefly in the dark. The road to which he will return does not lead to marriage or a second chance. It leads instead to glory, specifically to a later dinner with his commander General R. and a still later campfire around which he will tell his story. It leads, in other words, to infinite repetitions of such a mission in his new role as scout.

That, too, is generically instructive: where Old Homestead narratives formally repeated the figure of the house invaded and Romances favored the scenario of marital choice, Adventures consistently asserted a public stage, an open territory in which the number of possible dramas proliferated. Even if characters returned to the sites in which they began, they returned changed, as Charlie Leighton returns to camp after his first success in enemy territory. Many Civil War Adventures were similarly set in temporary male locales like an army camp or bivouac, though they might also include boarding house or smithy, cottage back door or Capitol Hill, pay office or Libby Prison. In their readiness to seize upon local details and unusual events, Adventure stories revealed the impulse to multiply, whereas Romances transformed and Old Homestead stories maintained. In so doing, Adventure stories were most likely to disregard the cultural legacy of the Revolution that Old Homestead stories shored up and to bypass the pressures of Reconstruction that Romances often represented; instead, they more nearly served the selective purposes of Redemption, not least in promoting the gender distinctions that would cost nineteenth-century women the right to vote.

Yet the public setting upon which Adventures generally insisted did not always keep wives and sisters tied to Old Homestead or Romance scenarios, and therefore out of sight. On modified terms heroines also left home, though they were more likely to enter narratives in a steamer cabin than on a ship's deck, in a hospital than on a battlefield, or in a carriage than on a street. Nonetheless, for women in popular narratives the available territory likewise seemed to open up, as it did on Capitol Hill during 1868 when the issue of suffrage took more decided shape as the Fifteenth Amendment. In Congressional debate and the journalistic response that suffrage occasioned, the role of women provoked the same questions that Captain Leighton raised over the "noble" Southern corpse: What was "fair"? What was "just"? As characters and citizens, women in the popular press also widely embodied "redemption," but on domestic terms that were more inclusively Christian than exclusively nationalistic. Theirs proved to be a salvation without irony and, ultimately, a solution without success.

More readily diverse than any other genre, Adventures were also more numerous, especially in the postwar years. Of 321 Civil War stories, some 77 were Adventures and another 70 combined Adventure strategies with those of other types, most often Romance. Altogether about 147 stories were Adventures of some sort, roughly 46 percent of the total. Only 60 of these appeared during the war; about 50 more were published by the end of the decade, and another 37 before the Centennial. Setting aside the considerable number of stories that were carried by *Harper's Weekly* before the war ended, the postwar vigor of the genre is even more striking: where 28 Adventure stories appeared in fifteen other American magazines before the war was over, a hefty 44 more were published by the end of the decade, and a remarkable 37 then appeared as Democratic state governments moved into place.

The surge in Adventures after 1865 owes a good deal to the founding of several postwar journals, for which Adventures were more often stock-in-trade. The *Southern Magazine*, for example, published 14 Adventures in the 1870s out of a total of 17 stories dealing with the Civil War, while only 5 Adventures out of some 19 stories appeared in the other four Southern magazines combined, most defunct by 1868. Adventure stories thus declined in number much more gradually over the period than stories of other types. In fact, no other genre was as substantially represented during the 1870s, when 23 Old Homestead stories and 25 Romances fell short of the 37 Adventures in print.

Stretching as they do across the Civil War years that ended with the Centennial, Adventure stories were more kaleidoscopic, more subject to marked shifts in tenor and direction than were stories of other types. Far likelier to chronicle what national service meant to men than to women, the stories generally engaged three problems: dutiful enlistment, protracted soldiering, and postwar adjustment. Sharing an emphasis on immediate detail and public service, Adventure stories nonetheless kept pace with the war and its aftermath in demonstrably different ways, depending on their focus. Richard Wolcott's "Hopeful Tackett—His Mark" (*Continental Monthly*, September 1862), for instance, represents the colloquial conviction of a young shoemaker who volunteers to defend "the Star-Spangle' Banger" and returns home after his leg is amputated. "A Night in the Wilderness" (*Galaxy*, May 1871), published anonymously, describes the eerie horror of the late battle of the Wilderness, as Grant pushed toward Richmond in 1864. A brief and unsigned account entitled "The Wounded Soldier and the Old Colored Woman" (*New National Era*, 9 June 1870) provides evidence of true postwar courtesy aboard a horsecar outside Boston. All three stories center on army service, all three underline battlefield courage, and all three foreground the progress of storytelling and the lessons learned in the war. Most important, all three stories acknowledge the inescapable mark of the war in the limbs that soldiers have lost, a sure sign that none returned home unchanged.

Yet each story delivers a different reading of the wounds that permanently maimed those who served their country. Hopeful Tackett's "mark" is his stump rather than his signature, and it is seen as "a mark of distinction," one of those "honorable scars" that unnoticed recruits willingly acquired in the field. By contrast, "A Night in the Wilderness" portrays a "slaughter-pen" in which weary columns march over "bodies chopped and hacked by balls," a grim terrain whose silent dead rise up. In part because of its brevity, "The Wounded Soldier and the Old Colored Woman" replaces battlefield details with careful note of the respect, gratitude, and blessing that the young soldier summons from strangers on a public conveyance, especially once they hear that he lost his foot at Fort Wagner. Furthering the distinctions in how mangled bodies should be read are the settings. Both "Hopeful Tackett—His Mark" and "A Night in the Wilderness" contrast the site of domestic order with that of wartime disruption; in Wolcott's story, a tension is thereby identified between "civil life" and the "rough, independent life in camp." Captain Turner's account of the fighting in the Wilderness substantiates that tension by noting that the "sense of loneliness and horrid helplessness" he describes is "the least like home experiences" though common among soldiers at the front. National service was thus separated from civility; the farther such stories got from the home and the longer they dwelt on battlefield engagements, the less viable the household was as a political model and the less potent was its domestic alternative to the "independence" of life with the troops.

All the more reason to recognize the refusal to segregate order and disruption in "The Wounded Soldier and the Old Colored Woman," which instead brings the two together on a horsecar at its most crowded, when an old woman climbs aboard. Set between departure and destination, the fall of Fort Sumter and the celebration of the Centennial, the story represents the unique accomplishment of an interstitial space in negotiating a seat for people of color on the national caravan. For that reason it is significant that the transaction takes place among a crowd of strangers, while Hopeful Tackett returns to his sweetheart in the shoemaker's shop and Captain Turner tells his story to fellow bachelors in a New York boarding house. At stake for Hopeful is his former engagement to the boss's daughter; for Captain Turner, the fate of his regiment. For the boy with one foot and his fellow passengers, however, the issue is whether an old colored woman can find a seat on the bus. Though the soldier gets out with a military salute shortly thereafter, he and his crutch leave behind "something finer than politeness" as the horsecar continues on its appointed route. Integrating blacks and whites, women and men, postwar problems and wartime losses demonstrated how amply the new "civil life" could be defined in popular narratives without surrendering individual initiative or personal liberty.

But "The Wounded Soldier and the Old Colored Woman" was the exception that proved the rule in contemporary journals that were not addressed to black readers, and that were not consistently attuned to the integrative message furthered by the *New National Era*. More common was the growing isolation of cultural oppositions based on gender distinctions, with pronounced thematic results: the emergence of humor to take the place of home, the alternative incivility of wartime action, and the subsequent need to depend on the kindness of strangers in reckoning publicly with national loss. Hopeful's cheerful resolution surfaces again in stories after the war, like the antic misfortunes of an inept mountaineer in Confederate Gray's "T.J.'s Cavalry Charge" (*New Eclectic Magazine*, April 1870), the unmasking of a phony German count in George E. Waring, Jr.'s "How I Got My Overcoat" (*Atlantic Monthly*, July 1871), and the recovery of a lost trunk in Louis A. Roberts's "The Romance of a Tin Box" (*Lippincott's*, February 1874). More disturbing are the further accounts of soldiering life: the Virginia militia's response to John Brown's raid at Harper's Ferry in Louise Mannheim's "The First Campaign of a Fat Volunteer" (*Southern Illustrated News*, 10 and 17 January 1863), the disintegration of a volunteer company in C. B. Lewis's "Fate's Choice" (*Galaxy*, April 1876), the battlefield scavenging at Chattanooga in "David Brown" (*Harper's Weekly*, 5 August 1865), and the disquiet of picket duty in Freeman S. Bowley's "A Dark Night on Picket" (*Overland Monthly*, July 1870). The consequences of trouble on the national road are felt in other tales of postwar adjustment: W. H. H. Murray's "A Ride with a Mad Horse in a Freight Car" (*Atlantic Monthly*, April 1869) set after the triumphal march up Pennsylvania Avenue, R. S. Sheppard's "Sentenced and Shot" (*Lakeside Monthly*, November 1870) set along the Gulf at war's end when General Custer's troops wanted to go home, and E. F. Terry's "Wanted: An Heir" (*Atlantic Monthly*, February 1871) set in a soldiers' home at which the Sanitary Commission doled out pensions to disabled veterans after the war. Together these stories indicate that the real war did at least get in the magazines, where the trajectory from Hopeful's "the lan dov the free-e-e" to Captain Turner's "procession of dead things" to the old colored woman's "thanky, dear, thanky" describes the bright promise, sore loss, and lasting revision that action on the battlefield brought about in American life.

On the whole, such stories displaced the pressure of national inheritance and an older generation of Americans by casting mainly young men. Hopeful Tackett does business with his boss, Herr Kordwaner, but he comes home to the boss's daughter Christina and to the newer and larger shop to be called "Kordwaner & Co." In the world of his story, the only thing old, "the dear old flag," is made young again by his "mark." The closest "A Night in the Wilderness" comes to age and older authority is the brigadier general who gives Captain Turner his orders, and the brigadier is out of ammunition. The horror in Turner's story is that the "Valley of Death" he describes is filled with corpses of the young. It is noteworthy, then, that the "youth" on the postwar horsecar headed for Brookline is questioned by an "old gentleman" to whom he tells his brief story. Rather than bow to the gray hairs of his senior, however, the soldier shames his fellow passenger into offering his seat and teaches the "true" gentleman's lesson in respect for the "old and poor and black." His parting salute compares with the new sign over Hopeful's shop and the "gray coals" to which Turner leaves his neighbors, a reminder that national service and battlefield courage helped to reinvent what was "fair" and "just" at the expense of a truncated youth.

The past nonetheless came to bear in Adventures, provocatively where they concerned slaves who wanted to be free and women who left their homes. Therein lay the problem for domestic rhetoric that elsewhere served to keep the past alive throughout the Civil War: if reform was to take place, it seemed necessary to carry the action outside the home, that site of descent and the backward glance. The result was that the further characters got from home the less the past mattered and the more sharply they felt the lessons they had learned once they returned. Heroines were thus round pegs in square holes, identified as they were with domestic stability. Yet they, too, entered public places and, implicitly, public life in the Civil War stories of the 1860s and 1870s, not only to discover but to personify what was "fair" and "just." They had less mobility, less independence in making their choices, and less explicit a national role, but the closer they stayed to the homes their men left the more available they became as characters to incorporate the collective past in the consensual future that emerged from political upheaval.

How much was at stake for women during the war is evident in Nora Perry's "Clotilde and the Contraband" (*Harper's Monthly*, May 1862), a story that significantly represents the shared plight of women who loved the Union and slaves who rushed to freedom in the wartime South. Like stories of enlistment and soldiering, the tale is organized around a sharp contrast between the republicanism that brought Clotilde's French father to New Orleans and the passionate embrace of slavery that brought her suitor's father to his Louisiana plantation after his slaves were freed in Martinique. Not only is the New World contrasted with the repressive monarchy across the Atlantic, but the land of opportunity is seen to deliver two versions of independence, producing freedom and slavery. The double contrast is heightened by the language in which Clotilde's suitors declare themselves: Archibald Ralston upholds the Union and offers his protection in English, while his rival Antoine Legrande markedly prefers French, the Confederacy, and the "subtle snare" he draws around Clotilde once she helps his slave to escape.

In this story, however, the pattern of contrasts produces a cracked family seal rather than an amputated limb, a challenge to an inherited rather than an embodied self. In the event, Clotilde would have been better off if the family seal had dissolved altogether, since by its motto on the letter that she gives to the runaway the slaveholder Legrande perceives her assistance and begins to plan his revenge. Still, she is given the chance to redeem the family name. Suddenly faced with the runaway while she is herself under scrutiny as a possible spy, Clotilde conceals him in the locked reliquary room where the "past splendors of the family" are stored. Thereby foisting freedom upon the special claims of continuity, "this outcast of men" into "this decaying grandeur," she acknowledges a seeming "reproach" for her choice. But as Perry presents the scene in the reliquary room, it is remarkably unclear whether the censure derives from the family legacy Clotilde will sully ("these carefully-preserved relics of an inheritance of rank and pomp") or from the slave ("one of God's creatures") whose liberty such an inheritance constrains. Poised at that transition and favoring freedom over family, Clotilde dresses the boy as a nun, a "soeur de charite," in a successful effort to meet any reproach by adapting domestic principles to a national cause.

In her turn, she is saved from the same "master" by Ralston, whom she does not initially love. Just as the reliquary room provided another interstitial space for transforming family ties into national service, however, Ralston's yacht provides the site for transforming the gratitude of a friend into the love of a wife, their mutual reward. As Clotilde sails away from her old home into "exile for the cause of freedom," she remembers the slave's earlier escape. Instead of casting her innocence and faith into doubt, as Captain Leighton does in the light of the tent, Clotilde retains both in liberating herself from Legrande's snare and her jaded lover from his cynicism ("I got back my faith again") by assisting the fugitive slave. In 1862, some years before emancipation's promise of justice and liberty was codified, "Clotilde and the Contraband" demonstrated how much of a national future for freedmen might depend upon the family inheritance to which women held the key.

Perry's early coupling of freedom for slaves with escape for women prefigured the pattern of Congressional debate when the Fifteenth Amendment was reported out of committee in January 1869. So, too, her preoccupation with transforming a Revolutionary inheritance would be central, though with consequences that kept latter-day Clotildes bound to reliquary rooms nationwide. Essentially dismantling the romance of a new union springing from "the cause of freedom," Congressional representatives would turn their attention to other Ralstons and Legrandes, to their manly fellowship that Perry's lover only pretends, and to the brotherhood that the disguised "soeur de charite" never knew. Once again, family seals would crack, but in 1869 they would serve as a badge of tyranny instead of a ticket to freedom.

Discussion of the Fifteenth Amendment opened in both the House and the Senate on 23 January, though each Judiciary Committee reported its own bill. In the House, George S. Boutwell of Massachusetts wrote and sponsored a narrow amendment that protected solely the

freedman's right to vote, while in the Senate William M. Stewart of
Nevada managed discussion of a broader amendment that also guaranteed the right to hold office and banned discrimination on the basis
of nativity, property, or creed as well as race, color, and previous condition of servitude. The marked differences in formulating the amendment's terms bespoke substantial disagreements about the privileges
of national citizenship in the wake of the Civil War, the previous Reconstruction amendments, and the growing public attention to women,
Indians, and the Chinese. Acutely felt, such disagreements complicated
the joint passage of either version of the amendment in Congress; only
after a Senate session running through the night of 8 February, a host of
unacceptable substitutions, a joint conference report, and further out-
cry was a single bill passed and delivered to the states. In its final form,
worded as the Senate preferred but with a much narrower application
and no sanction for the right to hold office, the Fifteenth Amendment
was declared ratified on 30 March 1870, after which all Southern states
were granted representation in Congress and the audacious control of
radical Republicans came to an end.[1] From 1870, Washington's authority legally supported suffrage for black men throughout the United
States, although the states soon discovered that literacy tests, property
restrictions, and poll taxes still fell within their domain.

Just as significant, however, were those who would not receive even
such minimal recognition for years to come. While the Fifteenth
Amendment pointedly included the right to vote in the "civil" rights
to be extended to black men, the Congressional debates of 1869 also
opened the constitutional door to universal suffrage and to several
lesser extensions of the elective franchise. Senator Ross of Kansas predicted universal suffrage or anarchy, Congressman Scofield of Pennsylvania spoke of putting the Declaration of Independence into the
Constitution at last, and Senator Warner of Alabama raised the issue
of those without means who were citizens nevertheless. "The question
before us," Warner declared, "is not one of negro suffrage. It is the
question of suffrage itself. It is the broad question who shall be the
voters of this country, in whose hands shall rest the political power."
Like some of his colleagues, Warner enthusiastically raised the issue

of class prejudice when he included "landless and dependent tenants" with "the great laboring, industrial classes" in his vision of American opportunity. Compounding class with gender, he argued as well on behalf of women as "the purest and best of God's creations," especially those like war widows who went unrepresented while they paid taxes.[2] Not labor alone but loyalty deserved its reward, as the economy of "Clotilde and the Contraband" had allowed.

But Warner also admitted that the hour for women's suffrage had not yet arrived and that "practical" considerations narrowed his support. So, too, other Republicans allowed the justice of granting the vote to women but fell back on judicial decisions that assumed women to be represented by husbands or brothers, though the same members of Congress regularly attacked the judgment that slaves could be represented by their masters.[3] More often it was Democrats who raised the possibility of woman's suffrage, as a viable challenge to extending the vote on any terms. Their conservative intransigence was occasionally served by continuing references to the innate inferiority of the "half-civilized colored man," who was "without history" and "incapable of self-government"; but these slights were dwindling, and they carried little weight in the face of widespread attention to the wartime service of the colored soldier.[4] In 1869, there was much more talk of the black soldier than there had been at the close of the war, when his wounds were fresh. "On staff and crutch he stands demanding his rights," said Congressman Whittlemore of South Carolina; "with scars and empty sleeves he pleads an equal franchise; with uplifted hands, which have borne the musket in defense of your altars and your homes, of that flag, emblem of freedom, of the future greatness of our Republic, he asks, not social, but political equality."[5] By comparison, women had few battlefield marks of their wartime dedication and thus little recognized "service" to reward.

The same was true of the Chinese, whose chances of obtaining suffrage paled when representatives from the West took the floor. Senator Williams of Oregon complained of their "political filth and moral pollution"; his colleague from Oregon, Senator Corbett, pointed to the pagan institutions that threatened to "supersede" Christian principles.

Not only were the Chinese unfit candidates for political responsibilities, said Cole of California, they had no intention of becoming citizens; even their dead were taken back to the Celestial Empire. Similarly apprehensive about the tide of immigrants of all sorts, Patterson of New Hampshire warned of the "incoming floods of ignorance and barbarism."[6] While the Declaration of Independence was invoked more than once as the territory of citizenship opened up, such fears about immigrants like the Chinese counted against universal male suffrage when it was proposed by Stewart in the Senate and Bingham in the House, neither of whom could dilute the continuing ire against Southern traitors or the suspicion of the Indians. While Senator Wilson of Massachusetts spoke eloquently for a constitutional amendment that would safeguard Catholics, the property-less, and the foreign-born, the result of steady debate in the Senate as well as the House was a much less comprehensive understanding of who should vote in the emerging nation and whose political power the Constitution should guarantee.[7]

That a nation was indeed emerging from the Civil War was a commonplace in 1869 where it had not been during Thirteenth Amendment debates just a few years before. Senator Morton of Indiana derided the "heresy of secession" when he declared that "the whole fallacy lies in denying our nationality." Senator Pomeroy of Kansas spoke of "this national Government, which will tower in its magnificence and stand forever," while Congressman Hamilton of Florida maintained that the "theory of centralization" propounded by Alexander Hamilton was no longer as "dangerous" as the theory of "arbitrary States rights in a national governement." Summing up the reigning party fervor in the House as the decade drew to a close, Blackburn of Louisiana observed: "It is the mission of the Republican party to see that the Government shall have a new and accelerated impetus under the new order of things, and be firmly organized and adjusted upon the idea of a great and overpowering nationality."[8] In the discussion of the Fifteenth Amendment, therefore, it was of particular moment how the Revolutionary "fathers" figured in the "free government" that Higby of California described and how the terms of citizenship within the Constitution were ultimately defined. Provocatively, the rhetoric of home and family employed in earlier constitutional debates did not simply lapse; it became instead a sign of decay.

Boutwell's opening remarks in the House set the tone for coupling domestic rhetoric with an aristocratic social order that was maintained through family control and at loggerheads with the democratic principle of suffrage. Thus cast, national citizenship was less likely to propel a "national household" or a "family of States." In Boutwell's formulation, the republic that the Constitution inaugurated was instead set against an aristocracy in which "the Government is in certain families made hereditary to the exclusion of others." The citizenship he imagined was then described as singular rather than cooperative; noting a Kentucky slavery case in 1822, he cited the court's opinion that *citizen* derives from *civis*, which led him not to a robust community but to its lone member as "one vested with the freedom and privileges of a city."[9] In the Senate, Ferry of Connecticut contrasted American government with the Greek preference for lineage dating back "through heroes and demi-gods" to Olympus, and with the priority given by the Jews to the Hebrew family of Abraham. Ross of Kansas warned that monarchy still threatened; if any single race made the country's laws, then a similar prerogative could fall to a single class, a single family, and a single individual, thereby confounding an American republicanism based on universal suffrage. Loughridge of Iowa condemned "the aristocracy of race" as the "last relic of the barbarism of slavery" in the House, where Mullins of Tennessee pointed to the sin of slavery as "the blood of Abel" rotting the house that the founders passed along. "We want a new house, for the old one fallen into decay," he insisted; "we want to repair and invigorate our constitution of government to meet the demands of the times." Not freedom but the crime of slavery, what Mullins called "the draft drawn upon us by our fathers," constituted the Revolutionary legacy as outspoken Republicans portrayed it in 1869.[10]

Therein lay the most pervasive realignment of postwar discourse that Constitutional debate was to engineer. Instead of celebrating the "Republican mother" who would welcome new "children" to the fold, those pressing for permanent reform now condemned the decayed "timber" of Revolutionary promise and indicted both founding fathers and the domestic rhetoric that assured their authority. There is ample evidence that striking at the "foundation" and removing the "corner stone" of the government, an attack on founding principles that Dixon of Connecticut condemned, is exactly what reformers had in mind. Not only the Constitution but the rhetorical sovereignty of the fathers, not only Revolutionary principles but the basic principle of inheritance, demanded closer scrutiny as support for expanding suffrage rights coalesced. "We have hauled up the old ark of the Constitution for repairs," said Pomeroy of Kansas on the Senate floor, after noting that the Constitution's framers had "sowed to the wind" in admitting slavery.[11] Neither his rhetorical gestures nor those of like-minded colleagues encouraged the filial obeisance or the homespun anxiety that antebellum oratory and postwar Democrats enjoined, gestures that assured the place of home and family in shaping earlier political debate.

The unexpected zeal with which domestic tropes were maligned suggests the shallow enthusiasm or downright misgivings in Congress about extending suffrage to the women associated with family affairs. As mothers and sisters and wives rather than as public speakers or wartime seamstresses, women were seen by Congressman Eldridge to be "educated, cultivated, and refined"; but they were too much "the priestess of the altar of the household," as Kentucky Senator Davis put it, to want the vote. Congressman Woodward of Pennsylvania saw the ballot as "a degradation to the female sex," and Senator Bayard of Delaware claimed that women vying for suffrage would be tempted "to unsex themselves" in deserting their maternal roles. That duties at home might spare women from national initiation was demonstrated when Senator Williams of Oregon drew an analogy to wartime service; voting women, he pointed out, "may come to feel like a romantic boy going to the war, dreaming of greatness and glory, but finding in the sufferings and sacrifices of the march, the camp, and the battle, a strong desire to go back to the quiet and happy home of his boyhood."[12] Hoping to curtail the privileges granted by an undesirable amendment, the conservative wing in Congress buttressed an appeal to Revolutionary forefathers by maintaining that their contemporary daughters were too virtuous to want the ballot and too bound to their children at home to vote. Of Indians and the Chinese the conservatives said little, since neither group was American or Christian or democratic enough to qualify as characters in the unfolding domestic drama.

Instead of the feminine ethos of the household that Chollet's Stella enabled or that Appleton's Ida Ridgely finally embraced, Congressional discussion of the rites of national citizenship in 1869 devolved upon "fellow citizens" joining in brotherhood to cement American democracy. The paradigm could promote or obscure the class distinction of "gentlemen," but it operated unmistakably to replace the stability of the home with the independence of free agency in a country to be governed by men. So Senator Wilson of Massachusetts stated: "I care not to what race a citizen of the Republic may belong, where he was born, what may be his possessions, what may be his intellectual culture, or his religious faith, I recognize him not only as a countryman, a fellow-citizen, but a brother, given by his Creator the same rights that belong to me." Congressman Hamilton of Florida likewise extended his hand to ex-slaves as "brothers in the family of mankind, equals in the brotherhood of men." Senator Fowler of Tennessee described the "freedom of the individual" as "all-absorbing," much like the "playmates of our boyhood hours, neighbors and associates."[13]

With "fellow-citizens" repairing "this house built by our fathers" and even supplanting "the altar of the household" among those who resisted extending the elective franchise, it was difficult to secure firm rhetorical ground upon which to claim the vote for women. Making what stand he could, Senator Pomeroy attempted to strip "woman" down to her citizenship, to promote her civil rights through rhetorical divestment. "I ask the ballot for woman," he claimed, "not on account of her weakness or on account of her strength; not because she may be above or below a man; that has nothing to do with the question. I ask it because she is a citizen of the Republic, amenable to its laws, taxed for its support, and a sharer in its destiny." That said, Pomeroy translated the comprehensive amendment he sought into "the dream of the fathers of a free and pure Republic," but his effort to bracket continuity with extended suffrage failed.[14] When the Fifteenth Amendment

finally made its ragged way through Congress, the "entire enfranchise-
ment" Pomeroy imagined had long since given way to "a rod of power"
in the hands of freed black men, before whom sponsor Stewart claimed
"all politicians quail." [15] Unfortunately, the freedmen would enjoy a
citizenship of the rod only as long as Reconstruction governments remained in office and Federal troops remained in the South.

Articulating the rights of citizenship along gender lines was a rhetorical practice outside the halls of Congress as well, since the status of
Revolutionary ideals was everywhere in doubt. The more fully political
privileges were coded as masculine, the more insistent was the break
with founding fathers. As early as 1867, Frederick Douglass equated
full citizenship with a new and resolute manhood in "An Appeal for
Impartial Suffrage" (*Atlantic Monthly*, January 1867), an essay that
bases the case for suffrage on the faithful service of black soldiers, the
need for the freedman's labor, and the urgency of enforcing national
interests upon the Southern states. His metaphor for the Reconstructive crisis suggests, in fact, that the domesticated romance of the Union
was bankrupt. Douglass writes: "We have thus far only gained a Union
without unity, marriage without love, victory without peace." Like Republicans in subsequent Congressional debates, he further undermines
domestic premises by representing the war as the inherited punishment for the Revolutionary sin of slavery, "the harvest of blood sown in
the spring-time of the Republic by your patriot fathers." His solution
is to replace family with national party, to redeem liberty by banishing "the bludgeon and the bowie-knife" from Congressional debate,
and to make the Negro "a man among men" by extending the vote
to all males. Though he repeatedly speaks of four million ex-slaves in
Southern states, which would include freed women with men, his brief
for gallantry, conquest, and flinty hearts bespeaks a male paradigm for
achieving power, which his sustained appeal to "statesmen of America"
reinforces.

The same readiness to cast national citizenship as a male prerogative
is central to R. W. Raymond's "National Characteristics" (*Overland
Monthly*, September 1869), a Western essay about the status of the
Chinese. Like Douglass, Raymond impugns the authority of inheri-

tance, here cast in scientific terms as an attack on natural selection in favor of human will. Raymond thereby pits classes, races, religions, and parties against individual responsibility, family and birthplace and tribe against personal liberty, and the aristocracy of birth against democracy. Faced with the Chinese traditions of dynasty, paganism, and monarchy, Raymond translates American freedom into a strategy for extending the ballot to eradicate racial barriers and promote individual autonomy. "Treat the particular Chang with justice," he observes, "and the collective John will not trouble you." Readier than Douglass to dispense with the strength of numbers ("There are very few things, indeed, that are true of four hundred million people"), Raymond severs all ties to family, history, and race in his effort to render the Chinaman "individually upright" and thus truly American.

Such a tendency to discover justice in liberty and thus distinctly outside the home allowed the marketplace greater play in defining citizenship and its privileges; Douglass, for instance, cites "enlightened selfishness" in claiming the vote for freedmen, and Raymond couples business with government in their mutual need for "honesty between man and man." Derived from the cultural readiness to segregate human activity into gendered spheres, such arguments for extended male suffrage also continued to draw support from conservative bastions like *Godey's* when Sarah Josepha Hale editorialized. In "Ought Women to Have the Right of Suffrage?" (October 1867), Hale similarly bracketed business and politics to argue against the competition of women, who reigned in the home. Drawing her authority from the Bible, she represents men as protecting and women as preserving, men as providing and women as inspiring, men as making laws and women as setting examples. "Our government," she states, "is based on man's authorities and woman's influences." Certainly the case for "true womanhood" was not new; but amid the debate over voting rights, Hale's widely disseminated endorsement of women's "moral goodness" separated from the "material things" of men and their "coersive" tactics served to ensure that citizenship, like suffrage, would develop as an exercise in power and industry, ostensibly influenced by the ascendancy of the good.

The more completely suffrage was thereby associated with what was manly and freestanding, the more difficult it became to imagine women at the ballot box or to identify the channels of Revolutionary inheritance with the brave new world of the postbellum nation. The rhetorical quandary that resulted for suffrage activists was apparent when Mary Olney Brown wrote an open letter to Douglass's *New National Era* ("The Right of Colored Women to Vote," 24 October 1872). After the magazine's exuberant response when the Fifteenth Amendment was ratified in 1870, few paused like Brown to reflect that "colored citizens" were now all male, in spite of the provisions of the Reconstruction amendments. In her short letter to the editor, Brown puts her finger on the problem for politicians ("In protecting the colored women citizens in the exercise of their right to vote, they are bound to protect the white women citizens in the exercise of the same rights, a step in advance which they were not quite ready to take") without dismantling or expanding the domestic sanctions that allowed Congress to restrict suffrage. Ultimately Brown replaces her recurring "women citizens" with the "mothers, wives, sisters, and daughters" who deserve the "protection" from "injustice" that full enforcement of the Fourteenth and Fifteenth Amendments would bring about, more an effort to gain the support of men than a full-scale redefinition of national privileges and immunities on domestic terms.

At greater length and in greater detail, however, Julia Ward Howe took up the challenge of imagining a more thoroughgoing democracy in "Women as Voters" (*Galaxy*, March 1869), which begins similarly by bracketing slaves and women as still marginalized in the political life that Perry had observed in 1862. Reconceiving their role, Howe confronts the disadvantages of domestic conventions head-on and then reasserts their civil function. Her specific target is the damaging argument that the family, as the foundation of society, should speak with a single voice; her strategy is to debunk the assumption of force and implicit contest between spouses as anachronistic and to replace contention with a more modern "process of reconciliation," the process by which parents reason with children, preachers convince their congregations, and representatives persuade their constituents. The new

society she foresees once women become voters is thus both individual-
istic and cooperative, just as an orchestra is both a unit and composed
of smaller units that make music together. Indicting the logic of conquest, Howe writes: "In the true family, each member is at once a unit
and part of a larger unit. It is a part of the old superstition of force to
believe that the perfection of the larger unity is to be attained only by
the mutilation of the smaller ones."

As the guardians of the national family, women must discard their
currently "mutilated" roles, according to Howe, and reach for "larger
liberties, larger work" in serving the public good. The reconstituted
ideal for Howe is not then the "particular Chang" or the "manhood of
a man" but the "eloquent matron," who will lead the nation's children
from the nursery to the "steps of State" as confidently as Kerber's Republican mothers led patriot children out of the Revolution. Instead of
separating virtue from enterprise as the home was separated from public life, instead of severing the individual from affiliations beyond the
self, Howe deliberately reconciles virtue with public service through
suffrage and thereby refigures national citizenship with the "charity,
patience, and modesty" that were widely associated with women and
widely divorced from the stringencies of Reconstruction policy.

As Howe's essay demonstrates, it was still possible after the military partition of the South to portray paramount national citizenship,
the premise guiding the Reconstruction Acts of 1867, in the household terms that *Uncle Tom's Cabin* had made familiar. Indeed, as the
additional essays by Brown and Hale corroborate, it was apparently difficult to imagine American women who were not principally mothers,
wives, sisters, and daughters concerned with reconciling their children's future to the past they preserved. As protagonists in Civil War
stories, they would always have at least one foot on the doorjamb of
Old Homestead promises, at least one other generation to safeguard.
In Adventure stories, consequently, they would take more baggage on
the road and thus be more vulnerable to wartime attack. Formally, as
Howe and Brown might have predicted, the women setting out in Civil
War stories faced the same strategic difficulty that hampered runaway
slaves in Old Homestead casts: how to get a move on when they were

generically bound to stay put. The solution they initiated, when it could be imagined, took a page from Romance models: they transformed the homestead itself and their roles in it on a national scale.

How bound they were to domestic premises was most evident when the violence that spurs Adventures was extreme; for example, the New York draft riots during July 1863 that erupt in Ellen Leonard's "Three Days of Terror" (*Harper's Monthly*, January 1867). Several days after a mother and daughter arrive to visit kin, the Irish rise up against the draft in what James M. McPherson has described as "the worst riot in American history" (610). In the streets of New York, 105 people were killed; in the streets of Leonard's story, buildings are fired, pedestrians beaten, brickbats thrown, and a Massachusetts man hung. Alarmed by the tumult, the visiting ladies hide behind closed blinds, the image of women who cannot move up the ladder to full citizenship because they cannot move out of the house. Barring their door, they run afoul of the systematic contrasts which gender distinctions encouraged and Leonard's story propounds. Where the streets are "dark, dirty, and crowded with ill-looking people" from the moment that the ladies dock, the house on East Twenty-second Street is seen as a refuge. When the riot breaks out ("a howling as of thousands of wild Indians let loose at once"), the family is enjoying afternoon siestas; when the "dangerous classes" degenerate into anarchy on the streets, the leisured few at home are maintaining calm.

The stage is thus set for invasion, which Leonard's story repeatedly imposes: the family's youngest son volunteers, the brother's wife rescues her husband from the mob, a wounded officer and his men seek shelter, the rioters knock and kick and threaten outside. "The war at the door," says a frightened narrator, "drowned the battle afar off." The problem for would-be tourists is that the house has become a prison and war zone ("We were bound, hand and foot, in this miserable neighborhood, unable to stir out of doors, and with the prospect of another night of horrors"); their solution is to turn it into a hospital for the wounded soldiers, which turns the ladies into nurses like Alcott's Miss Dane or De Forest's Mollie Prater in her schoolgirl days. They even face down the intruding mob with a quiet authority that convinces its leaders to desist, thus protecting the house from being burned.

But Leonard further reveals in "Three Days of Terror" what narrative circumstances in "The Brothers" and "Parole d'Honneur" tended to elide: the fact that the women still could not exit without an armed guard, nor could their rehabilitative influence extend beyond a cordon of muskets. In the story's final scene, the home regiments return from Gettysburg to rescue the "prostrate" city and the ladies march down Second Avenue surrounded by officers, policemen, and newspaper reporters. Augmenting the earlier image of imprisoned kin, this solemn parade suggests that women escape domestic premises only as docile wards of the state and escape that role in turn only with relief. The visiting ladies, "trunkless and bonnetless," take the next boat home. What they forfeit in their Old Homestead zeal to return is the irrevocable lesson that Adventures commonly posit at the end of the public road, the lesson that for heroines might well be closer to what was "fair" and "just" than mob leaders or army scouts could discover. Bound to the household for their credentials, however, heroines were unlikely to approximate the steady tramp that Leonard associates with the soldiers as "executives of law and government" or the "dispatches coming and going" that take couriers abroad.

Both elevated and hindered by their domestic functions, Civil War heroines confronted essentially two options in their bid for the "larger liberties" of public adventure. They could defy domestic restriction or enlarge its service. In war narratives, those who violated received conventions and reader expectations got caught, like the rebel spy Mrs. Heyward in "Trapped" or the disguised volunteer Jane Hemmings in "Colonel Charley's Wife." Reprisals lapsed only when the women were black and/or loyal to the Union; like Polly Pharaoh, they were then seen to reject a past they had not chosen for a future they could not share. At its most coercive, however, the domestic regard for continuity manifest in the home held heroines too close for comfort, as a single scene in "Em" (*Harper's Weekly*, 28 April 1866) reveals. Misjudged by her husband and locked in a remote tower of his plantation

house, the babyish Em at length decides to make her escape on a rope
of bedspreads that she ties around her waist. Then she jumps, out of
the house, out of the impossible role as wife, out of the doubtful loyalty to Virginia that her twin brother Stephie has already renounced.
But as she drops she strikes her head and breaks her arm so that she
swings just off the ground, "watching the whirling world grow black
around her, spinning in a vortex of fragments, and sensible of dissolu-
tion." From the home she chose upon her marriage, there is apparently
no escape, any more than there was for the visiting ladies stranded by
an Irish mob.

Like them, Em literally has limited prospects, positioned as she is
well off the ground of public activity. From their bedroom window, the
New Yorkers could see only row houses and rooftops, while a delirious
Em in her tower room sees the disembodied eyes that rebuke her transgression decades before another prisoner in an upstairs room would
see a woman in the yellow wallpaper. Even before she dangles from the
window as a hostage to the home, Em is hemmed in by accusations:
"the air was swarming with eyes, and as she tried to walk the weaker
ones down on the floor groaned and spat at her for treading on them."
In the simplest terms, female adventure in Civil War stories apparently
lay in getting out of the wrong house, but characters like Em did not
get far, and neither did their challenge to the domestic assumptions
that made them guardians of a mistaken past.

Longer lived and more versatile were heroines who carried their
homes with them or whose situations were already itinerant and public. Customarily, their dramas were played out in transitional spaces,
like the Maryland railroad car that a nurse rides in G. J. A. Coulson's
"Mrs. Spriggins, the Neutral" (*Southern Magazine*, February 1871), the
Tennessee hospital in which a Unionist family finds shelter in Elizabeth S. Phelps's "My Refugees" (*Harper's Monthly*, November 1864),
or the Florida plantation that a New England girl visits in Helen E.
Harrington's "In the Palmy Days of Slaveholding" (*Lakeside Monthly*,
July 1870). The climactic revelation such characters witness is not the
instability of domestic order in these Adventures, but its surprising
resilience: the "horspital nuss" finds a seat on the train when the cour-

teous Southern narrator offers his; the homeless Unionist pulls through an advanced case of typhoid when the doctor had given him hours to live; and the impressionable New England girl returns to the North so angered by slavery that she founds a Relief and Abolition Society and purchases her Southern friends.

Domestic imperatives thus break down disruptive agents instead of faltering when the war hits home. The nurse in border territory banishes sectional wrangling from her ward ("pollyticks don't make no difference to me"), the refugee wife softens her stony heart ("He's guv yer back, an' I won't never say hard things on Him agin!"), and the New England girl disdains Southern elegance ("I had no more admiration for Southern grace and loveliness") upon discovering that her friend has been whipped. While all three characters benefit from what R. W. Raymond would call the exercise of human will, they resist politics, desolation, and slavery on behalf of others. As Julia Ward Howe might put it, they join the chorus instead of piping an aria, even when the chorus is filled with people they do not know. Writes Phelps of the drummer boy who dies as the refugee wife gives thanks: "She was a stranger, but he took her in—in to his pure child's heart!" In phrasing a new national anthem, the women and children who expanded the household model discovered what was "right" and "just" by replacing the Adventure's road with its distant goal: the house redeemed.

The more popular alternative in the Civil War stories that veterans told was to stay on the road forever, from campfire to campfire and tale to tale. If they could not resolve the problem of dead faces in the moonlight, they could at least get further away. That is exactly what another scout over another moonlit body proposed in W.H.K.'s "The Sergeant's Little Story" (*Southern Magazine*, October 1873), as if in response to Captain Leighton's pause. Like the Northern captain, the Southern sergeant is on the road at night alone, now bringing dispatches across the Potomac to Lee's Virginia camp. He, too, finds himself standing over an enemy he has had to kill, now a Northern courier whose "wide-staring eyes" catch the light of the moon. He, too, pauses to consider what he has done, to consider "the purple spot in the pale forehead where the bullet went in and life came out." But his conclusion at length is a shrug and a drink. "Well, well, such is war—as the scout must wage it," he says to his fellow soldiers at table, and then: "Let's licker." Only the "melancholy laughter" of an owl stays with him and stays with his unfolding story as the owl flits from tree to tree until he is perched above the staring eyes.

The road to camp is long, however; this story's real excitement occurs when the sleeping sergeant is almost caught by Federal cavalry on an island in the Potomac. Hiding in the water, he escapes their notice, though not the saber that the Northern colonel unknowingly thrusts in his cheek. The point gives him a cavernous scar, a mark of the war like Hopeful Tackett's but one that keeps his face from the dashing good looks of Captain Leighton and his story from the wondering appeal of the Northern scout. The scar is a reminder of both the danger of the war and his escape. Sliding into the water "like a skilpot off a log," the sergeant stays alive among the animals: he breathes "as softly and steadily as a sleeping bull-frog" and then shakes himself like a dog ("a very primitive, Newfoundland mode of making the toilette, but quite refreshing and satisfactory under the circumstances"). Like all adventurers, he invents himself as circumstances demand; like other Civil War scouts, he is ready to kill, not just the first time on the road but again when two drunken soldiers stumble onto his island. Salvation for the sergeant lies in his bowie knife, "the only friend I could depend on now." Separated from family, regiment, and the safety of Hampton's Confederate cavalry, the sergeant draws his knife ("old 'Buck Horn,' friend and mess-mate!") to dispatch the men who keep him from the road.

As it happens, he does not have to "murder in cold blood" to get away; the soldiers turn out to be Hampton's men, as the sergeant acknowledges when his nephew interrupts his tale. His readiness to do what he must "under heavy provocation," however, reveals the danger and opportunity that lie down the adventurer's infinitely extendable road, above which a less resourceful Em dangles from her bedspreads. Where she goes down for the count, the bullfrog sergeant comes up for air. Where she bangs on a locked tower door, he gives a rebel yell on the banks of the Potomac. Where she cannot forget the violence the war has brought ("the tattered rags of those blue felt coats that had swung from the trees"), he shrugs and befriends it. The knife in his hands is his "rod of power," what suffrage was meant to be for black men in 1869 and what women on trains, in hospitals, and at relief societies never found as trustworthy as the laying on of hands. Where the sergeant draws his knife, Mrs. Spriggins catches the Southern narrator's coat, the Northern nurse touches the Unionist's hand, and the purchased slave husband and wife embrace in freedom. As Civil War adventure stories demonstrate, postwar citizens could likewise reach out a warm hand instead of a bowie knife if they chose, but they would be risking the anger of the mob, the snare of revenge, and the threat of accusing eyes from which there was no escape.

Against such odds, what binds "neutrals" and nurses and slaves to strangers is neither blood nor love but history, the force of circumstances to which they must respond and from which the meaning of a newly national citizenship would derive. How civilly strangers might greet the unexpected is the tacit subject of Homer's unbordered vignettes and the immediate question in a story Rebecca Harding Davis published amid the Centennial celebrations in Philadelphia, a story that opens in border territory on an autumn day in 1861. Stretching across some fifteen years to the months that followed Fort Sumter's fall, Davis's story challenges Homer's vignettes by testifying to the alarming circumstances that would also put women on the road, to the peculiar brand of independence they could also claim by 1876, and to the protean vitality that also makes adventure stories the most ideologically adroit of the three genres. How faithful heroines could remain to the domestic ties imprisoning Em is part of the problem Davis faced from the war's opening days in Wheeling, a town caught between union and secession while the "rod of power" was already held by an army blocking the roads out.

Rebecca Harding Davis,
"How the Widow Crossed the Lines"

(*Lippincott's*, December 1876)

ONE AFTERNOON IN October, 1861, a lady whom we shall here call Mrs. Potter was crossing a foot-bridge over a creek which emptied into the Ohio, cutting in two a straggling mill-town on the Virginia side. This town held, for the first year or two of the war, the key to an important position, and as the population was half rebel and half loyal, it had its full share of the hubbub, the stern tragedy and no less stern comedy of the time. It was made up of half a dozen streets of soot-blackened houses, stretching monotonously for three or four miles along a ledge between the hills and river, with here and there an iron- or glass-mill whose great chimney belched forth flame and smoke. There was nothing in the black streets to induce a sauntering habit in anybody, but Mrs. Potter paused on the foot-bridge and looked down to the Ohio shore. The water of the creek below was of a peculiar clear green: a heavy stone bridge crossed it just where it opened into the river, and the piers made piles and arches of soft shadow in it: beyond was the wall of Ohio hills flaming here and there into autumnal colors; a little steamboat with fluttering flag puffed up and down the muddy river; while overhead the clouds of bituminous smoke shut out the sinking sun with rolling masses of black, touched here and there with blood-red or purple splendor. Looking at these, the lady did not notice a confusion on the banks below her, which shelved down from the back yards of factories and sawmills, and were heaped with ashes and lumber. A few ragged children playing on the rafts began to cry out shrilly. Mrs. Potter heard them at last, and looking down saw a woman in the creek wading deliberately out into the deep current. No one as yet but these children had noticed her. The lady above could not scream: a kind of breathless horror seized her. There were the thumping, clashing mills, the broad daylight, the dirty banks, the children with their feeble little yells, and the woman calmly sinking deeper, step by step, into the water. She was quite composed: that added to the horror of it— a tidy, sober, young woman with a Scotch-Irish face, and hair so neatly dressed above her collar and blue cravat that it struck Mrs. Potter as oddly incongruous with the deed of death.

When the water reached her chin she knelt down. At that moment some workmen saw her and put off in a scow from shore. Before the lady could run across the bridge a crowd of men and boys had collected on the bank and were shouting out orders. She turned to go down to them: it seemed as if somehow the woman belonged to her.

"Elinor!"

It was her brother John, afterward Major Pomeroy of the Confederate service: indeed, he had his commission in his pocket at that minute, and had been secretly enlisting men all day to go with him across the lines. The Pomeroys, like all Virginians, laid down strict rules of decorum for their women. "Where *can* you be going, Elinor?"

"Oh, I beg your pardon, John. But there is a woman drowning. She looked at me—she called to me."

"She will be attended to. I'm not surprised that anybody should claim acquaintance with you. Your radical notions are the town's talk just now.—Here, Dickson!" beckoning a workman. "Take this money and see to that poor wretch. Come to me if more is needed. Mrs. Potter feels an interest in her."

"I doubt, zur, she'll want but a coafin, by the looks of her. And money woan't bring her what she needs if she do be a-livin'."

Major Pomeroy walked on, talking to his sister of the weather and like subjects. His heart burned hot within him. He was going into the Southern army, he might never come back, and his sister, whom he loved better than anybody in the world, had come out openly as an abolitionist. The society of the town (John Pomeroy's world) was moved with amazement and disgust. No wonder she rushed into a crowd of men after a drunken woman! Something there had always been in Elinor, he felt, of headstrong insubordination alien to a Virginia woman. She might have been a New England radical.

He turned into his mill. Mrs. Potter waited until he was out of sight, and then went swiftly back. "Dickson!" she called—"Dickson!" The man was a puddler in her brother's employ. "Is she dead? Where is she?"

"She's on the scow, ma'am. Whatever am I to do with the boss's money?"

"What is it she needs that money won't buy? You said that just now."

"Her baby. She's bin a-lookin' for it these three weeks. It's that that's drove her crazy and into the crik."

"Is the baby dead?"

Dickson had never heard that Mrs. Potter had lost a child, but he knew it now.

"No, it's not dead: it's bin tuk. She's a-loakin' for it all the time."

"Took? Go for a cab, and have her put into it, and driven to my house. She is recovering now."

"Your house? She's as wet as a fish. She'd better go to the jail," mumbled Dickson. "That's the place for mad people, by law."

"The laws will be altered soon in Virginia, thank God!" thought Mrs. Potter, hurrying away. She happened just then to pass some prisoners from the jail at work paving the streets, in chains. She smiled bitterly at this hint of the civilization in her native town. It was the outgrowth of slavery, though there were not twenty blacks in the county. Virginian though she was, she prayed God to crush the tyrant and traitor. She passed the gray stone custom-house, with the stars and stripes fluttering overhead: her heart swelled at the sight. Opposite, was a shambling old house intended for a theatre, but now used as a prison for rebels. It was guarded by a company of old fellows, volunteers who had probably never fired a gun in their lives, and who sat about the pavement in their shirt sleeves smoking or singing Methodist hymns.

As she passed, a young man wearing the uniform of the company came out of the prison-door. Mrs. Potter drew hastily back. She felt a sudden unaccountable antipathy to this man, though she had never seen him before. He was tall and lean, with small features set in red hair and whiskers. One of his thumbs was gone, she observed. Like other women, she believed that all her likings and sudden whims had some infallible divine reason to back them. Something would come of that! She would hear of the one-thumbed man again, she thought with a decisive nod.

Mrs. Potter's house was on a little island that lies between the Ohio and Virginia shores, and was occupied then by dwellings and market-gardens. Her husband was in Europe, and she could follow out her own vagaries in politics or hospitality uncontrolled.

About a week later she sent for her brother. They had not met in the mean time, and the alienation between them had been growing more bitter. The readiness with which love then turned to hate in families we can only comprehend by remembering that the whole atmosphere was charged with electric passions, and that the solid basis of daily business had crumbled away: employment of every kind had stopped with a sudden jar; a man had not the corrective of hard work for either his anger or his suspicion. In New England or Carolina he was swept along by an over-powering current of opinion, but in this border region he was in a dirty swirl or eddy: he saw little here of the lofty purpose of the war on either side, but he did see much of its savagery, its truculence, its mean trading spirit.

This man Pomeroy, for instance. While his brothers-in-arms were doing men's work under Ashby, he was forced to loiter in this mill-town, watched by spies, as he told his sister, at every step.

"I met Clingsby just now. He tells me my men are in disguise at Gallipolis. But I cannot cross to the Ohio side to join them, for Captain Poole has been following me for days."

"Poole the butcher, a Federal officer! Oh, John, I wish you were with the boys and Ashby. Perhaps they're wrong—I mean of course they're wrong. But they are gentlemen, at any rate."

"Be calm, Elinor. Tut! tut! child!" smiling, very well pleased. "I did not suppose your radical folly had left you so much sound judgment. Why did you send for me?"

"Have you been annoyed in any other way, John?" disregarding his question.

"Some mill-men—Welsh brutes!—fired at me the other evening.

But what can I do? The city is under martial law, and I dare not bring myself into prominent notice. I can leave it, however—shake the dust off my feet—for ever, I hope."

"And the Pomeroys built the miserable town!" The tears were in her eyes: she stroked her brother's hand, quite forgetting that he was one of the traitors and tyrants whom she had prayed God to crush.

"But you wanted me, Nell?"

"Yes," after a pause. "It was a story I heard—a woman that wants help. No, you needn't put your hand in your pocket: it is not money. She is a girl from some hill-county in Pennsylvania, who knows no more of the world than one of the sheep on her own farm. Three or four years ago a young man came to the neighborhood as teacher of the district school, courted and married her. They had one child—a boy christened John Knox, for the girl is an Old-School Presbyterian, after the straightest sect of her religion."

"Scotch-Irish?"

"Yes."

"I know the sort in Pennsylvania," nodding—"red-haired, high-cheekboned, obstinate as the devil—sure that their own kin are all booked for heaven, and calmly sending all the rest of the world to damnation."

"I'm afraid Margaret is of that stock. At any rate, the cast iron in her makes her hold the stronger on the only things she knows, her Church and her husband and child. About a year ago she received from New York proofs of her husband's marriage with another woman, still living. She is modest and clean-minded. I believe the sense of shame was as bitter as the loss, for she loved the man—loves him still. She left him, taking the child with her. He tried to make her give it up, that it should be brought up in the true faith, for it appears he is a Catholic."

"It's hardly fair to load the Church with every scoundrel that chooses to call her mother," said Major Pomeroy, whose Ritualism was of the highest.

"Well, that's not to the point. I suspect Margaret forgave him for his other wife more easily than for his Holy Mother. The man six months ago stole the child, and its mother, who is an ignorant country-girl, never out of her own county before, has worked or begged her way hundreds of miles, and seems to have lost all sense of fear. She heard that her husband was trying to make his way into the South—lost sight of him here: she was hopeless and starving, her reason gave way—"

"She was the woman who threw herself into the creek last week?"

"Yes: I brought her here. Will you see her, John?"

The little man ruffled his plumage: "Here? The hospital would have been the proper place of refuge. But we will see what can be done—we will see."

They went into the next room, where a homely, red-haired young woman sat mending stockings.

"Margaret, this is my brother, Major Pomeroy. He has come to advise you about your boy."

She looked up without any hope or lightening in her face.

"She is tired out," whispered Mrs. Potter.

"How have you looked for your son, madam?" said the major gently.

"Just walked up an' down, an' asked in every town if anybody had heard of a man called Peter Brodie. I told them of the boy too: nobody could have forgotten Johnny if they'd seen him. I doubt he's dead."

"His father may have put him in some Catholic institution," suggested Mrs. Potter.

"Margaret would rather believe him dead?"

"I would, sir," quietly. "I never saw much of the papists. But God is just: He would not give *my* child to the Scarlet Woman, drunk with the blood of the saints."

"Blood of the saints, eh? No doubt," with the patronizing nod which he reserved for women. "But to the matter in hand. You have a photograph of your husband?"

"I have, sir," taking an old-fashioned daguerreotype-case from her pocket. "I take shame to myself for keeping it. But Peter was very good to me."

"How like a woman to keep it! And how like a woman not to use it to find the man!"

"Why—why, I know this face!" stammered Mrs. Potter in her excite-ment. "Where did I see it? The man with one thumb! On the very day on which you came!—Among the guards of the prison, brother."

"I will see the provost-marshal then."

Now, for Major Pomeroy to see the provost-marshal was to run his head straight into the lion's jaws.

"Go to that man Rouse? Nothing of the kind!" cried Mrs. Potter. "You shall not risk your whole future for her or her child," thinking how John always had been a fool where a woman was concerned, no matter how old or ugly she was.

"Put on your bonnet, madam," said the little man quickly. "My buggy is at the door." In a few minutes they were driving to the prison.

This said Dick Rouse had been a bartender in Cleveland until six months ago, and, as far as Pomeroy knew, was a mere whisky-soaked brute. He prowled about the town, dogging silly school-girls who vented their Southern ardor by singing "My Maryland" or by pinning tiny Confederate flags to their petticoats out of sight. These foes did Rouse arrest every day and march down the street to take the test oath, with every mark of opprobrium and contempt.

The major remembered these things with bitterness of soul as he whipped up his horse. They entered the old theatre unchallenged by the guards, who were dozing on their benches as usual. To his aston-ishment, Margaret hurried on before him. He followed her to a large apartment used as a prison, the windows thick with dust, rows of wretched pallets on either side, and soldiers and prisoners gathered in a mob about the woman, who had just told the story to Rouse and given him the picture.

Dick beckoned a man aside, who, in answer to his question, said, "That is Red-haired Bob, beyond a doubt. But *he* had no child."

"The man has left you, then?" cried the major.

"Oh, that's you, is it, Pomeroy?" called out Rouse. "I've got a rod in pickle for you some day. Never mind now. If Bob had the child, he's killed it, and I haven't the courage to tell that poor critter that, sir. Jist look at her. Nary a woman comes here but is skeert with the looks of some of my men. But she don't see nothin' but her boy."

"It's not at all likely he killed the child," said Pomeroy.

Nothing short of murder would satisfy Rouse's excited sympathies: "I tell you, Mr. Pomeroy, there's a hankerin' for blood in that class that *we* can't onderstand. He'd think no more of plantin' that little one six feet deep than I'd think of smokin' killikinick."

"Bob told me one night he had a boy," said one of the men—"a very fine lad."

"Hillo! Where did he keep him? Why the devil didn't you ask him?"

"Because he told me—said he'd took it to Christiansburg, to an aunt or grandmother, and cleared the lines coming back. I couldn't understand why he come back."

"Because he was an infernal rebel spy," roared Rouse. "I had him in irons, but he got off to join Jim Brady on the Kanawha Salines."

The little major's eye twinkled at the mention of Jim Brady, a devil-may-care Irishman who had elected himself colonel of a rebel gang that haunted the shores of the Ohio, with as much fun as ferocity in their mad raids.

"She can't reach Christiansburg without a pass," said Rouse anxiously. "Passes by Fortress Monroe was cheap enough a month ago, but now it's onpossible." He scribbled something on a piece of paper which he held against the stove, and turned to the major, who was looking at him as he might at a wild beast that had suddenly revealed members of a human body: "See here, Pomeroy! You Southern sympathizers," winking significantly, "has a way of running an underground railroad through the lines. Now, this woman's excited a sort of interest in me. I ask no questions. If she kin git through without trouble from your side, this scratch of writin' will ensure her agin' interference from mine."

The major nodded gravely. Rouse, who had looked for gratitude and applause, slapped him with his dirty diamonded paw: "Say, Pomeroy! That don't mean that I've let up on you, my man. You walk devilishly straight, or I'll slip Peter Brodie's irons on you." He grinned as the little major shook him off contemptuously and left the room with Margaret. "I've got them high-flyers well under my thumb. But I hope he'll pull the woman through. It's a cursed pity of her."

When Mrs. Potter heard the major's report, she smiled scornfully:

"It is all a ruse of that man Rouse to tempt you to run the blockade. The first step you make they will shoot you down like a dog."

"My duty is plain, Elinor. I must run the blockade at once, to help both my State and this woman."

"State, indeed! What has the State done for you that you should put your neck in a halter for it? Have you ever been elected to a single office that you wanted? As for the woman—go in, Margaret: tea is ready— I'll find her child for her. I wish you would appeal to logic on this subject, John, and you'd think as I do. Read the *Impending Crisis* or the *Tribune*, and you would see that the abolitionists—"

"Logic? From a woman?" jumping into the buggy. "And there comes the Widow Van Pelt! This is too much. I shall call to-night and tell you my arrangements."

Now, Mrs. Van Pelt was one of those human pudding-stones, remarkable only as accretions of queer little particles, common in our Western and Southern towns, where idiosyncrasies, small as well as great, develop unchecked by strict social limitations. She was enormously fat, ruddy, and from head to foot an airy flutter of lace, ribbons and glittering Turkish jewelry. Brisk little Mrs. Potter greeted her as "Euphemia, my dear child," seated her, and dealt with her on the whole very much as if she had been a giantess weak in the brain and tottering in the knees.

"Was that your brother John who drove from the door? I wanted to show him a letter which came to me this morning, smuggled through— Heaven knows how. Frank La Geyere, you know—chief of the Mississippi Tigers—shot through the heart. I thought John would like to hear it. Old classmates at Charlottesville. Dear! dear! All those young men that I've nursed in their petticoats dead and gone? It's no wonder I'm a Southern sympathizer. Tea? Oh certainly. What lovely old Leeds ware! Where do you pick it up, Elinor? No, indeed! Euphemia Van Pelt's political opinions are well known, thank Heaven! in spite of all your Rouses."

"I should think you would have some regard for the principles of liberty, Euphemia. Now, Charles Sumner says—"

"Principles of liberty! Bah!" filliping her thumb. "Didn't I live ten years in Carolina? I think I should understand the subject a little better than your Sumners or Garrisons. Didn't my sister Sarah marry in Louisiana, and die there, leaving eight children running wild this blessed day over the plantation? How would they have got along with French bonnes and Irish nurses, I'd like to ask your abolition leaders. I should think you'd be ashamed to take part with poor Frank's murderers, anyhow, Elinor. Lord! what a dancer he was! In the Spanish quadrilles— do you remember? And Charley too. But I forgot to tell you the letter was from Charley—Sarah's eldest boy, you know? Lying dangerously wounded at the plantation; father in the army; children running headlong to the devil with the blacks. I'm going to them, of course. Upon my word, I think every minute I hear their mother crying, 'Up, Euphemia, up! go to my little ones!' Sarah always had a queer stagey turn of expression: she was very fond of plays and play-actors."

"You mean to run the blockade, and you came to me to help you to do it?" said Mrs. Potter, putting down the cream-jug in a calm despair.

"Precisely! Joe wanted to ask Secretary Stanton for a pass. But I said, 'I've no time to go round by Fortress Monroe. I'll risk the lines, and I know a clever little abolitionist who will help me.'"

Mrs. Potter's pretty little face flushed angrily. She prided herself on her loyalty, and here were two rebels depending on her to help them in their machinations against the government! And more: she knew that she would help them. As she drank her tea in silence the widow ran airily on: "Why, I'm not a fool! I'd be searched at Fortress Monroe, and it's not their Aunt Euphemia alone these children want."

"What, then?"

Mrs. Van Pelt cast a searching glance at Margaret: "I'll trust her: the Scotch tell no tales." She jumped up, lifted her gauzy skirts, and made a waltzing step. "Do you see that petticoat—jupon, eh? Silk, quilted: warm for this weather? Now, you think it is cotton-batting inside there? Pins, needles, yeast-powders, hair-nets, all the new patterns and pounds of quinine! No more ague for Sarah's poor little children, thank the Lord! Yes, it will be warm while I'm running the blockade," reflectively, "but I'll think there's life in it for those little chaps, and trot along."

A sudden idea came to Mrs. Potter. Here was a chance to save her brother. "Euphemia," Mrs. Potter drew her aside, "I have a story to tell you." It was Margaret's story. "I'll help you to go, but you must take her with you," she added at the close: "there is no danger that *you* will be shot."

Mrs. Van Pelt's eyes were running over with tears. She ran and kissed Margaret with effusion. Johnny's mother turned aside, wiped the pearl-powder from her lips, and said nothing; but when Mrs. Potter left the room, she rose suddenly and stood tall and grim before the fluttering widow: "I am going into the South, but I'll do it unbeknownst to that lady or her brother. I'll drag them into no trouble. You'd be wise to do the same."

Mrs. Van Pelt regarded her, her head on one side like a contemplative macaw: "Now, do you know, there's a great deal of sense in that! Heaven knows, *I* don't want to implicate Elinor with that Rouse: Rouse is a beast."

She turned away and sat down to the piano. When Elinor came in she was deafened by the rattling jigs and marches. "Something softer, Euphemia," she begged.

But Mrs. Van Pelt shook her head: "I can always think best in a clatter, and I'm laying plans." Presently, with a farewell clang, she rose: "I have it. Good-night, Nell. Let your guest walk to the gate with me: I must say good-bye to her."

When she was out of hearing, she said to Margaret, "The sooner we go the better. No baggage, mind, woman! You must leave all your fineries behind. If we reach there with our lives, we may thank God. I'd like to wear a disguise, but, Lord bless you, child! everybody in the county knows *me*. My plan is this: we'll just put on our bonnets, and hire a stupid fellow I know to drive us down the Ohio side of the river to Gallipolis. Then we'll cross in a bateau, and hide in some farm-house until Jim Brady comes along. He'll take us to the Kanawha Salines, and from there—"

"My husband is with a man named Jim Brady: I must find him, and then my boy," said Margaret, who had heard the first part of the harangue with an utterly vacant face.

"Oh, no doubt. Now, no finery!" sharply.

The next morning at daybreak some Federal officers met the gay widow taking a constitutional walk across the bridge which spanned the Ohio, accompanied by a hard-featured servant-maid carrying a bundle tied in blue check. Euphemia was happy, having her daily dram of excitement. She had a keen eye for color too: noticed the brown rushing water below; the twinkling yellow lights of the factories still burning; the pale moon fading in the morning light. But Margaret saw a stout little boy in a check apron such as those she carried. "I misdoubt they'll be too small for him," she thought one minute, and the next that somewhere beyond that line of misty hills he might be lying dead. She stopped short, looking up. Before, she had always prayed to Jehovah, the terrible God wrapped in clouds more awful than those of Sinai. Now, it was the Child Jesus she saw in His mother's arms. "I want my boy!" she said. "You loved your own mother: Johnny needs me, Lord," with her hands on her breast, which ached for the child, and the tears rolling down her cheeks.

Just at that moment the tramp of cavalry sounded like thunder on the plank road behind her: it was the bodyguard of General Rosencrans (then commanding the Mountain Department) going to morning drill. Mrs. Van Pelt put on her eye-glasses to look critically at the carriage and grooming of the horses. But it was Margaret's first contact with soldiery. They pressed her back against the wall; their uniforms glittered; each horse kept step and obeyed the orders of the bugle. To Margaret it was the terrible war-horse of Job, "whose neck is clothed with thunder, which smelleth the battle afar off, the noise of the captains, and the shouting."

An ambulance went by filled with rebel prisoners: one was wounded near to death.

This was war. It gave her a vague idea of great masses of human beings pushing each other into yawning graves. She began to repeat one of the Psalms in metre used by her Church:

> But who is He that is the King
> Of glory? Who is this?

The Lord of hosts, of Zion Lord,
Who strong in battle is.

But the battle and Zion, and the awful Lord of hosts who reigned there, seemed to be far-off dumb shows to her, while close beside her were her boy Johnny and a Babe resting quietly in His mother's arms. "If Mary could see me, *she* would have pity," thought the bigoted Presbyterian. "The sword pierced her soul also."

THE CONSPIRATORS found the open farm-wagon which Mrs. Van Pelt had hired waiting in a secluded spot, and climbing into it unmolested, quietly drove down the river on the Ohio side. She had brought an ample lunch-basket. No halt was needed. About noon the next day they reached a small village of two or three dozen houses nearly opposite to Parkersburg. There was apparently an unusual excitement in the muddy town, all the men of the population having gathered on or about the porches of the little inn. They drove into the barnyard, and the women made their way unnoticed to the inn-parlor. The windows of the room, hung with green paper blinds, opened on to the porch. Mrs. Van Pelt established herself on a chair at a convenient crack in the paper.

"One must be on guard here," she said. "That is a Union officer outside, and these people are all secessionists, though they had the ill-luck to be born on the Ohio side."

But Margaret sat stolid as usual, her bundle on her lap.

"The Union officer is young Joe Camp," cried Mrs. Van Pelt in an excited whisper—"and a major, as I live! Great Heavens! of what stuff are heroes made! A mere boy, and a silly, vain boy at that! Listen! He has been sent to pay the troops in Parkersburg to-morrow, and he's drinking with this crowd, and bragging of the amount strapped about his waist. Take my word for it, there will trouble come of it," as she stepped down from the chair.

The trouble soon came. A small boy had disappeared five minutes before down the muddy road which served as a street, and now came in sight followed by a dozen men, the foremost of whom, a stout, broad-faced fellow of fifty, came up on the porch with a quizzical laugh: "How d'ye do, Major Camp?" nodding familiarly.

The young fellow drew back with dignity: "Good-morning. I remember you, I think. A man who worked for my father."

"Yes: cleaned the boss's stables many a time. Colonel James Brady now, sir—of the Confederate service."

The young officer had pluck in spite of his smooth cheeks. He laid his hand on his sword and glanced quickly about him: "This is your gang, eh?"

"Yes, if you like that name for 'em. Don't wear no uniform—as yet: go it on our own hook, this regiment does. But I'm a reg'lar commissioned officer, Camp, and I arrest you as sich. I'll trouble you for that belt under yer waist-coat. Can't allow aid and comfort to go to the enemy."

Mrs. Van Pelt, at the window, was in a perpetual paroxysm of excitement, exultation and pity: "Well done, Jim! Poor little Joe! It is too bad, too bad! Positively, the tears are in his eyes, and he is as white as his shirt. But he's had to hand over the money."

"Very well, major," said Jim calmly. "Now I'll trouble you for your parole."

"Never!" with an oath. "I'll not be ousted from the service by my father's stableman!"

"Then you'll hev to take sich treatment as the stableman kin giv. Better think twice, Joe."

"Well done, Jim Brady!" yelled the crowd. Margaret had not heard the name before, having remained listless and immovable during the uproar outside. She rose now, and without a word went out and made her way through the furious crowd up to Brady. He and Camp had drawn their revolvers and were facing each other when she pushed Brady's pistol down: "My husband is with you."

"Damn your husband!" dashing her aside.

Margaret came up, faced him again on the instant, neat, patient, obstinate: "His name is Peter Brodie."

The name arrested him: "You're Pete's wife, eh? Well, stand aside, my good woman.—Your parole, Camp, or—"

One against a village, with Brady at its head, were odds to which the gallant little major yielded at last. He gave his parole, and quickly disappeared in the inn. Jim turned to Margaret: "Thar's a good day's job!—I've got no good news to give you of Pete, ma'am. We left him up the Kanawha Salines. He's—he's attendin' to biz thar. You'd best go home, my good woman."

"I will go up the Kanawha: I must see him."

"Good Lord! You *can't* see him: he's dead—shot in a scrimmage last Monday. Thar! thar now!—God knows I didn't want to tell her! He's no loss to any woman, anyhow."

Mrs. Van Pelt was out by this time, but Margaret did not heed nor hear her. She stood quite still, staring into Brady's face. It was a long time before she could speak: "Johnny? He had my boy."

Jim looked at the men bewildered: "Never hearn tell of Pete's havin' a boy. None along of him, anyhow."

One of the gang came forward a step and gave him a significant look: "The poor woman better be took inside, and I'll talk a bit to this lady yer."

The usually hard lines of Margaret's face grew harder: "I'll hear it myself, sir. You've got word of my boy: I can stand it."

The fellow shuffled, hesitated. Brady moved away: Mrs. Van Pelt, when she could do nothing else to help Margaret, patted her shoulder and purred like a motherly cat.

"Pete told me, ma'am—it may hev bin a lie: he was an awful liar—that he'd run off from his wife and kerried away the boy." Mrs. Van Pelt nodded vehemently. "He said he wished he hadn't done it."

"I knew he'd be sorry for me," said Margaret.

"Yes, ma'am, because—He left the child with some kin of his up the Salines—old folks. There was a skirmish nigh thar, and the house was burned, and the old man and woman got off."

"Johnny—?"

"Well, ma'am, I—I 'spose they sort of forgot the child, for Brodie said when they went back next day the house was burned to the ground, and there was only one or two little bones in the ashes."

She turned to Mrs. Van Pelt, quite calm, with a silly smile: "If he's dead I'll just go back to the farm;" and then suddenly slipped down in a heap on the ground.

"It's worse than murder! You're a butcher, you fellow!" cried the widow, stooping over her, while the women from the house crowded out.

In the afternoon Mrs. Van Pelt sent for Brady and held a shrill, vigorous colloquy with him: "It's my only chance, Jim—colonel. I must go to my dying nephew. You can send a detachment with me up the Kanawha and put me safely inside the lines."

Jim fumbled his hat sheepishly. In the presence of Mrs. Van Pelt he felt himself all the stable-boy: "Well, mum, jist as you say. About this poor woman?"

"Oh, she asked to be sent back to Mrs. Potter, and Major Camp offered to take her up by rail from Parkersburg. Poor Joe on parole, eh? Well, he was always a kind-hearted boy, but he's in the wrong: he must take his punishment. I am glad, James, you have had discretion to know on which side the Lord is fighting."

The end of the affair was that the mortified, miserable little major took the night-train with Margaret, and two hours later Brady sent a guard with Mrs. Van Pelt to cross the river below Parkersburg and essay the blockade, now closely established through the south-western counties.

Margaret remained with Mrs. Potter until spring. She spoke at times of her father and mother on the farm in Centre county, and of how it was her duty to be with them. But her iron will was broken: she was weak in both body and mind. Mrs. Potter humored her, petted her as a child, and the treatment was healthful.

One day in June she took her on a long drive through the upper part of the town, where the gardens of the houses slope down to the river. The roses were in bloom, gayly-dressed children played in the yards, the low hills were green with pawpaw bushes.

"That is a hospital under the care of the Sisters of St. Joseph," pointing to a large house surrounded by trees and built on the bank of the broad glancing river. "I used to go there often, but avoided it this winter, knowing your prejudice against the Catholics."

"I have heard they were good women," said Margaret gently. "I used to be sure I knew who were right and wrong, but I am not sure of anything now, except—"

"Except what, child?"

"I know that He is taking care of Johnny."

"Yes! yes!" hastily. "Shall we go in? They *are* good women."

She thought the sight of the sick, the blind and the orphans, and their tender nurses, might help to restore Margaret's mind to a healthier tone. But she listened dully while the sisters eagerly told Mrs. Potter of their patients and their winter's work. "We have one case in which you will be sure to be interested," said the Mother—" 'Le fils du regiment,' we call him—a boy found by the Second Virginia in a burning house, and taken by them through the winter's campaign: they brought him up the river here a month ago, and left him with us—"

She stopped, looking at Margaret, who stood speechless before her, her lips moving without sound.

"Yes! yes!" cried Mrs. Potter: "where is the child?—Oh, Margaret, if it can be!"

The nun was a woman, after all: she guessed much of the truth, ran before them across the hall, and threw open the door of the chapel. A little fellow was placing flowers on the altar. "John! here, John!" she cried.

But his mother sank on her knees, holding out her arms, and could not reach him.

He was a big, stout boy—a thorough boy—and he hugged and kissed and shouted and tugged at her until she could neither faint nor cry, but had to come back to life in a hurry.

When she had risen to her feet, her quick mother's eye ran over the boy's strong limbs, his carefully-brushed hair and neat clothes. Then she looked up to the other woman and took her hand. The sister understood her, though she did not say a word. "Tut! tut! that was a trifle," she said. "You would have done just the same. We are all His children," crossing herself, whereat John Knox crossed himself too. There was a blue ribbon about his neck from which hung a cross, and above the altar which he had been trimming with flowers a picture of the Infant Jesus with His mother's arms about him.

Margaret took up the cross about Johnny's neck, but did not remove it. "When I was looking for my boy," she said to the sister, "it was of the Child Jesus I thought, and of His mother."

It is time to end our sketchy recollections of war-times in the old border town. Mrs. Van Pelt, we know, reached her journey's end safely, for she visited the Exposition in October, and was on the grand stand to witness the Southern tournament, larger and airier than ever, the bride of an ex-Confederate general. She is a rebel still at heart, sniffed the air as she passed West Virginia's noble exhibit and building, and would eat nowhere but at the Southern Restaurant. General Pomeroy, on the contrary, hobbled about on his wooden leg (he lost one in the Wilderness), full of zeal for "our reunited country." He was a Southern commissioner, and so has been dined and wined into hearty good fellowship with his Northern brethren.

Margaret is living on the farm now with her old father, a happier, healthier woman than before her trouble. She is a devout United Presbyterian still, though when she tells John Knox of his namesake she "doubts but that he was a hard man, and not as well acquainted with the Catholics as them whose opportunities have been better."

"Thunder on the Plank Road"

IN THE AUTUMN that followed the battle of Bull Run, the mountains of western Virginia were remote from everything but the war. Wheeling, where Rebecca Harding grew up, had more mills than academies, more prisons than theaters, and more settlers going west than politicians going south, since there was no easily passable road to Richmond over three hundred miles away. Serving the city's iron foundries and steel mills was the Baltimore and Ohio Railroad, which provided access along the Ohio River to the Mississippi. To protect that conduit as well as the arsenals of state firearms in the mountains beyond Harper's Ferry, both McClellan and Lee moved into the area during the summer of 1861. In skirmishes and pitched battles, Federal troops fighting under Rosecrans and Cox prevailed, banishing all but the ubiquitous bushwhackers who marauded to the east and south. With Wheeling and the vicinity secured, mountain loyalists met to propose statehood for "New" Virginia and to secede from Secessia.

Set during the fighting in western Virginia, "How the Widow Crossed the Lines" represents wartime conflict as a series of contrasts, which underline the political tensions in a town "half rebel and half loyal" from the war's earliest days.[16] Suitably aligning personal identity with political struggle, Davis presents Margaret Brodie's search for her son as a contest that pits husband against wife, man against woman, South against North, and guerrilla warfare against domestic stability. Notably, it is a contest that Margaret's husband precipitates when he steals Johnny and thus any hope of a future the family might have had together. As is customary in the adventures recounted by army veterans, Davis's story apparently favors clear choices, gender distinctions, and a road on which the protagonist has "worked or begged her way hundreds of miles." Personal identity, national politics, and literary form all thus derive from conflict, which is readily accepted by the Federal scout who yells "Tallahassee" to startled rebel pickets.

But Davis's story further establishes a third site, a border within border country, by opening on the footbridge between Virginia and Ohio where Elinor Potter unexpectedly pauses. Her gesture is emblematic: between opposing factions, "How the Widow Crossed the Lines" will ultimately promote a mediating alternative, an interstitial space similar to Perry's reliquary room in "Clotilde and the Contraband." Here, however, the space is discovered by traveling women and able to transform apparent confrontation into a Christian paradigm for national recovery. Just as her diverging characters finally reconvene in Philadelphia for the Centennial Exposition, so Davis's story posits new life for the nation whose widows share the bridge.

None of this is clear to the woman walking into the creek, so near the Ohio River over which Stowe's Eliza Harris had raced to freedom just a decade before. Wading into the water that cuts the mill town in two, Margaret Brodie sinks under the strain of the seeming irreconcilables that the story draws out. Where her husband is Catholic, she is Protestant. Where he is nomadic, first as a district teacher and then as a member of Jim Brady's gang, she was born and bred in the hill country in Pennsylvania. Where he has married before in New York and has long been sliding south, she is upright, Northern, and deliberate, even as she wades to her death.

Their gendered antagonism is underscored in the story's opening paragraphs by a choreography of oppositions between other characters. Mrs. Potter is set against her brother Major Pomeroy, since he favors loyalty to his state and she insists on abolition. Elaborating that political tension, the hotheaded Mrs. Van Pelt later defends the home in Carolina and the sister's family in Louisiana that bind her sympathies to the South, while Mrs. Potter argues for the "principles of liberty" that are widely associated with Sumner and Garrison in New England. The personal cum political standoff is apparent again on the streets of the town, where Mrs. Potter contrasts the sight of prisoners paving in chains with the flutter of the stars and stripes atop the customhouse. Therein lies a contrast between work without pay and regulated trade, ultimately between the slavery of the South and the free market of the North. As though to typify the growing national presence in local affairs, the contest is finally cast as a distinction between the jail belonging to the state and the prison in which enemies of the Union are lodged. With so many instances of the contest on hand, the impending confrontation between warring factions seems about to be met head-on.

But the creek that cuts the town in two is also the beginning of borderland salvation. While Margaret Brodie sinks under the burden she cannot resolve, Mrs. Potter stands above her on the bridge that joins the creek's two banks, a privileged site whose liminal status is further suggested by the autumnal season and Mrs. Potter's pause. Throughout the story, that space between recurs, and significantly it is occupied by women and children: for example, by Mrs. Potter's house on the island and by the children on rafts who first spot the drowning woman. Motherhood is central to Davis's wartime vision; the widow's story begins with a woman whose child has "bin tuk" and ends beneath a picture of the Child Jesus. Between the creek and the chapel fall the hardship of Johnny's "death" up the Salines and the miracle of his return to the nuns, tellingly cast as the death of a grandson and the return of the *fils du regiment*. Both death and rebirth are signified by the cross that hangs around the boy's neck, as well as by the bridge that all three women will traverse. In Johnny's absence, the violence that threatens him is made visible as the "dirty swirl or eddy" in which Margaret nearly drowns, and then amplified as the "great masses of human beings pushing each other into yawning graves" that Margaret imagines while the bodyguard of General Rosecrans thunders past her on the bridge.

That Mrs. Potter's house, to which Margaret is first taken, is situated on an island in the great Ohio is doubly revealing. Not only does her home substantiate the family claim on liminal and regenerative sites, it also suggests the outskirts where Hester Prynne resides in Hawthorne's *The Scarlet Letter*. Davis was an ardent reader of Hawthorne, whom she met in 1862 when she visited Boston in the midst of her literary success with *Life in the Iron Mills*.[17] In "How the Widow Crossed the Lines" the references to Hawthorne's novel are repeated: the presence of the customhouse certainly, the "stern" doctrinal rigor of Margaret's faith, even the "cast iron in her" that finally breaks. In her first appearance, Margaret walks into the water with the same "outward calm" that Hester brought from the prison to the scaffold, while her inward turmoil is suggested by Mrs. Potter's horror just as Hester's is suggested by Pearl's anguished cries. In Davis's hands the geography of moral choice is also familiar: Mrs. Potter's house is situated between the town of Wheeling (Davis's Boston in more senses than one) and the "wilderness," here the Kanawha Salines where bushwhackers skirmish and later the battle of the Wilderness in which Major Pomeroy would lose his leg.

Just as place establishes the map of a moral universe, for Davis as well as Hawthorne, their similar claims on time suggest its historical import. In both narratives, the future is bound up in children (Pearl and Johnny), the compassion and tolerance they will finally embody, and the human mediation their mothers will provide as a model for communal action. Challenging the "strict rules of decorum" that Virginia imposed on women in a latter-day echo of strictures in Puritan Massachusetts, Davis's women transform the world made by soldiers as surely as Hester transformed the meaning of the scarlet letter she wore.

Yet invoking Hawthorne, even peripherally, also suggests where Davis has parted company with his example. The customhouse, which functioned for Hawthorne as the place from which to look backward to the Puritan errand, serves Davis as the place from which to look forward, literally to the prison opposite and prefiguratively to the one-thumbed man whom Margaret pursues. Since Mrs. Potter will later recollect this moment when she holds Margaret's daguerreotype, the narrative's strategy suggests that feminine intuition is prophetic and feminine recollection the basis for future action. The resulting events produce little of the "gloom" that sent Mrs. Hawthorne to bed with a headache when her husband read his novel's final pages. Instead, "stern tragedy" mixes with "stern comedy" in Davis's story of national "errand." Furthermore, with the shift from Boston to Wheeling, the "cast iron" of Margaret's will does not rust over time as in the Surveyor's Salem but breaks to be refashioned, arguably into the tempered steel that Wheeling's mills were even then turning out.[18]

Hawthorne's moral geography is likewise reconstituted in West Virginia. While the town remains a place where rebels like Major Pomeroy are watched, much as the colonial governor watched Hester and Chillingworth watched Dimmesdale, the wilderness is a place where people are killed, hardly the shady forest in which Hester let down her hair. Again, the brook in Hawthorne's forest that murmurs of the trouble it has seen is a dividing line that Pearl refuses to cross; but the creek that eddies through Wheeling like the war itself presents no obstacle to Davis's women. Margaret deliberately wades into it and Mrs. Potter casually saunters over it. If Pearl metaphorically refuses to step into time and human sorrow until the signs are right, the wading Margaret is virtually baptized in history (Davis thereafter names her character) and Mrs. Potter appears to rise above it at the story's commencement. From that position, she effectively displaces the Puritan authorities whom Hawthorne installed above Hester's scaffold; in Davis's opening scene, the "crowd of men and boys" remains down below and is largely unnamed, like the women outside Hester's prison door.

The greater latitude of Davis's female characters is further evident in the want of authority given male pronouncements. Whereas Hester is firmly imprisoned for her sin, Margaret sees neither the "coafin" nor the jail that Dickson indicates, and she escapes the hospital that Major Pomeroy would prefer; she is instead taken home to recuperate by Mrs. Potter's order. Indeed, throughout the story Elinor Potter, Margaret Brodie, and Euphemia Van Pelt among them direct the action, a three-part replacement for the roles played in Hawthorne's narrative by Hester and Pearl. Their greater mobility and social resourcefulness is at least in part owing to the fact that they have none of them sinned. Mrs. Potter's sorest transgression is her "headstrong insubordination," Mrs. Van Pelt's her idiosyncratically "queer little particles," and Mrs. Brodie's her "bigoted" Presbyterianism, all of which enable these women to take charge of events. In the older world that Hester Prynne helped to create, Pearl eventually had to learn her lesson; but Davis's women are free to create a world in which Johnny teaches his, as the Child Jesus did before him.

Their collaborative efforts build on Mrs. Potter's initial pause to produce a restorative space between the warring camps claimed by men. Between the provost marshal's office where Margaret hears of Jim Brady and the inn where she finds him is the bridge she crosses with Mrs. Van Pelt. Between the "twinkling yellow lights" of the mills and the "thunder on the plank road" when the Federal bodyguard passes are the "mother's tears" that Margaret sheds, the ambulance and wounded soldiers that she imagines, and the "sword" she shares with Mary, the biblical model she sees supplanting Jehovah and Job. As the women move south, the site of transformation shifts again to the village porches opposite Parkersburg, which are located between the barnyard that the travelers cross and the inn parlor out of which they peer.

The further they go the more permeable become the terms of confrontation: the farm wagon passes through the barnyard without getting noticed and Mrs. Van Pelt makes use of a crack in the parlor blinds without getting caught. Instead, motherly intercession becomes more dynamic; from the inn parlor, Margaret breaks into the "furious crowd" much as Mrs. Potter earlier "rushed into a crowd of men" on the banks of the creek, but this time Northern major and Southern colonel have drawn their weapons. By pushing down Brady's revolver, Margaret dispels the mounting tension and effectively saves Joe Camp's life. She in turn is restored to health by the ministrations of Mrs. Potter, who "petted her as a child" when she returned to Wheeling on her way back to the farm. Confirming the restorative capacity of women is the story's closing scene, in which the *fils du regiment* is returned to his rightful mother in a hospital staffed by nuns.

The family that Peter Brodie disrupted and that the "old folks" up the Salines failed to protect is thereby reunited and the story's failed romance is essentially canceled by Peter's death and Margaret's return to Pennsylvania. The lawlessness of the Kanawha Valley ("one or two little bones in the ashes") is also brought under control, not by Rosecrans's Mountain Department or even by the Second Virginia, who rescue Johnny from the burning house offstage some months before the Mother Superior credits their care. Instead of arriving on the pommel of a saddle, Johnny is restored to his mother in the ever more sequestered spaces of domestic security: inside a hospital, inside a chapel, beside an altar, beneath a picture of "the Infant Jesus with His mother's arms about Him."

Less an appeal to the "preindustrial past" that Bernard Bowron has described, Davis's solution to the "savagery" of the Civil War is to extend the province of the home in Margaret Brodie's footsteps, to challenge the "logic" of state loyalty in favor of Elinor Potter's principles, and to mount the bridge over troubled waters for Euphemia Van Pelt's liberating "constitutional."[19] Although Joe Camp cannot defy the man who cleaned his father's stables, the "airiest" of women can turn a gang leader into a "stable-boy" simply by insisting on her duty to her sister's dying son. Like Lincoln in his Second Inaugural Address calling for "malice toward none" and "charity for all," Davis seeks to "bind up the nation's wounds" by tending to the widows and orphans that the war left behind.

In a reconstructive echo of Lincoln's words, editor John Foster Kirk welcomed just such contributions to *Lippincott's* when the magazine first appeared in 1868. Noting that Philadelphia remained the City of Brotherly Love ("with hatred to none and with charity to all"), Kirk called for "common ground where all who love the Union (and none others) can meet" (*Lippincott's*, January 1868), the very ground that Davis's public bridges and inn parlors and hospitals identify. By the 1870s, after an influx of Old Homestead and Romance narratives had taken up the national problems of continuity and reunion, Kirk's magazine had settled into Civil War Adventures, often with a formal twist: for example, the anxiety about family homesteads in stories like Davis's earlier border tale, "The Yares of the Black Mountains" (July 1875), encouraged the generic ingenuity of grafting the adventures of women onto the maintenance of the home. Generally speaking, the Old Homestead and Romance narratives in *Lippincott's* came from women, the Adventures from men. Therefore, the appearance of a female Adventure extending domestic territory is a significant step toward cultural engagement and formal complexity, an indication that newer magazines might rival the prestige of the *Atlantic Monthly* and might complicate the ways in which the war would be remembered.

Their pages reveal that Old Homestead anxieties were strategically bound to Adventures for women by the time the nation celebrated the signing of the Declaration of Independence in 1876. For Davis, the generic move toward national restoration became a form of female invention so that Revolutionary promise was paradigmatically recharged. Indeed, respect for the founding ideals of liberty and justice actually promoted rather than restricted female adventure, since widows like Margaret Brodie and near widows like Elinor Potter effectively extended the public domain that domestic priorities could monitor. Unlike army scouts on midnight roads, heroines like Euphemia Van Pelt would always arrive at the homes they resuscitated, while soldiers around a campfire need only live to fight another day.

Founded in the year that the Fifteenth Amendment was first proposed, *Lippincott's* thus offered a cultural forum in which the Congressional debates on women's civil status could be continued and in which
domestic tropes and the alternative endings they imagined for national
dramas could persist. Where the scarred Confederate courier makes
every effort to get off his island and onto the sectional road leading
south, Mrs. Potter makes the island her home and makes home the
redemptive site toward which all centennial roads lead at last. What
Davis's several heroines learn along the way, "them whose opportunities have been better," is that what is "fair" is tolerance and what is
"just" will set them free.

CODA

From Uncle Tom
to Uncle Remus and Beyond

DURING THE YEARS following the fall of Fort Sumter and then the peace negotiated at Appomattox, the operations of domestic rhetoric effectively strained the generic limits of Civil War stories written amid political crisis, mindful as the popular press was of the continuing public genuflexion to the founding fathers. Magazines as divergent as the *Atlantic Monthly* in Boston and the *Southern Magazine* in Baltimore, the *Lakeside Monthly* in Chicago and the *New National Era* in Washington provided cultural arenas in which readers traced how much disruption the old homestead might endure, how much resistance the romance of national union might overcome, and how much claim to the open road of postwar opportunity those back home might exert. Richer, more sustained, and more kaleidoscopic versions of "news from the war," popular narratives elaborated the gendered code upon which Winslow Homer had relied in organizing his early composite drawing for *Harper's Weekly*; but they also put women in camps, on horseback, and aboard trains to test how secure once segregated American promises would be in postwar circulation. As "How the Widow Crossed the Lines" demonstrated in 1876, the women who arose from Homer's rocking chair after the war struck home could carry a good deal more than their knitting under their skirts.

Walking emblems of the motherly love that takes them abroad, Euphemia Van Pelt and Margaret Brodie recall the antebellum Eliza Harris in *Uncle Tom's Cabin*, the slave mother who ran away from the Shelby plantation to save her son Harry from being sold. Clutching the boy on the ice floes as she crossed the Ohio, Eliza likewise stretched the claims of domestic values into a hostile environment for thousands of antebellum readers, as Euphemia later does in loading her petticoat before she crosses the bridge to hurry south. In fact, both women are explicit in remembering whom they were bound to protect once they put their feet on the road. "No more ague for Sarah's poor little children, thank the Lord!" exclaims the widow, much the same sentiment Eliza had uttered twenty-five years earlier while she rested with her son ("Harry darling! mother can't eat till you are safe") in the public house on the river's banks. Crossing over to a new life, both women bring with them as much of the life they leave behind as they can carry.

By 1876, however, more heroines were spending more time on the road, as the bonds of true motherhood were extended by the war and the accumulating patterns of wartime stories. Eliza's earlier travels were comparatively brief before she arrived at Senator Bird's kitchen and later the Quaker settlement; white mothers like Mrs. Bird, Mrs. Shelby, and Mrs. St. Clare did not leave home at all in Stowe's novel, since their function in the 1850s was to maintain the stability that the fugitives sought. By the 1870s, the itinerant domesticity of slave women like Eliza had been surpassed by the perpetual relocations of white women fending off the war: the Mrs. Van Pelts going to nurse those in need, the Mrs. Brodies going to find those who had been lost, and the Mrs. Potters going to attend to those local misfortunes that their men ignored. While the road to adventure remained offstage for black women like Twain's Aunt Rachel, who resembles Stowe's Eliza in arriving instead at one household after another, the women in Davis's story spend almost no time at home. Beyond Mrs. Potter's house, the story reveals the Adventure's predilection for public settings: the provost marshal's office and prison, the open farm wagon, the inn parlor, the Catholic hospital, and the Centennial Exposition. While traveling women were not yet seen trumpeting their message like the star-spangled soldier in Homer's *News from the War*, neither were such characters in popular magazines shut behind the windows of distant homes. Some traveled laden ("pins, needles, yeast-powders, hair-nets, all the new patterns and pounds of quinine") and some traveled light ("No baggage, mind, woman!"), but they had come a long way since 1862, most without sacrificing their tie to liberty in justice and all without receiving the vote.

Their greater mobility, however, also revealed that the war and emancipation had undermined the homes that traditionally gave heroines their rhetorical command. Like the Widow Van Pelt, they were freer to leave because there was less to defend. Like Mollie Prater on her horse, they were discovering that the war had produced more Old Ponder Mejunkin places, not homes forever but only for the time being. In the North as well as the South, protagonists in Civil War stories were less frequently going home again as Hopeful Tackett did; instead, they surfaced at narrative boarding houses like Captain Turner or boarded horsecars like the wounded veteran of Fort Wagner. Beginning mid-war, more homes more often were found vacated, like the "mons'us big house" that Aunt Rachel occupies with the Federal troops or the derelict homestead that Doctor Leroy Prater and his gang claim before they are caught. Even the recovering M'Call household in De Forest's story is narratively abandoned; by the end of "Parole d'Honneur," Alec and the boarding Yankee captain are still a long way off. Auguring badly for the reconstructive sway of domestic rhetoric, this unsettled state is actually typified less in contemporary stories by the women who travel than by their sons who wander like Johnny Brodie, stolen from his mother, deposited by his father, attacked with his grandparents, found by the Second Virginia, and left with the Sisters of St. Joseph. In being passed from hand to hand, Johnny has little in common with the son to whom Eliza Harris successfully clung; his relocations are more reminiscent of the sketchy travels that Aunt Rachel reports after her son Henry escapes, then barbers, and then ransacks the South in search of her. On the road of historical crisis and opportunity, other mothers like Margaret Brodie seemed too susceptible to the swirl of contemporary events or too bound to domestic responsibilities to hitch their wagons to the North Star.

The modest number of women on the road, coupled with the early lapse in cross-sectional romance, thus compromised the postwar impact of a feminized model in reinventing the national household. For every laden widow, there were too many couriers who traveled unencumbered, and so there was a marked tendency to neglect the example of Hassy Few's women who rarely forgot in favor of Alec M'Call's men who rarely remembered. As a result, the way was narratively opened for the "money and emigration" that De Forest's men recognized as necessary for rebuilding the South. But the generic promise of conservative transformation that resulted when women ventured out of the home, whether for the bridge to freedom or for the new homestead of marriage, subsided during the Reconstructive years with disquieting implications for the true hold of Revolutionary justice on Redemptive liberties. Faced with the narrative burden of carrying a confederated past into a national future, the inclination of Old Homestead stories was to shore up traditional loyalties and local cohesion at the expense of new arrivals. Adventures, by contrast, opened the narrative road of opportunity with greater generosity but with no guarantee that new citizens would arrive at anything more than perpetual motion. The model of sanctuary thus held tight while the model of wanderlust hung loose; in effect, neither of the genres that remained numerically vigorous after the Reconstruction amendments were ratified was intrinsically receptive to the political rights of the newly enfranchised freedmen, much less to the rights of the disparate groups whose chance at full citizenship temporarily flickered in the halls of Congress. In the pages of contemporary magazines, the open road's promise of invention finally served less often to revitalize founding ideals than homebound nostalgia served to undergird the corporate adventurism of the gilded age.

In fact, the sustained generic competition between Old Homestead stability and Adventure spunk metamorphosed after Centennial celebrations into a startling alliance that traveling widows never anticipated. Impecunious during the barren 1870s, Southern writers discovered a decade later that the profitable literary marketplaces of the North were opening at last, beyond the settled receptivity of *Lippincott's* or the *Galaxy*. At a greater distance from Confederate defeat and Reconstructive demands, writers like Grace King and Thomas Nelson Page tapped into the resurgent demand for plantation ease once manufactured to confound abolitionists, at the same time that Northern capital in Southern cities was making distinct headway. Nor were the two impulses now at odds in the South; what Twain would shortly call "the jejune romanticism of an absurd past" or "Lost Cause" was increasingly peddled by his "brisk" and "energetic" purveyors of a new Southern order, and nowhere more briskly and energetically than in the Northern press. As Paul Gaston has observed in *The New South Creed*, "the romance of the past was used to underwrite the materialism of the present. The names and signatures of Confederate generals were everywhere in demand by railroad companies and corporations." With reconciliation foremost on both sides of the Mason-Dixon line, magazines also spawned a generic reorientation that retreated still further from the advent of liberty and justice for all.[1]

As Stowe had demonstrated well before emancipation, neither the cabin of Uncle Tom nor the road of George Harris would secure both freedom and a home for those who had once been enslaved. In other hands, the Old Homestead paradigm, which had provided Stowe with her domestic power and encouraged the figure of a "national household" in the Congressional resolve to end slavery, would cease even to gesture toward conservative reform. On the one hand, household priorities enabled a postwar retreat to the "happy darkey" who fostered a national lien on domestic serenity; on the other, the pull of blood invited the "tragic mulatto" who signified the internal threat of a Southern house divided. In neither case were there to be many subsequent Aunt Rachels standing their ground. In the conciliatory 1880s, the "house liberated" would instead fade as a narrative gesture, to be decisively replaced by the cross-sectional romances that circulated once again during Centennial preparations and the years that followed.

Pushing Confederate fathers offstage and shunning the vengeance of section and kin, newly issued Mollie Praters would opt to be "comfortable for life" in the parlors that their Northern captains refurbished and that their servants tended with silent discretion. Not even the further adventures of sergeants and civilians rivaled the popularity of Southern women who accepted the Captain Humphreys with money to invest.

The melding of plantation nostalgia and venture capital also coincided with a growing reliance upon "divided kinsmen" as an apt measure of wartime tensions. Recollecting the contest between domestic anxiety and venturesome escape in the popular stories of the 1870s, the now "fratricidal" war figuratively abandoned widows with petticoats for the battle between Chollet's Jack and Dix, a battle fought without her earlier mothers or fathers or Tom Lodownes once the continuing claims of family structure were fictively bent to the urge of masculine competition. A gendered shift away from the issues of parental authority and kitchen stability that had governed wartime households in print, the emerging preference for brothers like Jack and Dick over mothers like Stella made masculine will central and pointedly relocated the new nation in onetime border territory.

The process of dismantling a feminized ethos, even in the Civil War homesteads that still appeared in popular magazines, was begun as early as 1877, when Federal troops were officially withdrawn by President Hayes.[2] They were replaced by the ascendancy of "home rule" as Democrats claimed the remaining statehouses in South Carolina and Louisiana, part of the negotiated political settlement that put a Republican rather than a Democrat in the White House during the disputed election of 1876. That same year, the fledgling *Atlanta Constitution* changed hands, and Henry W. Grady accepted the vacant position as editor of the newspaper that would soon be proclaiming the gospel of hard work to the "New South" of the 1880s. Chapter and verse the gospel of the Republican Party since the 1850s, Grady's campaign for recovery through industrial progress encouraged the North to rest easy about Southern affairs, especially once newcomer Joel Chandler Harris began experimenting with an "old time Negro" who reassured

Northern and Southern readers alike that the bonds of love forged on antebellum plantations still tied freedmen to the white households they refused to leave.[3]

The particular narrative course by which a little white boy and an old black man arrived at their perennial fireside demonstrates how ready the New South was to employ the popular scenarios that had previously served the North. Harris's unnamed boy is the son of Miss Sally and Captain John Huntington, a Yankee soldier turned Atlanta lawyer upon his marriage. When the Yankee's story first appeared in the *Atlanta Constitution* in 1877, it served to fill out the character of the talkative Uncle Remus by showing him to be more fond of his white family than of his own freedom; when Sherman's army swept into rural Georgia from Atlanta, Uncle Remus took gun in hand and brought down the Yankee sharpshooter who was drawing a bead on Miss Sally's brother, Mars Jeems. In "Uncle Remus as a Rebel: How He Saved his Young Master's Life" (14 October 1877), the faceless Yankee died. But in 1880, when Harris brought out his first collection of Uncle Remus stories in New York, the fallen sharpshooter was given a name, a sister Theodosia from Vermont, and a willing nurse in Miss Sally, whom he loved and then married. Retitled "A Story of the War," the narrative was among the first to imitate the Northern remedy of cross-sectional love and marriage in a hitherto unreceptive South.[4]

National romance and reconciliation thus replaced the violent postwar challenge of Southern intransigence, but only after an unrepentant Uncle Remus reiterated the choice he had to make between family and freedom. "W'en I see dat man take aim, en Mars Jeems gwine home ter Old Miss en Miss Sally," he says, "I des disremembered all 'bout freedom en lammed aloose." More than the reconstructive Romance, it was these Old Homestead credentials that caught the national imagination and positioned Uncle Remus to replace the Southern boy's distant father in Harris's tales, just as he replaced Mars Jeems's overseer in managing the plantation during the war. Proven loyal to his white family rather than to his own interests or his Yankee "friends," Uncle Remus thus became the unexpected guarantor of continuity, safety, and restoration in a united national family. Fully reconstructed already,

Harris's storyteller was an instant success in the North, where *Uncle Remus: His Songs and His Sayings* sold three thousand copies in its first two days and passed through four editions in as many months.[5] In nine further books appearing into the next century, Uncle Remus would sit with Miss Sally's boy of an evening, as yams roasted in the cabin fire and he told the stories that older slaves had told him.

Postponing his chance for emancipation as readily as Uncle Tom once set aside his free papers to remain with the unregenerate St. Clare, the figure of Uncle Remus recalls Stowe's effort to incorporate slaves into a domestic creed that subordinated individual freedoms to communal stability. Small wonder, then, that Harris would declare in the *Atlantic Monthly* how much he owed to the author of *Uncle Tom's Cabin* or that the tales Uncle Remus told would soon rival the antebellum popularity of Stowe's novel.[6] Departing in "Uncle Remus as a Rebel" from the minstrel show's patter on topical issues, Harris initiated the narrative return to plantation stability that would serve Southern writers in the Democratic 1880s as successfully as such domestic tropes had previously served the Republican Stowe, one reason why critics like James Baldwin have expropriated the example set by Uncle Tom.[7]

More recently, however, Darwin Turner has noted the maternal solicitude of Uncle Remus toward Miss Sally's boy and the return of what he calls "a world centered on familial love."[8] Like Stowe, Harris draws attention to a child, though his boy is a Little Eva who never dies, a George Shelby whose Uncle Tom is never sold. Like Stowe, Harris means for the domestic scene to orient a national drama; as Robert Hemenway has observed, "Uncle Remus in the quarters was intended to serve as a sign-post on America's 'road to reunion,' a uniting symbol for South and North."[9] Like Stowe in describing the Quaker settlement, Harris sets his idyll where food is prepared, a reminder of the repast to come, of its Christian import, and of the social exchange that meals and their preparation represent. By the cabin fireside as in Stowe's Quaker kitchen, two generations convene, the image of stability that domestic rhetoric had proffered during political crisis for more than thirty years.

But Harris disturbs the serenity of the antebellum hearth in subversive ways, most evident when Uncle Remus's cabin is contrasted with the Quaker settlement that Jane Tompkins has read as Stowe's emblematic scene. Instead of day for Harris's readers, it is night. Instead of Eliza visiting the homes of white women, Miss Sally's boy visits the freedman's cabin. Instead of white hands, black voices guide the action, so that sorting peaches in the Quaker kitchen gives way to telling stories by the freedman's fire. Instead of feminine work, masculine leisure prevails, both in Uncle Remus's cabin and in the stories he tells. Pointedly, the world of the early Uncle Remus stories is almost uniformly male, from the frame that Harris establishes to the folklore he recounts; even the plantation witches are brothers. Miss Sally, a later version of Mrs. Shelby or Mrs. St. Clare, is seen from the first as listening outside the cabin window, beyond the light that the fire throws. Where Stowe's novel endeavors to restore the feminine preserve by rescuing Eliza from the river and attempting to rescue Uncle Tom from Legree, Harris's stories invent alternatives to domestic order, nowhere more flagrantly than in Brer Rabbit's insistence on flinging back sass. The result is that the "spirit of mutual cooperation" that Tompkins describes in the settlement kitchen is replaced by a stratified animal kingdom, an anarchic territory in which the security of home is undercut, survival is uppermost, and pretense is key. In the world that the kindly Uncle Remus shows the little white boy, it's every brer for himself.[10]

Most attuned to this newly liberating role that domestic rhetoric could assume in the 1870s is the story Uncle Remus tells of the tar-baby, the first tale that Harris published after he had established his plantation frame and still his best remembered. In Harris's version, an irate Brer Fox sets a doll made of tar on the road, and in nothing flat Brer Rabbit has taken her silence for undeserved airs and walloped her sticky hide ("I'm gwinter larn you howter talk ter 'specttubble fokes") until he is pinned, head, hands, and feet. Debating how to dispose of Brer Rabbit permanently ("You been runnin' roun' here sassin' after me a mighty long time"), Brer Fox finally throws him in the brier patch he says he most fears, whereupon Brer Rabbit takes off ("Bred en bawn in a brier-patch!") as lively as ever. Hugh Keenan has pointed out that there are divergent ways in which his wily escape could have been read in the 1870s: as a tactic for winning black liberty from white clutches or as a model for dodging "the Negro question" altogether in an unreconstructed South.[11] But whether Brer Rabbit stands in for the freedmen who refused to get tarred with a stereotypical brush or for the Confederates who finally went their own way once Reconstruction ended, his modus operandi is a fast word and a quick wallop, which not even the gutsy Mollie Prater could deliver when she had the knife in her hand.

Like the Southern scout on his island in the Potomac, Brer Rabbit is most interested in staying alive. In "How Mr. Rabbit Was Too Sharp for Mr. Fox," the second half of the tar-baby story as Harris tells it, staying alive means getting altogether unstuck: from the tar baby, from her silence, and even from his own preoccupation with a neighborly "howdy" that the tar-baby refuses to give. Begging the fox not to throw him in the brier patch, Brer Rabbit is already working his way loose from the silence of the tar-baby, to which enfranchised black men need no longer be stuck when Joel Chandler Harris began telling his tales. Brer Rabbit is a Tom Lodowne who talks, a Robert Dane divorcing himself from the arresting power of the feminine.

In the frame story that Harris has contrived, the little white boy is actually given a moral choice: between the ruthless invention that gets scouts and rabbits back on the road and the homely kindness that makes the boy welcome in the black man's cabin or safe at night in his own bed. What Brer Rabbit does not offer and the boy cannot choose is romance, the easy transition from one household to another, one family to another, one childhood to another. Although Brer Rabbit declares he was "bred en bawn" in the brier patch, he seems to be the only rabbit there, and he does not stay long. Whereas Uncle Remus never seems to go far from his cabin, Brer Rabbit is always sprinting ("lippity-clippity, clippity-lippity") down the road. Robert Bone has therefore called the brier patch "an eloquent image of the uses of adversity."[12] It is also, evidently, the male replacement for female romance, the site of transformation where the young grow up and the fettered cut loose. As a substitute for the romance of union and national reconstruction that "A Story of the War" was meant to ratify, the brier patch suggested a thorny redemptive future which only the crafty could welcome.

The exuberance of Brer Rabbit throughout the postwar years testifies to the failure of popular domestic rhetoric to promote a cooperative alternative: in the opportunities that a more tolerant Margaret Brodie recommends to her son, in the mercy that a desperate Mollie Prater begs for her father, or in the security that an auctioned Aunt Rachel rises to claim from "de man." Out of what they lost came liberty for all and justice for some, most radically in the Constitutional amendments that secured emancipation with the promise of civil and political rights for black men. Even they, however, would have to wait for the promise to be fully redeemed through enforcement, as black and white women would have to wait for the voting rights that a newly paramount national citizenship might have won. The decline of a feminized ethos was accelerated by the outbreak of renewed violence in events like the B & O Railroad's wildcat strike of 1877 and the labor unrest that loosed class antagonisms previously hidden. If postwar American culture was not yet the jungle that Upton Sinclair would describe in 1906, neither was it the Quaker settlement that Stowe had earlier imagined. For the thousands of readers who beseiged Harris with requests for "The Wonderful Tar-Baby Story" in 1879, the American future lay not down "de big road" of amended opportunity or up to the "big house" of Revolutionary splendor but in the brier patch, out of which more vigorous, more ornery, and more disturbing popular narratives had already begun to emerge.

The waning command of the household as a model for political change was sharply revealed toward the end of the nineteenth century with the *Plessy v. Ferguson* decision in 1896, the Supreme Court's mutation of Reconstruction promises into the discriminatory policies of Jim Crow. Acknowledging that the Thirteenth Amendment's ban on involuntary servitude had been successfully extended to Mexican peonage and the Chinese coolie trade, Justice Henry Billings Brown wrote in the majority opinion that the most pressing issue before the court was nonetheless the liberty of the states, in this case Louisiana's authority to regulate railroad commerce by segregating passenger seating. To support a decision favoring state jurisdiction, Brown called upon the respect for continuity, safety, and restoration that domestic rhetoric had traditionally advanced. "In determining the question of reasonableness," he wrote of the Louisiana legislature, "it is at liberty to act with reference to the established usages, customs and traditions of the people, and with a view to the promotion of their comfort, and the preservation of the public peace and good order." Instead of challenging the legislative transgression of cabin customs as Stowe had or promoting "the sacred right of family" as Senator Sumner had later done on the slave's behalf, Brown and the court quietly eradicated cabin life from "the public peace" and freed families from "the people," a reactionary move that Karen Sanchez-Eppler has seen lurking in sentimental abolitionism from the outset. Even John Marshall Harlan's resonant dissent in his lone minority opinion did not reenlist domestic affiliations in civil guarantees but sorrowed for the "personal liberty" and the "equality of rights which pertains to citizenship" that the Thirteenth Amendment was meant to win. Where Constitutional reform in 1865 had hovered between the domestic relations that permitted slavery to flourish and the reinvention of liberty and justice that would reconstruct the national household, the *Plessy v. Ferguson* retreat demonstrated, especially in opposing "established usages" to "personal liberty," that the conservative appeal of national restoration could no longer deliver a Revolutionary legacy to heirs who were not white.[15]

In this century, the once revolutionary alliance between domestic rhetoric and the campaign for civil rights only continued to fray. When the "separate but equal" doctrine was subsequently overturned, in fact, it was not black "sons" or "daughters" but "citizens" whose rights were at last recognized by the Supreme Court. In *Brown v. Board of Education of the City of Topeka*, decided in 1954, Reconstruction promises were again recalled in evaluating the status of black Americans, in this case schoolchildren who had every reason to be represented as the Harry Harrises on the ice floes of a later era. But after investigating Fourteenth Amendment debates, which the court found inconclusive, Chief Justice Earl Warren observed that public education was less an

extension of the family than an extension of the state, "the very foundation of good citizenship" and "a principal instrument in awakening
the child to cultural values." Where earlier lawmakers consulted by the
court had helped to define paramount national citizenship in the language of subjection and obedience that child rearing as well as gender
relations had allowed, Warren's consolidated opinion almost a century
later spoke of "minors of the Negro race," of "Negro students," and
of "children in public schools," a telling sign of the diminished role
that family relations had come to play in public debate. If political
change were to reinvigorate Revolutionary ideals, Warren concluded,
the clock could not be turned back to 1868 or 1896; nor, apparently,
could the older language of home and family effect a national continuity that Reconstruction Congresses and the Warren Court ultimately
abandoned.[14]

Because of the inescapable restrictions that domestic rhetoric seems
to have signaled, it is worth turning for a moment to the debates engendered by the Nineteenth Amendment, which in 1920 finally granted
all women the right to vote. In the House, where discussion was most
agitated, the mesh between women's political rights and the domestic
claims with which they had long been identified was easily reasserted.
Those who argued for suffrage often spoke of widening the sphere
of women and their purifying influence, while those who opposed
the measure once again worried about both contaminating woman's
natural role in the home and inviting what Scott Ferris of Oklahoma
derisively called "the fear of petticoat domination." Just as familiar
were the apostrophes to the Declaration of Independence by those who
favored extending rights, while the guardians of the status quo looked
back to the original Constitution and then to the forced ratification
of the Fifteenth Amendment, which Senator Ellison DuRant Smith of
South Carolina was to condemn as "a crime against the civilization of
the white men of America." Unusual in this struggle for domestic turf,
however, was the rhetorical transformation of homemaker into citizen,
so that mother became a "peer," wife became an "equal," and marriage
became a "partnership" when recast on the national stage. In the same
way that enlistments had substantiated the claims of black men to the

ballot after the Civil War, the industry of women in factories, counting
rooms, and workshops made them more likely candidates for voting
rights after World War I and revolutionized the rhetoric their advocates
could invoke. William E. Cox of Indiana spoke of recognizing women
as citizens "armed with the ballot," a soldierly metaphor that recalled
Charles Sumner's "mighty army" of abolitionists and anticipated Congressional readiness to grant women "America's most effective weapon,
the ballot," in the ringing words of Ohio's Simeon D. Fess.[15]

Although congressmen like Frank Clark of Florida still warned that
voting rights would disrupt the home ("which in America is the foundation stone of the Republic"), supporters of woman suffrage relocated
democracy's rhetorical base in the citizen ready to vote. They thereby
redefined national citizenship as individual yet comprehensive, self-
reliant yet public-spirited, masculine yet feminine. As James Cantrill
of Kentucky put it, "Right, justice, liberty, and democracy have always
been, and will always be, safe in the tender care of American womanhood. From this day on, let the men and women of America be equal
and united, citizens all, for the common good of our beloved Nation and
for the welfare of all mankind." In joining domestic sanctity to national
citizenship, Congressional representatives effectively reclaimed "established usages, customs and traditions" in the battle for political rights,
recollected the universal vision of Fifteenth Amendment radicals, and
revitalized the ideals of liberty and justice to which Americans had
been swearing allegiance.[16]

It was thus fitting that, in 1954, the Supreme Court tied the education of "Negro citizens" to "the performance of our most basic public
responsibilities," a recognition of cooperative service that departed remarkably from the "enforced separation of the races" and the "police
power" awarded to the states in 1896, when the national continuity
signaled by domestic order proved more restrictive than liberating. In
each instance, as in the years following the Civil War, the rhetoric of
home and family bespoke an anxiety about the resilience of Revolutionary ideals and at least a tentative paradigm for how liberty and justice
might be renewed. For Stowe's readers in the years before Fort Sumter
fell, Uncle Tom offered the example of a redemptive domestic revolu-

tion. For Harris's readers in the years after the Centennial was held, Uncle Remus suggested a revolutionary underside to the restoration of home rule.

But neither Stowe nor Harris provided a vision of cultural reconstruction that *Harper's Monthly* essayed in 1867 by publishing Mary Hose's "Bushy and Jack," an earlier version of the tar-baby story that fit Brer Rabbit into the kind of feminized domestic frame that later Supreme Court Justices would eschew. Instead of Harris's unnamed white boy center stage, Hose introduced a family of Georgia women escaping Sherman's advance. Instead of an aging freedman as titular hero, Hose preferred a young black "responsibility" named Bushy, who tells the tale in his capacity as general factotum to the refugee household. Both Hose's frame and Bushy's tale propose a thoroughly domesticated territory, from Miss Fanny's evening teacup and sleeping baby to the pease patch that Bushy's old man is trying to protect and the family that Brer Rabbit finally rejoins ("See me yeye yer! dis war all my family lib!") in the brier patch. Joining Stowe's kitchen government to Harris's brier patch gumption, Hose momentarily suggested that the newly liberated had every reason to stay down on the farm if they were given a voice in its management. "Bushy and Jack" thus posited an escape into home, of which only the memory ("Bred en bawn in a brier-patch!") remained for Harris's trickster.

In failing to return to the fireside frame as Harris always did, however, Hose left unresolved the difficulty of perpetually reinventing a Revolutionary past, the trick of keeping liberty and justice alive that "buckra" like Miss Fanny would eventually learn from a "teef" like Brer Rabbit. Only when "armed with the ballot" could "peers" equal "fellow-citizens" on the road of reconstructed opportunity. The trick of staying alive with baggage, of making a home in the brier patch, was taught only fleetingly and at length unsuccessfully in popular Civil War narratives. But the allegiance to liberty and justice, which Americans were to swear, had a great deal to do with whether Winslow Homer's white boy with a trumpet or Mary Hose's black boy with a tale would be heard, as black schoolchildren in Topeka nearly a century later would insist.

NOTES

Preface: Popular Narratives and Civil Crisis

1. For thoughtful reflections on media studies as culturally charged, see George Lipsitz, " 'This Ain't No Sideshow': Historians and Media Studies," *Critical Studies in Mass Communications* 5 (1988): 147–61; Ian Connell and Adam Mills, "Text, Discourse and Mass Communication," in *Discourse and Communication: New Approaches to the Analysis of Mass Media*, ed. Teun A. van Tijk (New York: Walter de Gruyter, 1985), 26–43; Joseph Turow, "Cultural Argumentation Through the Mass Media: A Framework for Organizational Research," *Communication* 8 (1985): 139–64; and Paul DiMaggio, "Market Structure, the Creative Process, and Popular Culture: Toward an Organizational Reinterpretation of Mass-Culture Theory," *Journal of Popular Culture* 11 (1977): 436–52. For the rapprochment between intellectuals and popular culture, from the hostility of the Frankfurt School and the New York Intellectuals toward mass culture and kitsch, to the sixties celebration of pop and camp, to the current influence of the British Marxist Raymond Williams and the Birmingham Center for Cultural Studies, see Andrew Ross, *No Respect: Intellectuals and Popular Culture* (New York: Routledge, 1989), especially 1–14.

2. The elegant reference to a collective "subjunctive" mood is actually Victor Turner's; see Michael Schudson, "The New Validation of Popular Culture: Sense and Sentimentality in Academia," *Critical Studies in Mass Communication* 4 (1987), 57. On the importance of narrative conventions, see M.J. Birch, "The Popular Fiction Industry: Market, Formula, Ideology," *Journal of Popular Culture* 21 (1987): 79–102; Clinton R. Sanders, "Structural and Interactional Features of Popular Culture Production: An Introduction to the Production of Culture Perspective," *Journal of Popular Culture* 16 (Fall 1982): 66–74; and

Richard A. Peterson, "The Production of Culture: A Prolegomenon," *American Behavioral Scientist* 19 (1976): 669–84. For a view of cultural work as the text's "terministic screen" through which readers see their own experience emplotted, see Barbara Warnick, "A Ricoeurian Approach to Rhetorical Criticism," *Western Journal of Speech Communication* 51 (1987): 227–44, as well as Christopher Pawling, "Popular Fiction: Ideology or Utopia?" in *Popular Fiction and Social Change*, ed. Christopher Pawling (London: Macmillan, 1984), 1–19; Robert A. White, "Mass Communication and Culture: Transition to a New Paradigm," *Journal of Communication* 33 (1983): 279–301; and Raymond Williams, "Communications as Cultural Science," *Journal of Communication* 24 (1974): 17–25. For the role of the popular press in solidifying national identity during the years surrounding the Civil War, see Edward Caudill and Susan L. Caudill, "Nation and Section: An Analysis of Key Symbols in the Antebellum Press," *Journalism History* 15 (Spring 1988): 16–25; William J. Gilmore, "Literacy, the Rise of an Age of Reading, and the Cultural Grammar of Print Communications in America, 1735–1850," *Communication* 11 (1988): 23–46; and, above all, James W. Carey, *Communication as Culture: Essays on Media and Society* (Boston: Unwin Hyman, 1988), especially 1–9. Questioning the simple transmission model that has long characterized mass media studies, Carey has substituted a ritualistic view of communication that celebrates the narrative contest through which culture has been manufactured, circulated, maintained, and reproduced.

3. See David Paul Nord, "A Republican Literature: Magazine Reading and Readers in Late-Eighteenth-Century New York," in *Reading in America: Literature and Social History*, ed. Cathy N. Davidson (Baltimore: Johns Hopkins University Press, 1989), 114–39; Mary P. Ryan, *Cradle of the Middle Class: The Family in Oneida County, New York, 1790–1865* (New York: Cambridge University Press, 1981), 230–42, together with Stuart M. Blumin's greater emphasis on working-class adjustments to the domestic ideal in *The Emergence of the Middle Class: Social Experience in the American City, 1760–1900* (New York: Cambridge University Press, 1989), 179–91. For a sketch of the New York *Ledger*'s "innocuous" fare and stunning success among the less leisured, see Frank Luther Mott, *A History of American Magazines* (Cambridge: Harvard University Press, 1938–68), Vol. 2: 356–63.

4. See Carey, *Communication as Culture*, 153–56. Also useful are Caudill and Caudill, "Nation and Section"; Gilmore, "Literacy"; and Sanders, "Structural and Interactional Features of Popular Culture Production."

5. William Charvat has noted that as early as the 1840s Boston had also emerged as a center for publishing cheap fiction like temperance novels, a sign of the class tensions in the city that literary magazines tended to ignore. It is similarly worth noting that not everyone in Boston embraced the Republican Party or the war effort, as the local draft riot in July 1863 revealed. But the Civil War stories that came out of Boston were not told by rioters, nor was the city's anti-Republican sentiment generally acknowledged in Southern magazines. For an assessment of Boston's publishing economy, see William Charvat, *Literary Publishing in America, 1790–1850* (Philadelphia: University of Pennsylvania Press, 1959), 19–20, 27–35; and Mott, *A History of American Magazines*, Vol. 1: 202–5, 378–80.

6. Of the numerous and substantial treatments the magazine has received, the most helpful are Mott, *A History of American Magazines*, Vol. 2: 493–515; Irving Garwood, *American Periodicals from 1850 to 1860* (Macomb, Ill.: Commercial Art Press, 1931), 73–76; John Tebbel, *The American Magazine: A Compact History* (New York: Hawthorn Books, 1969), 110–12; M. A. DeWolfe Howe, *The "Atlantic Monthly" and Its Makers* (Boston: Atlantic Monthly Press, 1919), 42–69; and Ellery Sedgwick's sketch in *American Literary Magazines: the Eighteenth and Nineteenth Centuries*, ed. Edward E. Chielens (Westport, Conn.: Greenwood Press, 1986), 50–57. See, too, Louis J. Budd, "Howells, the *Atlantic Monthly*, and Republicanism," *American Literature* 24 (1952): 139–56; and Ellery Sedgwick III, "The Early Years of the *Atlantic Monthly*," *American Transcendental Quarterly* 58 (December 1985): 5–30. Southern response to the *Atlantic*'s antislavery stance may be found in the *Southern Literary Messenger* 25 (December 1857): 472.

7. Circulation figures are unavailable, but see Mott, *A History of American Magazines*, Vol. 2: 540–43.

8. Carey, *Communication as Culture*, 153. The vigor of Democratic partisanship at home was also evident in the violent draft riots that broke out on New York streets in the summer of 1863, when largely Irish workers attacked a black orphanage and Horace Greeley's Republican *Tribune* rather than the more conservative Harper establishment. Information on the politics of publishing in New York appears in Charvat, *Literary Publishing in America*, 19, 21–29, 47–53; and Mott, *A History of American Magazines*, Vol. 1: 375–77.

9. See informative observations by Mott, *A History of American Magazines*, Vol. 2: 383–405; Algernon Tassin, *The Magazine in America* (New York: Dodd, Mead, 1916), 232–55; Tebbel, *The American Magazine*, 107–9; Jay B. Hubbell,

The South in American Literature, 1607–1900 (Durham, N.C.: Duke University Press, 1954), 730; Eugene Exman, *The House of Harper: One Hundred and Fifty Years of Publishing* (New York: Harper and Row, 1967), 69–79; and Barbara M. Perkins's sketch in Chielens, *American Literary Magazines*, 166–71. See, too, *Harper's Monthly*'s own "A Word at the Start" (June 1850): 1–2, and the "Advertisement" at the beginning of the magazine's first bound volume.

10. For further information, see Mott, *A History of American Magazines*, Vol. 2: 469–87; Exman, *The House of Harper*, 80–93; and Tebbel, *The American Magazine*, 109–10.

11. See overviews by Mott, *A History of American Magazines*, Vol. 2: 428–30; Tassin, *The Magazine in America*, 205–31; and Kent Ljungquist's sketch in Chielens, *American Literary Magazines*, 328–33. In *Putnam's*, see C. F. Briggs's "The Old and the New" (January 1868): 1–8, and his "The First Volume" introducing the first bound issues of the new series.

12. Useful information appears in Mott, *A History of American Magazines*, Vol. 3: 361–81; Tebbel, *The American Magazine*, 121–23; and Edward Chielens's sketch in Chielens, *American Literary Magazines*, 139–44. Also see Robert J. Scholnick, "The *Galaxy* and American Democratic Culture, 1866–1878," *Journal of American Studies* 16 (1982): 69–80; and Justus R. Pearson, Jr., "Story of a Magazine: New York's *Galaxy* 1866–1878," *Bulletin of the New York Public Library* 61 (1957): 217–37, 281–302.

13. For information on Philadelphia's rise and decline as the biggest center of publishing and printing in the country, see Mott, *A History of American Magazines*, Vol. 1: 201, 208–10, 377–78. On Mathew Carey's enterprise, see Charvat, *Literary Publishing in America*, 26–27, 38–60, and *The Profession of Authorship in America, 1800–1870*, ed. Matthew J. Bruccoli (Columbus: Ohio State University Press, 1968), 18–20, 37–39; as well as David Kaser, "Carey and Lea," in *Publishers for Mass Entertainment in Nineteenth Century America*, ed. Madeleine B. Stern (Boston: G. K. Hall, 1980), 73–80.

14. Of the numerous available introductions, most informative are Mott, *A History of American Magazines*, Vol. 1: 580–94; Tassin, *The Magazine in America*, 102–8; James Playsted Wood, *Magazines in the United States*, 3d ed. (New York: Ronald Press, 1971), 49–54; Allison Bulsterbaum's sketch in Chielens, *American Literary Magazines*, 144–50; Ruth E. Finley, *The Lady of 'Godey's': Sarah Josepha Hale* (Philadelphia: Lippincott, 1931), especially 174–278; and Joseph N. Satterwhite, "The Tremulous Formula: Form and Technique in *Godey's* Fiction," *American Quarterly* 8 (1956): 99–113.

15. While background material is not extensive and the magazine itself withheld circulation figures, brief sketches appear in Mott, *A History of American Magazines*, Vol. 3: 396–401; and Tebbel, *The American Magazine*, 124–25. Also useful are Kirk's inaugural comments in "Our Monthly Gossip" (January 1868): 107, 114.

16. Calling for a new Confederate literature and securing a Southern reading public were not, however, the same thing. As the editor of the *Southern Literary Messenger* observed in 1860: "Southern patriotism never was proof against Northern newspapers and picture magazines. If the angel Gabriel had gone into the very heart of the South, if he had even taken his seat on the top of the office of the Charleston Mercury and there proclaimed the immediate approach of the Day of Judgment, that would not have hindered the hottest secessionist from buying the New York Herald and subscribing for Harper's Magazine." Cited in Hubbell, *The South in American Literature* (568), whose extended treatment of early publishing ventures in Richmond (236, 363–69, 534–35) deserves note. Figures on manufacturing resources are taken from John Tebbel, *A History of Book Publishing in the United States* (New York: R. R. Bowker, 1972–81), Vol. 1: 474, information usefully augmented by Mott, *A History of American Magazines*, Vol. 1: 629–30, Vol. 2: 107–10.

17. The most extensive of several overviews are Mott, *A History of American Magazines*, Vol. 1: 629–57; Tassin, *The Magazine in America*, 186–90; David T. Dodd's sketch in Chielens, *American Literary Magazines*, 390–95; Sam G. Riley, *Magazines of the American South* (Westport, Conn.: Greenwood Press, 1986), 233–37; and Benjamin Blake Minor, *'The Southern Literary Messenger,' 1834–1864* (New York: Neale Publishing, 1905), especially 209–36.

18. Little information is available on the *Southern Illustrated News*, for which neither the editor nor the circulation is known. The best sources are Richard Barksdale Harwell, "A Confederate View of the Southern Poets," *American Literature* 24 (1952): 51–61; and the newspaper's own "Prospectus" (13 September 1862): 8.

19. The circulation of the magazine is unknown, as is the editor. Other data are available in Mott, *A History of American Magazines*, Vol. 2: 111; Tebbel, *The American Magazine*, 99; and Riley, *Magazines of the American South*, 247–49. In addition, the *Southern Monthly* published germane comments anonymously in "Southern Literature" (September 1861), "Our Reception" (October 1861), "Opinions of the Press" (November 1861), "To Contributors" (December 1861), and "Our Sanctum" (February 1862, April 1862).

20. The most extensive coverage appears in Riley, *Magazines of the American South*, 97–99; and Ray M. Atchinson, "The *Land We Love*: A Southern Post-Bellum Magazine of Agriculture, Literature, and Military History," *North Carolina Historical Review* 37 (1960): 506–15. See, too, the magazine's outspoken editorials, particularly those for August 1866 and October 1866.

21. The fullest sketch is Ray M. Atchinson's in Chielens, *American Literary Magazines*, 395–99, which may be usefully supplemented by Hubbell, *The South in American Literature*, especially 717–18; and Mott, *A History of American Magazines*, Vol. 3: 46.

22. Of the several extensive treatments of Bret Harte and the journal he brought to international recognition, see Mott, *A History of American Magazines*, Vol. 3: 402–9; Franklin Walker, *San Francisco's Literary Frontier* (New York: Knopf, 1939), 256–83; Richard O'Connor, *Bret Harte: A Biography* (Boston: Little, Brown, 1966), 97–133; and Ernest R. May, "Bret Harte and the *Overland Monthly*," *American Literature* 22 (1950): 260–71. Also helpful is Harte's opening volley in his "Etc." column (July 1868): 99–100.

23. For substantial introductions, see Michael Hackenberg's sketch in Chielens, *American Literary Magazines*, 199–203; Mott, *A History of American Magazines*, Vol. 3: 413–16; Herbert E. Fleming, "The Literary Interests of Chicago," *American Journal of Sociology* 11 (1906): 377–408; and "The Life-Story of a Magazine," *Dial* 54 (16 June 1913): 489–92.

24. Although no circulation figures are available and attention to the *New National Era* in general has been spotty, useful remarks appear in Penelope L. Bullock, *The Afro-American Periodical Press, 1838–1909* (Baton Rouge: Louisiana State University Press, 1981), 53; Roland E. Wolseley, *The Black Press: U.S.A.* (Ames: Iowa State University Press, 1971), 23; Martin E. Dann, ed., *The Black Press, 1827–1890: The Quest for National Identity* (New York: Putnam's, 1971), 91–99; Constance McLaughlin Green, *The Secret City: A History of Race Relations in the Nation's Capital* (Princeton, N.J.: Princeton University Press, 1967), 94–113; Mott, *A History of American Magazines*, Vol. 3: 283–84; and Frederick Douglass, *Life and Times of Frederick Douglass, Written by Himself* (1881; rpt. Secaucus, N.J.: Citadel Press, 1983), 407–8. In the *New National Era*, see "Our Journal" (13 January 1870): 2, "Prospectus of the New Era! A Colored American National Journal" (13 January 1870): 3, "Salutatory of the Corresponding Editor" (27 January 1870): 2, and "What the Press Say of the New Era" (3 February 1870): 2.

25. Gilmore, "Literacy," especially 23–29. Weighing the quid pro quo that

bound the republican message to the new medium of magazines, Dana Nelson [Salvino] has recently observed: "Printers and editors had a crucial role in the dissemination of the literacy ideology; while they played a publicly acknowledged moral function, they also had a fundamentally economic interest in the enterprise of literacy." See "The Word in Black and White: Ideologies of Race and Literacy in Antebellum America," in *Reading in America*, 145. Also useful are Dorey Schmidt, "Magazines in American Culture," in *The American Magazine; 1890–1940*, ed. Dorey Schmidt (Wilmington: Delaware Art Museum, 1979): 6–9; and Tebbel, *A History of Book Publishing*, Vol. 1: 207.

26. James F. Klumpp and Thomas A. Hollihan, "Rhetorical Criticism as Moral Action," *Quarterly Journal of Speech* 75 (1989): 88; Celeste Michelle Condit, "Interpellating Rhetoric, Politics, and Culture: 'Hail' or 'Greetings'?" *Communication* 11 (1990): 248. On the cultural significance of reading rhetoric, see, too, Maurice Charland, "Rehabilitating Rhetoric: Confronting Blindspots in Discourse and Social Theory," *Communication* 11 (1990): 253–64; Christine Oravec, "The Sublimation of Mass Consciousness in the Rhetorical Criticism of Jacksonian America," *Communication* 11 (1990): 291–314; Karlyn Kohrs Campbell and Kathleen Hall Jamieson, *Deeds Done in Words. Presidential Rhetoric and the Genres of Governance* (Chicago: University of Chicago Press, 1990); 1–13; and Walter R. Fisher, "Narration as a Human Communication Paradigm: The Case of Public Moral Argument," *Communication Monographs* 51 (March 1984): 1–22.

27. James Boyd White, *When Words Lose Their Meaning; Constitutions and Reconstitutions of Language, Character, and Community* (Chicago: University of Chicago Press, 1984), vi. For further comment on the rhetorical dimensions of the law and the respect for convention that law and literature share, see Brook Thomas, *Cross-Examinations of Law and Literature: Cooper, Hawthorne, Stowe, and Melville* (New York: Cambridge University Press, 1987), 1–18; Robert A. Ferguson, *Law and Letters in American Culture* (Cambridge, Mass.: Harvard University Press, 1984), 1–10; Robert W. Gordon, "New Developments in Legal Theory," in *The Politics of Law: A Progressive Critique*, ed. David Kairys (New York: Pantheon, 1982), 281–309; Sanford Levinson, "Law as Literature," *Texas Law Review* 60 (March 1982): 373–403; and Stephen C. Yeazell, "Convention, Fiction, and Law," *New Literary History* 13 (1981): 89–102.

Introduction

1. The most informative examination of *News from the War* appears in David Tatham, "Winslow Homer at the Front in 1862," *American Art Journal* 11 (1979): 86–87. In other drawings for *Harper's Weekly*, Homer relied upon similar conventions for organizing his figures and the composite story they told. For an excellent discussion of *Pay-Day in the Army of the Potomac* (*Harper's Weekly*, 28 February 1863), see Peter H. Wood and Karen C. C. Dalton, *Winslow Homer's Images of Blacks: The Civil War and Reconstruction Years* (Austin: University of Texas Press, 1988), 41–46. Here, too, Homer segregates men and women into spheres as though into "opposite sides of the same coin" and then suggests the greater freedom of camp in the detail of the circulating canteen. Rarely again, however, do his figures confront one another across a gendered or sectional divide; even during the contest between radical Republicans and the postwar South, Homer's concern was to lie significantly with the lives of black Americans and the consequences of emancipation, only suggested in *News from the War* by the sidelong glance of the burdened slave. For a bold conflation of gender and race imperatives in the reconstructive task of protecting the freedmen by subduing the rebels, see Thomas Nast's "Would You Marry Your Daughter to a Nigger?" (*Harper's Weekly*, 11 July 1868): 444, in which the Chief Justice of the Supreme Court marries the representative freedman to the Democratic Party as a reluctant white bride.

2. For information on how male reading habits changed dramatically during the long stretches of free time in camp, thereby fueling the postwar magazine boom, see David Kaser, *Books and Libraries in Camp and Battle: The Civil War Experience* (Westport, Conn.: Greenwood Press, 1984), 77–125.

3. The "little lady who made this big war," in Abraham Lincoln's reported phrase, has received keen critical attention of late, as has her success in attacking slavery on domestic grounds. See Mary Kelley's observations on "the power of womanhood *and* its boundaries" in Jeanne Boydston, Mary Kelley, and Anne Margolis, *The Limits of Sisterhood: The Beecher Sisters on Women's Rights and Woman's Sphere* (Chapel Hill: University of North Carolina Press, 1988), 154–63; Philip Fisher's attention to the "restructuring of the national home" in *Hard Facts: Setting and Form in the American Novel* (New York: Oxford University Press, 1987), 87–127; Brook Thomas's evaluation of "contradictory social structures" coexisting in the market and the domestic economy of the home in *Cross-Examinations of Law and Literature*, 113–37; Karen Halttunen's read-

ing of Legree's "haunted house" in "Gothic Imagination and Social Reform: The Haunted Houses of Lyman Beecher, Henry Ward Beecher, and Harriet Beecher Stowe," in *New Essays on "Uncle Tom's Cabin,"* ed. Eric J. Sundquist (New York: Cambridge University Press, 1986), 107–34; Jane Tompkins's critique of "household economy" in *Sensational Designs: The Cultural Work of American Fiction, 1790–1860* (New York: Oxford University Press, 1985), 122–46; Gillian Brown's architectonics of liberation beginning with "the careless condition of the Southern kitchen" in "Getting in the Kitchen with Dinah: Domestic Politics in *Uncle Tom's Cabin,"* *American Quarterly* 36 (1984): 503–23; and George B. Forgie's discussion of "the domestic scene" in *Patricide in the House Divided: A Psychological Interpretation of Lincoln and His Age* (New York: Norton, 1979), 159–99.

4. As Poovey observes, the pressure of competing social distinctions explains both the apparent vigor of gender differences in the nineteenth century and their systematic instability. She writes: "Only because the differences of class, race, and national identity produced real, if occluded, effects, in other words, could sexual difference seem decisive and the anchor of all social relations." See *Uneven Developments: The Ideological Work of Gender in Mid-Victorian England* (Chicago: University of Chicago Press, 1988), 199. Also useful on "the politics of domesticating culture" in the rise of the eighteenth-century novel is Nancy Armstrong, *Desire and Domestic Fiction: A Political History of the Novel* (New York: Oxford University Press, 1987), especially 3–27. On more recent narrative investment in "the configuration of home, identity and community," see Biddy Martin and Chandra Talpade Mohanty, "Feminist Politics: What's Home Got to Do with It?" in *Feminist Studies/Critical Studies*, ed. Teresa de Laurentis (Bloomington: Indiana University Press, 1986), 191–212.

5. There is some confusion about identifying the wounded veterans, particularly since Homer did not submit the brief explanation of his drawing that was customary among other special artists in the field. David Tatham has persuasively argued that the wounded men are Confederate soldiers and that the ragged "CAVALRY" placard above their heads is an ironic comment on Confederate illusions of glory (letter to the author, 14 August 1990), a conclusion with which Wood and Dalton agree (118, fn121). The fact that Homer stations his unguarded figures in the open air certainly supports their view. But in the absence of comment from the artist, *Harper's Weekly* clouded the issue by manufacturing the necessary explanatory paragraph, which follows the illustration's vignettes from the "tender hearts" stricken by unwelcome

news through imprisoned Unionists and wounded veterans to the freer soldiers in camp "who hear, with half-suppressed jealousy, of glories they did not share" (*Harper's Weekly*, 14 June 1862, 378). It is fair to say that the uniforms the men have on, the lack of cordiality among the figures, and the theme of "war news illustrated" that Northern readers evidently sought all combine to suggest that the wounded men are Federal soldiers, from which the women stand apart. Homer's biographer, William Howe Downes, substantiates such a reading when he refers to the anxiety about news of prisoners that Homer's *From Richmond* illustrates. See *The Life and Works of Winslow Homer* (1911; rpt. New York: Dover Publications, 1989), 44. At the very least, this confusion suggests how simple it would be in later years to represent the confrontation between North and South as a gendered tension, which popular romances did not always resolve.

6. See Francis Bellamy, "The Story of The Pledge of Allegiance to The Flag," *University of Rochester Library Bulletin* 8 (Winter 1953): 29–39; Margaret Butterfield, "Francis Bellamy, '76," *University of Rochester Library Bulletin* 8 (Winter 1953): 25–28; and "National School Celebration of Columbus Day. The Official Programme," *Youth's Companion* 66 (8 September 1892): 446–47. Bellamy's original pledge ran to just twenty-two words: "I pledge allegiance to my Flag and the Republic for which it stands: one Nation indivisible, with Liberty and Justice for all." In the early 1920s, the opening phrase was reworded slightly to accommodate larger numbers of immigrant children in public schools; in 1954, the phrase "under God" was added from Lincoln's Gettysburg Address in a conscious effort to rebut communism. See the United States House Report from the Committee on the Judiciary, *Amending the Pledge of Allegiance to the Flag of the United States*, 83d Cong., 2d sess., H. Rept 1693 (1954); and the *Congressional Record*, 83d Cong., 2d sess., 7 June 1954, 7757–61.

7. See Werner Sollors, *Beyond Ethnicity: Consent and Descent in American Culture* (New York: Oxford University Press, 1986), especially 208–36.

8. Linda K. Kerber, "The Republican Mother," in *Women's America: Refocusing the Past*, ed. Linda K. Kerber and Jane De Hart-Mathews (New York: Oxford University Press, 1987), 84, 90.

9. As used here, the term *household* offers a quantifiable version of the home that family and servants were thought to treasure in common, a sublimation of class priorities and racial distinctions that popular magazines routinely made less suspect than it ought to have been. For a more sociologically respectable

use of the term, see Elizabeth Fox-Genovese, *Within the Plantation Household: Black and White Women of the Old South* (Chapel Hill: University of North Carolina Press, 1988), 31–32.

10. See Karen Sanchez-Eppler, "Bodily Bonds: The Intersecting Rhetorics of Feminism and Abolition," *Representations* 24 (Fall 1988): 28–59; Gertrude Reif Hughes, "Subverting the Cult of Domesticity: Emily Dickinson's Critique of Women's Work," *Legacy* 3 (Spring 1986): 17–28; and Joanne Dobson, " 'The Invisible Lady': Emily Dickinson and Conventions of the Female Self," *Legacy* 3 (Spring 1986): 41–55. Such revisionary critiques, among others, demonstrate that the operations of a domestic model are now thought to have been wider in scope than a simple "cult" would suggest and its agents more complex in their motivations and ambitious in their agendas than Barbara Welter's "true women" first seemed.

11. For a measured evaluation of the perennial effort to discover what adopters intended, see Paul Brest, "The Misconceived Quest for the Original Understanding," *Boston University Law Review* 60 (1980): 204–38. Perhaps the most energetic proponent of original intent is Raoul Berger, who writes in *Government by Judiciary: The Transformation of the Fourteenth Amendment*: "Even Humpty-Dumpty did not carry it so far as to insist that when Alice 'used' a word *he* could dictate what *she* meant" (Cambridge, Mass.: Harvard University Press, 1977), 371. For more recent misgivings about straightforward recovery, see David Zarefsky and Victoria J. Gallagher, "From 'Conflict' to 'Constitutional Question': Transformations in Early American Public Discourse," *Quarterly Journal of Speech* 76 (1990): 247–61, together with Yeazell, "Convention, Fiction, and Law"; Levinson, "Law as Literature"; and Howard Jay Graham, *Everyman's Constitution: Historical Essays on the Fourteenth Amendment, the "Conspiracy Theory," and American Constitutionalism* (Madison: State Historical Society of Wisconsin, 1968), 337–38.

Chapter One: Domestic Narrative and National Stability

1. George B. Forgie points out that Lincoln reimagined the threat of the "house divided," though neither the "literature of fratricide" that Forgie surveys nor more recent historiographical references to Lincoln's speech in 1858 have regularly noted the alternative threat that was sustained in popular narratives. See *Patricide in the House Divided*, 201–81.

2. *History and American Society: Essays of David M. Potter*, ed. Don E.

Fehrenbacher (New York: Oxford University Press, 1973), 64. To support his point, Potter cites social scientist Morton Grodzins, who observes in *The Loyal and the Disloyal*: "Populations are loyal to the nation as a by-product of satisfactions achieved within non-national groups, because the nation is believed to symbolize and sustain these groups. From this point of view, one is loyal not to the nation but to family, business, religion, friends. One fights for the joys of his pinochle club when he is said to fight for his country" (Potter, 74). State sovereignty drew upon these ties in the years following the Revolution, a pattern that persisted in the South longer than it did elsewhere.

3. See also the poetic invocation in "The Gathering of the Southern Volunteers" (*Southern Literary Messenger*, June 1861), to be sung to the tune of "La Marseillaise"; William H. Holcombe's "Sic Semper Tyrannis" (*Southern Literary Messenger*, October 1861); William Gilmore Simms's other "Odes, Sonnets and Songs, for the Times" (*Southern Literary Messenger*, February & March 1862); and Col. Beuhring H. Jones's "My Southern Home" (*Land We Love*, January 1868).

4. One of the first to respond to Lincoln's subsequent call for 300,000 more troops was abolitionist James Sloane Gibbons, who wrote the poem that became a rallying song in the hands of several composers, Stephen Foster among them. Close to two million copies of different tunes for "We Are Coming Father Abra'am" were sold by the time the Civil War ended, as more and more Northerners sang words like these: "We are coming, Father Abra'am, / three hundred thousand more, / From Mississippi's winding stream and from New England's shore; / We leave our plows and workshops / our wives and children dear, / With hearts too full for utterance, with but a silent tear; / We dare not look behind us, but steadfastly before— / We are coming, Father Abra'am— / three hundred thousand more!" The lyrics were mistakenly attributed at first to William Cullen Bryant, editor of New York's *Evening Post* in which the poem appeared on 16 July 1862. See Charles Hamm, *Yesterdays: Popular Songs in America* (New York: Norton, 1979), 239; and Richard Crawford, ed., *Civil War Songbook: Complete Original Sheet Music for 37 Songs* (New York: Dover Publications, 1977), vii, 30–33.

5. For the development of the plantation tradition in antebellum literature as both a response to abolition and a pledge to Revolutionary ideals, see Drew Gilpin Faust, *The Creation of Confederate Nationalism: Ideology and Identity in the Civil War South* (Baton Rouge: Louisiana University Press, 1988), 1–21; George Dekker, *The American Historical Romance* (New York: Cambridge University Press, 1987), 272–81; Anne Firor Scott, *The Southern Lady: From Ped-*

estal to Politics, 1830–1930 (Chicago: University of Chicago Press, 1970), 3–21; William R. Taylor, *Cavalier and Yankee*, especially 145–76; Buck, *The Road to Reunion*, 327–41; and Francis Pendleton Gaines, *The Southern Plantation: A Study in the Development and the Accuracy of a Tradition* (New York: Columbia University Press, 1925), 18–35.

6. *Congressional Globe*, 38th Cong., 1st sess., 9 February 1864, 536.

7. Once the Senate settled on the language of the Northwest Ordinance, which had prohibited slavery in the territories since 1787 and thus provided familiar legal phraseology for those intent on abolishing slavery, the Thirteenth Amendment assumed the form in which it would eventually be ratified:

> Section 1. Neither slavery nor involuntary servitude, except as a punishment for crime whereof the party shall have been duly convicted, shall exist within the United States, or any other place subject to their jurisdiction.
>
> Section 2. Congress shall have the power to enforce this article by appropriate legislation.

In his landmark study of Thirteenth Amendment debates and the earlier antislavery movement, Jacobus tenBroek argues that Northern victories on the battlefield and Republican victories at the polls in 1864 had effectively put an end to the institution of slavery, with the result that the "free nation" he attributes to the amendment's first section engendered far less dispute than the "revolution in federalism" provoked by the enforcement power secured to Congress in the amendment's second section. See *Equal Under Law: The Antislavery Origins of the Fourteenth Amendment* (New York: Collier Books, 1965), 157–97. For competing views on the tenor and implications of Thirteenth Amendment debates during 1864 and 1865, see Eric Foner, *Reconstruction: America's Unfinished Revolution, 1863–1877* (New York: Harper & Row, 1988), 60–68; Philip S. Foner, *History of Black Americans*, Vol. 3: *From the Compromise of 1850 to the End of the Civil War* (Westport, Conn.: Greenwood Press, 1983), 458–72; Harold M. Hyman and William M. Wiecek, *Equal Justice Under Law: Constitutional Development, 1835–1875* (New York: Harper and Row, 1982), 386–438; Herman Belz, *A New Birth of Freedom: The Republican Party and Freedmen's Rights, 1861 to 1866* (Westport, Conn.: Greenwood Press, 1976), 113–37; G. Sidney Buchanon, "The Quest for Freedom: A Legal History of the Thirteenth Amendment," *Houston Law Review* 12 (October 1974): 1–34; and Harold M. Hyman, *A More Perfect Union: The Impact of the Civil War and Reconstruction on the Constitution* (New York: Knopf, 1973), 263–306.

8. In the *Congressional Globe*, see remarks by Clarke (N.Y.), 38th Cong.,

1st sess., 31 March 1864; Sumner (Mass.), 38th Cong., 1st sess., 8 April 1864, 1479–81; Kellogg (Mich.), 38th Cong., 1st sess., 14 June 1864, 2955; and Ashley (Ohio), 38th Cong., 1st sess., 6 January 1865, 138.

9. *Congressional Globe*, 39th Cong., 1st sess., 318. Cf. remarks by Saulsbury (Del.), 38th Cong., 1st sess., 31 March 1864, 1366; Powell (Ky.), 38th Cong., 1st sess., 8 April 1864, 1483; Pruyn (N.Y.), 38th Cong., 1st sess., 14 June 1864, 2939; Wood (N.Y.), 38th Cong., 1st sess., 14 June 1864, 2941; and Mallory (Ky.), 38th Cong., 2d sess., 9 January 1865, 178.

10. *Congressional Globe*, 38th Cong., 2d sess., 6 January 1865, 139.

11. *Congressional Globe*, 38th Cong., 1st sess., 8 April 1864, 1484; 38th Cong., 2d sess., 6 January 1865, 143; 38th Cong., 1st sess., 9 February 1864, 536.

12. *Congressional Globe*, 38th Cong., 1st sess., 8 April 1864, 1481; Appendix, 38th Cong., 2d sess., 6 December 1864, 3. Lincoln reiterated his concern for widows and orphans in his Second Inaugural Address, delivered on 4 March 1865. But on 11 April, in his last public speech, he employed the sort of national metaphor that again brought the Union into the domestic fold. Identifying reconstruction as "the reinauguration of the national authority," Lincoln urged that the debate over the "legal" secession of Southern states be set aside. "Finding themselves safely at home," he observed, "it would be utterly immaterial whether they had ever been abroad." By reasserting the single national "home" to which states were bound, Lincoln underlined the conservative appeal of a union to which Southern states would at length return. See *Collected Works of Abraham Lincoln*, Vol. 8: *1864–65*, ed. Roy P. Basler (New Brunswick, N.J.: Rutgers University Press, 1953), 332–33, 399–405.

13. *Congressional Globe*, 39th Cong., 1st sess., 30 January 1866, 499.

14. There were four stories told by or about slave protagonists: "Tippoo Saib" (*Harper's Weekly*, 2 April 1864), Mrs. E. P. Campbell's "Edmund Brook" (*Atlantic Monthly*, October 1868), Sarah B. Cooper's "Old Uncle Hampshire" (*Overland Monthly*, November 1872), and George Cary Eggleston's "My Friend Phil" (*Galaxy*, December 1875). Ample slave characters play subsidiary parts in the remaining four stories: "Adventures of a Teacher in Dixie" (*Harper's Weekly*, 5 April 1862), Helen W. Pierson's "In Bonds" (*Harper's Monthly*, September 1864), Mary Hose's "Bushy and Jack" (*Harper's Monthly*, May 1867), and Kate P. Kereven's "Dr. Aar" (*Lippincott's*, November 1868).

15. The five stories published in *Harper's Monthly* include Mary E. Dodge's "Our Contraband" (August 1863), Helen W. Pierson's "Chip" (July 1865), M. Schele De Verre's "The Freedman's Story" (October 1866), John Hay's

"The Foster Brothers" (September 1869), and Lizzie W. Champney's "Polly Pharaoh" (July 1876). The enthusiastic *Atlantic Monthly* published four stories that were generally more polished in their execution and more daring in their challenge to fictive conventions: Rebecca Harding Davis's "John Lamar" (April 1862), Louisa May Alcott's "The Brothers" (November 1863), J. W. De Forest's "A Gentleman of the Old School" (May 1868), and Mark Twain's "A True Story, Repeated Word for Word As I Heard It" (November 1874). Also of note are "Old Levert's Grave" in *Harper's Weekly* (21 April 1866) and Theoda Foster Bush's "Clar's Choice: A Word to the Freedwomen" in the *New National Era* (24 March 1870). As verbal efforts to find roles for ex-slaves in an American household, all of these stories deserve fuller attention than they have received to date.

16. In his covering letter to Howells, Twain wrote: "I enclose also "A True Story" which has no humor in it. You can pay as lightly as you choose for that if you want it, for it is rather out of my line. I have not altered the old colored woman's story, except to begin it at the beginning, instead of the middle, as she did—and traveled both ways (cited in Paine, Vol. 2: 514). Wrote Howells in reply, "This little story delights me more and more; I wish you had forty of 'em!" See Henry Nash Smith and William M. Gibson, eds., *Mark Twain–Howells Letters* (Cambridge: Harvard University Press, Belknap Press, 1960), 25. For later remarks by Twain and Howells on "A True Story," see James D. Wilson, *A Reader's Guide to the Short Stories of Mark Twain* (Boston: G. K. Hall, 1987), 267–78; Kenneth E. Eble, *Old Clemens and W.D.H.: The Story of a Remarkable Friendship* (Baton Rouge: Louisiana State University Press, 1985), 67; and Louis J. Budd, *Critical Essays on Mark Twain, 1867–1910* (Boston: G. K. Hall, 1982), 39.

17. Herbert A. Wisbey, Jr., provides further and welcome details in "The True Story of Auntie Cord," *Mark Twain Society Bulletin* 4 (June 1981): 1, 3–5. Also see Albert Bigelow Paine, *Mark Twain: A Biography* (New York: Harper and Row, 1912), 514–15. Likewise useful are Twain's own comments in "A Family Sketch," largely unpublished, composed around 1896; photocopy in DeVoto 226, pp. 38–39, Mark Twain Papers, General Library, University of California, Berkeley.

18. On the many uses of Auntie Cord, see Arthur G. Pettit, *Mark Twain and the South* (Lexington: University Press of Kentucky, 1974), 54. On Twain's connection with the *Buffalo Express*, see Louis J. Budd, *Mark Twain: Social Philosopher* (Bloomington: Indiana University Press, 1962), 87, 92.

19. In the wake of Daniel Patrick Moynihan's *The Negro Family: The Case for National Action*, published in 1965, scholars have both condemned the perpetuation of Aunt Jemimas, Sapphires, and Amazons, and endorsed the female strength that such figures have promoted. Alert to issues of political control that have rarely favored blacks, for example, Bell Hooks has observed: "In a sense whites created in the mammy figure a black woman who embodied solely those characteristics they as colonizers wished to exploit." See *Ain't I A Woman: Black Women and Feminism* (Boston: South End Press, 1981), 84. For further responses to what Bettina Aptheker has called the "matriarchal mirage" (black women as "all-powerful, domineering, sexually permissive, and aggressive"), see Marcia Ann Gillespie, "The Myth of the Strong Black Woman," in *Feminist Frameworks: Alternative Theoretical Accounts of the Relations Between Women and Men*, 2d ed., ed. Alison M. Jaggar and Paula Rothenberg Struhl (New York: McGraw-Hill, 1984), 32–36; Bettina Aptheker, *Woman's Legacy: Essays on Race, Sex, and Class in American History* (Amherst: University of Massachusetts Press, 1982), 129–51; John H. Bracey, Jr., August Meier, and Elliott Rudwick, eds., *Black Matriarchy: Myth or Reality?* (Belmont, Calif.: Wadsworth, 1971), 160–84; and Robert Staples, "The Myth of the Black Matriarchy," *Black Scholar* 1 (January–February 1970): 8–16, which comments most fully on "the literary castration of the black male." Among the first to indict the uses to which the matriarchal figure has been put in monitoring American race relations, Angela Davis nonetheless proposed that the black woman also became "the custodian of a house of resistance," a more complex reading of the emerging stereotype that Twain's narrative supports and that Joanne Braxton's more recent emphasis on "the outraged mother" elaborates. See Angela Davis, "Reflections on the Black Woman's Role in the Community of Slaves," *Black Scholar* 3 (December 1971): 2–15; and Joanne M. Braxton, "Harriet Jacobs' *Incidents in the Life of a Slave Girl*: The Re-Definition of the Slave Narrative Genre," *Massachusetts Review* 27 (1986): 379–87. Also useful are Valerie Smith, *Self-Discovery and Authority in Afro-American Narrative* (Cambridge: Harvard University Press, 1987), 28–43; and Houston A. Baker, Jr., *Blues, Ideology, and Afro-American Literature: A Vernacular Theory* (Chicago: University of Chicago Press, 1984), 50–56.

20. The full text in the King James version reads: "Thus saith the Lord; A voice was heard in Ramah, lamentation, and bitter weeping; Rahel weeping for her children refused to be comforted for her children, because they were not. Thus saith the Lord; Refrain thy voice from weeping, and thine eyes from

tears: for thy work shall be rewarded, saith the Lord; and they shall come again from the land of the enemy. And there is hope in thine end, saith the Lord, that thy children shall come again to their own border." In describing both exile and return, Jeremiah's account of Rachel's woe falls easily within the purview of Old Homestead stories about the Civil War.

21. See *Witnessing Slavery* (Westport, Conn.: Greenwood Press, 1979), 82–87.

22. For the influence of Twain's early "Jim" tales, see Wilson, *A Reader's Guide to the Short Stories of Mark Twain*, 268.

23. For the unenviable role of slaves in Western humor, see Wilson, *A Reader's Guide to the Short Stories of Mark Twain*, 267–70; Everett Emerson, *The Authentic Mark Twain: A Literary Biography of Samuel L. Clemens* (Philadelphia: University of Pennsylvania Press, 1984), 77; Pettit, *Mark Twain and the South*, 35–55; and Philip S. Foner, *Mark Twain, Social Critic* (New York: International Publishers, 1972), 253–58.

24. Twain wrote in September: "I amend dialect stuff by talking & talking & *talking* it till it sounds right—& I had difficulty with this negro talk because a negro sometimes (rarely) says "goin'" & sometimes "gwyne," & they make such discrepancies in other words—& when you come to reproduce them on paper they look as if the variation resulted from the writer's carelessness. But I want to work at the proofs & get the dialect as nearly right as possible" (Smith and Gibson, *Mark Twain–Howells Letters*, 26).

25. For analysis of the antebellum convention of representing slavery as disrupting families, see Wilson, *A Reader's Guide to the Short Stories of Mark Twain*, 270; James Grove, "Mark Twain and the Endangered Family," *American Literature* 57 (1985): 377–94; Frances Smith Foster, "'In Respect to Females . . .': Differences in the Portrayals of Women by Male and Female Narrators," *Black American Literary Forum* 15 (Summer 1981): 66–70; and Foster, *Witnessing Slavery*, 129–39.

26. See Harriet A. Jacobs, *Incidents in the Life of a Slave Girl, Written by Herself*, ed. Jean Fagan Yellin (Cambridge: Harvard University Press, 1987), xxvi.

27. Frances Smith Foster has pointed out that the "broken-family motif" in evidence before the Thirteenth Amendment abolished slavery was the price paid for the stature slave heroines would achieve. "The viability of the slave family," Foster writes, "had to be denied to increase the pathos of the homeless victim" (*Witnessing Slavery*, 135). The more regularly female slaves adopted the domestic mainstays that served white women in print, the more apparent it

became that slave families often struggled without the fathers who elsewhere assumed financial responsibility for the home.

28. See "Distrust of the Reader in Afro-American Narratives," *Reconstructing American Literary History*, ed. Sacvan Bercovitch (Cambridge: Harvard University Press, 1986), 300–322.

Chapter Two: The Romance of Union as National Metaphor

1. In bringing her case before the Supreme Court, Bradwell contended that the State of Illinois had abrogated her right to earn a livelihood, the same argument made by the butchers of New Orleans in the more familiar Slaughter-House Cases decided the same day in 1873. Both Bradwell and the butchers lost; deciding against them, the Supreme Court curbed national jurisdiction so sharply that the "privileges and immunities" clause of the Fourteenth Amendment was permanently sapped. Just as noteworthy was Justice Bradley's reasoning against Bradwell in his concurring opinion joined by Justices Field and Swayne. "The paramount mission and destiny of woman," Bradley wrote, "are to fulfil the noble and benign offices of wife and mother. This is the law of the Creator" (16 Wall. 130 [1873], 141). For coverage of the case and the implications of the verdict against Mrs. Bradwell, see Karen Berger Morello, *The Invisible Bar: The Woman Lawyer in America, 1630 to the Present* (New York: Random House, 1986), 14–21; Judith A. Baer, *Equality Under the Constitution: Reclaiming the Fourteenth Amendment* (Ithaca, N.Y.: Cornell University Press, 1983), 106–7; Eleanor Flexner, *Century of Struggle: The Woman's Rights Movement in the United States*, rev. ed. (Cambridge: Harvard University Press, Belknap Press, 1975), 122–23; Robert M. Spector, "Woman Against the Law: Myra Bradwell's Struggle for Admission to the Illinois Bar," *Journal of the Illinois State Historical Society* 68 (1975): 228–42; and Charles Fairman, *History of the Supreme Court of the United States*, Vol. 6: *Reconstruction and Reunion, 1864–88: Part One* (New York: Macmillan, 1971), 1364–68.

2. In its final form, as passed by both Houses of Congress and ratified by the states, the Fourteenth Amendment reads:

Section 1. All persons born or naturalized in the United States, and subject to the jurisdiction thereof, are citizens of the United States and of the State wherein they reside. No State shall make or enforce any law which shall abridge the privileges or immunities of citizens of the United States; nor shall any State deprive any person of life, liberty, or property, without due process of law; nor deny to any person within its jurisdiction the equal protection of the laws.

Section 2. Representatives shall be apportioned among the several States according to their respective numbers, counting the whole number of persons in each State, excluding Indians not taxed. But when the right to vote at any election for the choice of electors for President and Vice President of the United States, Representatives in Congress, the Executive and Judicial officers of a State, or the members of the Legislature thereof, is denied to any of the male inhabitants of such State, being twenty-one years of age, and citizens of the United States, or in any way abridged, except for participation in rebellion, or other crime, the basis of representation therein shall be reduced in the proportion which the number of such male citizens shall bear to the whole number of male citizens twenty-one years of age in such State.

Section 3. No person shall be a Senator or Representative in Congress, or elector of President and Vice President, or hold any office, civil or military, under the United States, or under any State, who, having previously taken an oath, as a member of Congress, or as an officer of the United States, or as a member of any State legislature, or as an executive or judicial officer of any State, to support the Constitution of the United States, shall have engaged in insurrection or rebellion against the same, or given aid or comfort to the enemies thereof. But Congress may by a vote of two thirds of each House, remove such disability.

Section 4. The validity of the public debt of the United States, authorized by law, including debts incurred for payment of pensions and bounties for services in suppressing insurrection or rebellion, shall not be questioned. But neither the United States nor any State shall assume or pay any debt or obligation incurred in aid of insurrection or rebellion against the United States, or any claim for the loss or emancipation of any slave; but all such debts, obligations and claims shall be held illegal and void.

Section 5. The Congress shall have power to enforce, by appropriate legislation, the provisions of this article.

Constitutional scholarship on the Fourteenth Amendment is awesome, as is the amount of litigation based upon its provisions, especially the guarantees of Section 1. Most germane for understanding the intent of contemporary rhetorical maneuvers are Michael Kent Curtis, *No State Shall Abridge: The Fourteenth Amendment and the Bill of Rights* (Durham, N.C.: Duke University Press, 1986), 18–91; Daniel A. Farber and John E. Muench, "The Ideological Origins of the Fourteenth Amendment," *Constitutional Commentary* 1 (Summer 1984): 235–79; Hyman and Wiecek, *Equal Justice Under Law*, 386–438; John A. Kaczorowski, "Searching for the Intent of the Framers of the Fourteenth Amendment," *Connecticut Law Review* 5 (Winter 1972–73): 368–98; and Joseph H. Taylor, "The Fourteenth Amendment, the Negro, and the Spirit of the Times," *Journal of Negro History* 45 (1960): 21–37.

3. In the *Congressional Globe*, see remarks by Stevens (Pa.), 39th Cong., 1st sess., 8 May 1866, 2459; Thayer (Pa.), 39th Cong., 1st sess., 8 May 1866, 2467; and Schenck (Ohio), 39th Cong., 1st sess., 8 May 1866, 2470.

4. *Congressional Globe*, 39th Cong., 1st sess., 8 May 1866, 2470.

5. *Congressional Globe*, 39th Cong., 1st sess., 9 May 1866, 2471, 2472.

6. *Congressional Globe*, 39th Cong., 1st sess., 9 May 1866, 2503.

7. *Congressional Globe*, 39th Cong., 1st sess., 10 May 1866, 2544.

8. *Congressional Globe*, 39th Cong., 1st sess., 4 June 1866, 2938.

9. *Congressional Globe*, 39th Cong., 1st sess., 8 June 1866, 3031.

10. *Congressional Globe*, 39th Cong., 1st sess., 23 May 1866, 2766.

11. *Congressional Globe*, 39th Cong., 1st sess., 24 May 1866, 2802.

12. *Congressional Globe*, 39th Cong., 1st sess., 30 May 1866, 2891–93.

13. *Congressional Globe*, 39th Cong., 1st sess., 8 June 1866, 3033, 3034.

14. *Congressional Globe*, 39th Cong., 1st sess., 8 June 1866, 3037.

15. In the *Congressional Globe*, see remarks by Congressmen Stevens (Pa.) and Johnson (Pa.), 39th Cong., 1st sess., 13 June 1866, 3148.

16. *Congressional Globe*, 39th Cong., 1st sess., 4 December 1865, 78.

17. *Congressional Globe*, 39th Cong., 1st sess., 20 July 1866, 3975.

18. *Congressional Globe*, 39th Cong., 1st sess., 21 July 1866, 3988.

19. *Congressional Globe*, 39th Cong., 1st sess., 21 July 1866, 3989.

20. *Congressional Globe*, Appendix, 39th Cong., 2d sess., 28 January 1867, 80.

21. *Congressional Globe*, 40th Cong., 2d sess., 8 May 1868, 2393.

22. *Congressional Globe*, 40th Cong., 2d sess., 8 May 1868, 2395.

23. *Congressional Globe*, 40th Cong., 2d sess., 1 June 1868, 2395.

24. *Congressional Globe*, 40th Cong., 2d sess., 28 May 1868, 2633.

25. In addition to his own magazine essays, collected in *A Volunteer's Adventures* and *A Union Officer in the Reconstruction*, see summaries of De Forest's government service and Reconstruction policies in James A. Hijiya, *J. W. De Forest and the Rise of American Gentility* (Hanover, N.H.: University Press of New England, 1988), 53–93; Aaron, *The Unwritten War*, 164–69; James H. Croushore and Davis Morris Potter, Introduction to *A Union Officer in the Reconstruction* by John W. De Forest (New York: Archon Books, 1968), v–xxvi;

and E. R. Hagemann, "John William De Forest and *The Galaxy*: Some Letters, 1867–1872," *Bulletin of the New York Public Library* 59 (April 1955), 179.

26. The striking substitution of Alec for Mollie, essentially a substitution of the Adventure's independence for the Romance's transformation, is the story's most incisive gesture, particularly if a trace of gender confusion forces a Romance plot on M'Call. As a representative of the postwar South, he is then simultaneously the "educated veteran" that Daniel Aaron follows in *Miss Ravenel's Conversion* and "the girl" that Edmund Wilson sees as epidemic in late nineteenth-century American fiction, including De Forest's last novels. See Aaron, *The Unwritten War*, 173; and Wilson, *Patriotic Gore*, 708–9. In the contemporary drama of Reconstruction, such a representative could choose without submitting, but only until the Federal detail disperses. Even he, however, is pursued by the specter of an unmollified past.

Chapter Three: The Adventure of National Initiation

1. Like the Thirteenth Amendment permanently abolishing slavery, the Fifteenth Amendment that determined how far suffrage would be extended was finally brief:

Section 1. The right of citizens of the United States to vote shall not be denied or abridged by the United States or by any State on account of race, color, or previous condition of servitude.

Section 2. The Congress shall have power to enforce this article by appropriate legislation.

For a detailed analysis of the Congressional jockeying that produced this minimal formulation, see William Gillette, *The Right to Vote: Politics and the Passage of the Fifteenth Amendment* (Baltimore: Johns Hopkins Press, 1965), 46–78. Gillette argues that the true aim of the amendment was to enfranchise black men in the crucial northern states that Republicans needed to carry, rather than the freed slaves of the South whose voting rights were already protected by the Fourteenth Amendment. For recently competing views on the genuine Congressional effort to legislate racial justice, see Hyman and Wiecek, *Equal Justice Under Law*, 463–72; and Michael Les Benedict, *A Compromise of Principle: Congressional Republicans and Reconstruction 1863–1869* (New York: Norton, 1974), 325–36.

2. In the *Congressional Globe*, see remarks by Ross (Kans.), 40th Cong., 3d

sess., 8 February 1869, 982; Scofield (Pa.), 40th Cong., 3d sess., 29 January 1869, 725; and Warner (Ala.), 40th Cong., 3d sess., 4 February 1869, 861, 862.

3. See remarks in the *Congressional Globe* by Senators Welch (Fla.), 40th Cong., 3d sess., 8 February 1869, 982; Sawyer (S.C.), 40th Cong., 3d sess., 8 February 1869, 998; and Edmunds (Vt.), 40th Cong., 3d sess., 8 February 1869, 1001.

4. Racial slurs came from Congressman Eldridge (Wis.), *Congressional Globe*, 40th Cong., 3d sess., 27 January 1869, 643; Senator Fowler (Tenn.), *Congressional Globe*, Appendix, 40th Cong., 3d sess., 8 February 1869, 196; and Senator Davis (Ky.), *Congressional Globe*, 40th Cong., 3d sess., 8 February 1869, 998.

5. *Congressional Globe*, Appendix, 40th Cong., 3d sess., 28 January 1869, 93.

6. For attacks on the Chinese, see the *Congressional Globe* for remarks by Senators Williams (Oreg.), 40th Cong., 3d sess., 5 February 1869, 901; Corbett (Oreg.), 40th Cong., 3d sess., 6 February 1869, 939; and Cole (Calif.), 40th Cong., 3d sess., 8 February 1869, 1008; as well as Patterson (N.H.), 40th Cong., 3d sess., 9 February 1869, 1037.

7. *Congressional Globe*, 40th Cong., 3d sess., 17 February 1869, 1307.

8. In the *Congressional Globe*, see remarks by Senators Morton (Ind.), 40th Cong., 3d sess., 8 February 1869, 990; and Pomeroy (Kans.), 40th Cong., 3d sess., 29 January 1869, 709; Congressmen Hamilton (Fla.), Appendix, 40th Cong., 3d sess., 29 January 1869, 102; and Blackburn (La.), Appendix, 40th Cong., 3d sess., 30 January 1869, 241.

9. *Congressional Globe*, 40th Cong., 3d sess., 23 January 1869, 557, 559.

10. For remarks in the Senate, see Ferry (Conn.), *Congressional Globe*, 40th Cong., 3d sess., 4 February 1869, 858; and Ross (Kans.), *Congressional Globe*, 40th Cong., 3d sess., 8 February 1869, 982. In the House, see Loughridge (Iowa), *Congressional Globe*, Appendix, 40th Cong., 3d sess., 29 January 1869, 200; and Mullins (Tenn.), *Congressional Globe*, Appendix, 40th Cong., 3d sess., 5 February 1869, 128, 129, 130.

11. For Dixon's condemnation, see *Congressional Globe*, 40th Cong., 3d sess., 28 January 1869, 706; for Pomeroy's response, see *Congressional Globe*, 40th Cong., 3d sess., 29 January 1869, 709.

12. Women were thoroughly domesticated in the remarks of Congressman Eldridge (Wis.), *Congressional Globe*, 40th Cong., 3d sess., 27 January 1869, 643; Senator Davis (Ky.), *Congressional Globe*, Appendix, 40th Cong., 3d sess., 8 February 1869, 289; Congressman Woodward (Pa.), *Congressional Globe*,

Appendix, 40th Cong., 3d sess., 20 February 1869, 207; Senator Bayard (Del.), *Congressional Globe*, Appendix, 40th Cong., 3d sess., 6 February 1869, 169; and Senator Williams (Oreg.), *Congressional Globe*, 40th Cong., 3d sess., 5 February 1869, 901.

13. For the emerging rhetoric of brotherhood, see remarks in the *Congressional Globe* by Senator Wilson (Mass.), 40th Cong., 3d sess., 17 February 1869, 1307; Congressman Hamilton (Fla.), Appendix, 40th Cong., 3d sess., 29 January 1869, 102; and Senator Fowler (Tenn.), Appendix, 40th Cong., 3d sess., 8 February 1869, 196.

14. *Congressional Globe*, 40th Cong., 3d sess., 29 January 1869, 710.

15. *Congressional Globe*, 40th Cong., 3d sess., 26 February 1869, 1629.

16. For a brief overview of the war's initial events and how they affected Davis in Wheeling, see Jean Fagan Yellin, "The 'Feminization' of Rebecca Harding Davis," *American Literary History* 2 (1990): 203–19. Only acknowledged in this tale's clash of loyalties is the fate of the slaves, which prompted Davis's subsequent attack on social inequalities in *Waiting for the Verdict* (1867) as well as her attention to sudden violence in "John Lamar" (*Atlantic Monthly*, April 1862). But social justice was not quite abolition for the young Rebecca Harding, despite her nod here to Elinor Potter's principles. "My family lived on the border of Virginia," Davis later wrote. "We were, so to speak, on the fence, and could see the great question [of Abolition] from both sides. It was a most unpleasant position. When you crossed into Pennsylvania you had to defend your slave-holding friends against the Abolitionists, who dubbed them all Legrees and Neros; and when you came home you quarreled with your kindly neighbors for calling the Abolitionists 'emissaries of hell.' The man who sees both sides of the shield may be right, but he is most uncomfortable." *Bits of Gossip* (Boston: Houghton Mifflin, 1905), 165–66.

17. See Davis, *Bits of Gossip*, 30–31, 55–64. For Hawthorne's significance to Davis, see Jane Atteridge Rose, "The Fiction of Rebecca Harding Davis: A Palimpsest of Domestic Ideology Beneath a Surface of Realism" (Ph.D. Diss., University of Georgia, 1988), 71–72; Tillie Olsen, "A Biographical Interpretation," in *Life in the Iron Mills and Other Stories* by Rebecca Harding Davis (New York: Feminist Press, 1984), 71, 89; and Gerald Langford, *The Richard Harding Davis Years: A Biography of Mother and Son* (New York: Holt, Rinehart and Winston, 1961), 26–27.

18. For a quick summary of the Bessemer process in the context of its military uses and Davis's industrial concerns, see Jean Pfaelzer, "Rebecca Hard-

ing Davis: Domesticity, Social Order, and the Industrial Novel," *International Journal of Women's Studies* 4 (1981): 234–44.

19. Bernard R. Bowron, Jr., "Realism in America," *Comparative Literature* 3 (1951), 281. The "feminizing" of Christ's redemptive example is bolstered by the names Davis assigns her characters, all of which may be traced to the True Cross. Most intriguing is the unusual choice of Euphemia for the title character, since St. Euphemia is seen by some as the "Muse of mellifluous speech" who was "protected by so stern a taboo that even early Christians feared to violate it." See Walker, *The Woman's Encyclopedia of Myths and Secrets*, 26–27. Jacobus de Voragine notes that Euphemia miraculously survived numerous assaults in prison, until an executioner thrust a sword in her side. See *The Golden Legend* (New York: Longmans, Green and Co., 1941), Vol. 1: 553. St. Helena, from whose name Elinor is derived, is believed to have been responsible for unearthing the True Cross around 335 on a pilgrimage to Calvary; in Christian iconography, her emblem is the cross. See David Hugh Farmer, *The Oxford Dictionary of Saints*, 2d ed. (New York: Oxford University Press, 1987), 102, 202; and Donald Attwater, *The Penguin Dictionary of Saints*, 2d ed. (New York: Penguin, 1983), 163. St. Margaret of Scotland, an appropriate namesake for the iron-willed Presbyterian, brought to Edinburgh as part of her dowry the Black Cross, which was thought to have been taken from the cross on which Christ died. See Kathleen Parbury, *Women of Grace* (Boston: Oriel Press, 1985), 64. While Davis never confessed to forethought in naming her characters, the singular orientation of these three references to the Cross may buttress the motif made explicit by the blue ribbon around Johnny's neck.

Coda: From Uncle Tom to Uncle Remus and Beyond

1. Mark Twain, *Life on the Mississippi* (New York: Harper and Brothers, 1929), 375, 328; Paul M. Gaston, *The New South Creed: A Study in Southern Mythmaking* (New York: Knopf, 1970), 172. The popularity of the Southern plantation revival after 1880 is examined in C. Vann Woodward, *Origins of the New South, 1877–1913* (Baton Rouge: Louisiana State University Press, 1971), 155–69; Gaston, *The New South Creed*, 167–86; Lively, *Fiction Fights the Civil War*, 42–71; Hubbell, *The South in American Literature*, 701–33; Smith, *The Civil War and Its Aftermath in American Fiction*, 30–44; and Gaines, *The Southern Plantation*, 62–94.

2. As Eric Foner has noted in *Reconstruction*, Hayes did not completely re-

move Federal troops from the South; he recalled them to their barracks and thus retired them from action (580).

3. Louis D. Rubin, Jr., has observed that Harris and Grady at the *Atlanta Constitution* were "marketing the same product—reunion," a cause that Edwin De Leon had advanced in his essays on the "New South" published by *Putnam's, Harper's Monthly*, and the *Southern Magazine* a few years earlier. See "Uncle Remus and the Ubiquitous Rabbit," *Critical Essays on Joel Chandler Harris*, ed. R. Bruce Bickley, Jr. (Boston: G. K. Hall, 1981), 158. For the tranquilizing effect of the Uncle Remus stories in the North, see Hugh T. Keenan, "Twisted Tales: Propaganda in the Tar-Baby Stories," *Southern Quarterly* 22 (Winter 1984), 58; Robert Hemenway, "Author, Teller, Hero," in *Uncle Remus: His Songs and His Sayings*, by Joel Chandler Harris (1880; rpt. New York: Penguin, 1982), 20; Gaston, *The New South Creed*, 180–81; and Joseph M. Griska, Jr., "Uncle Remus Correspondence: The Development of Joel Chandler Harris' Writing, 1880–1885," *American Literary Realism* 14 (1981): 26–37.

4. Eric L. Montenyohl gives a full account of Harris's key alterations between 1877 and 1880 in "Joel Chandler Harris's Revision of Uncle Remus: 'The First Version of 'A Story of the War,' " *American Literary Realism* 19 (Fall 1986): 63–72.

5. For statistics on sales, see Robert Bone, *Down Home: A History of Afro-American Short Fiction from Its Beginnings to the End of the Harlem Renaissance* (New York: Putnam's, 1975), 28; Hemenway, "Author, Teller, Hero," 7; and Eric L. Montenyohl, "The Origins of Uncle Remus," *Folklore Forum* 18 (Spring 1986), 160.

6. As Jay Hubbell has indicated, Harris first read *Uncle Tom's Cabin* while serving as a printer's apprentice at Joseph Turner's plantation in Putnam County, where he also began to collect the tales he heard from the slaves. See *The South in American Literature*, 786.

7. For a careful study of how the faithful family retainer developed out of the minstrel dialogue that the *Atlanta Constitution* and its readers had previously favored, see Montenyohl's "The Origins of Uncle Remus."

8. Darwin T. Turner, "Daddy Joel Harris and His Old-Time Darkeys," in *Critical Essays on Joel Chandler Harris*, ed. R. Bruce Bickley, Jr. (Boston: G. K. Hall, 1981), 119, 123. In "Uncle Remus and the Ubiquitous Rabbit," Rubin has noted the "happy darkey" stereotype that domesticated both Uncle Tom and Uncle Remus (159–60); George R. Lamplugh has further commented upon the postwar absence of plantation mistresses and the number of Confederate wid-

owers in popular magazine fiction. See "The Image of the Negro in Popular Magazine Fiction, 1875–1900," *Journal of Negro History* 57 (1972), 177–89.

9. Hemenway, "Author, Teller, Hero," 19–20.

10. Tompkins, *Sensational Designs*, 141.

11. Keenan, "Twisted Tales," 60–61.

12. Bone, *Down Home*, 39.

13. Justice Brown's remarks may be found in *Plessy v. Ferguson*, 163 U.S. 537 (1896), 550; Justice Harlan's dissenting comments follow, 555. See, too, "Bodily Bonds," in which Karen Sanchez-Eppler observes: "For abolitionists, the domestic values that ostensibly offer a positive alternative to the mores of plantation society simultaneously serve to mask slavery's exploitations behind domesticity's gentle features" (46).

14. For Warren's rhetorical maneuvers, see *Brown v. Board of Education of the City of Topeka*, 37 U.S. 483 (1954), especially 493.

15. In the *Congressional Record*, see remarks by Ferris (Okla.), 65th Cong., 2d sess., 10 January 1918, 779; Smith (S.C.), 66th Cong., 1st sess., 4 June 1919, 618; the "peer of man" allusion made by Dill (Wash.), 65th Cong., 2d sess., 10 January 1918, 805; the reference to woman as "your equal, your companion in the battle of life" made by Hersey (Maine), 65th Cong., 2d sess., 10 January 1918, 778; President Wilson's proposal of a "partnership of privilege and of right" in his speech to the Senate, 65th Cong., 2d sess., 30 September 1918, 10929; Cox (Ind.), 65th Cong., 2d sess., 10 January 1918, 795; and Fess (Ohio), 65th Cong., 2d sess., 10 January 1918, 799.

16. In the *Congressional Record*, see remarks by Clark (Fla.), 65th Cong., 2d sess., 10 January 1918, 785; and Cantrill (Ky.), 65th Cong., 2d sess., 10 January 1918, 765.

BIBLIOGRAPHY

Aaron, Daniel. *The Unwritten War: American Writers and the Civil War*. New York. Oxford University Press, 1973

Aptheker, Bettina. *Woman's Legacy: Essays on Race, Sex, and Class in American History*. Amherst: University of Massachusetts Press, 1982.

Armstrong, Nancy. *Desire and Domestic Fiction: A Political History of the Novel*. New York: Oxford University Press, 1987.

Atchinson, Ray M. "The *Land We Love*: A Southern Post-Bellum Magazine of Agriculture, Literature, and Military History." *North Carolina Historical Review* 37 (1960): 506–15.

Attwater, Donald. *The Penguin Dictionary of Saints*. 2d ed. New York: Penguin, 1983.

Baer, Judith A. *Equality Under the Constitution: Reclaiming the Fourteenth Amendment*. Ithaca, N.Y.: Cornell University Press, 1983.

Baker, Houston A., Jr. *Blues, Ideology, and Afro-American Literature: A Vernacular Theory*. Chicago: University of Chicago Press, 1984.

Baldwin, James. "Everybody's Protest Novel." *Partisan Review* 16 (1949): 578–85.

Bell, William R. "The Relationship of Joel Chandler Harris and Mark Twain." *Atlanta Historical Journal* 30 (Fall–Winter 1986–87): 97–111.

Bellamy, Francis. "The Story of The Pledge of Allegiance to The Flag." *University of Rochester Library Bulletin* 8 (Winter 1953): 29–39.

Belz, Herman. *A New Birth of Freedom: The Republican Party and Freedmen's Rights, 1861 to 1866*. Westport, Conn.: Greenwood Press, 1976.

Benedict, Michael Les. *A Compromise of Principle: Congressional Republicans and Reconstruction 1863–1869*. New York: Norton, 1974.

Berger, Raoul. *Government by Judiciary: the Transformation of the Fourteenth*

Amendment. Cambridge, Mass.: Harvard University Press, 1977.

Bickley, R. Bruce. "Joel Chandler Harris and the Old and New South: Paradoxes of Perception." *Atlanta Historical Journal* 30 (Fall–Winter 1986–87): 9–31.

Birch, M. J. "The Popular Fiction Industry: Market, Formula, Ideology." *Journal of Popular Culture* 21 (1987): 79–102.

Blumin, Stuart M. *The Emergence of the Middle Class: Social Experience in the American City, 1760–1900.* New York: Cambridge University Press, 1989.

Bone, Robert. *Down Home: A History of Afro-American Short Fiction from Its Beginnings to the End of the Harlem Renaissance.* New York: Putnam's, 1975.

Bowron, Bernard R., Jr. "Realism in America." *Comparative Literature* 3 (1951): 268–85.

Boydston, Jeanne, Mary Kelley, and Anne Margolis. *The Limits of Sisterhood: The Beecher Sisters on Women's Rights and Women's Sphere.* Chapel Hill: University of North Carolina Press, 1988.

Bracey, John H., Jr., August Meier, and Elliott Rudwick, eds. *Black Matriarchy: Myth or Reality?* Belmont, Calif.: Wadsworth, 1971.

Braxton, Joanne M. "Harriet Jacobs' *Incidents in the Life of a Slave Girl*: The Re-Definition of the Slave Narrative Genre." *Massachusetts Review* 27 (1986): 379–87.

Brest, Paul. "The Misconceived Quest for the Original Understanding." *Boston University Law Review* 60 (1980): 204–38.

Brown, Gillian. "Getting in the Kitchen with Dinah: Domestic Politics in *Uncle Tom's Cabin*." *American Quarterly* 36 (1984): 503–23.

Buchanon, G. Sidney. "The Quest for Freedom: A Legal History of the Thirteenth Amendment." *Houston Law Review* 12 (October 1974): 1–34.

Buck, Paul H. *The Road to Reunion, 1865–1900.* Boston: Little, Brown, 1937.

Budd, Louis J. *Critical Essays on Mark Twain, 1867–1910.* Boston: G. K. Hall, 1982.

———. "Howells, the *Atlantic Monthly*, and Republicanism." *American Literature* 24 (1952): 139–56.

———. *Mark Twain: Social Philosopher.* Bloomington: Indiana University Press, 1962.

Bullock, Penelope L. *The Afro-American Periodical Press, 1838–1909.* Baton Rouge: Louisiana State University Press, 1981.

Butterfield, Margaret. "Francis Bellamy, '76." *University of Rochester Library Bulletin* 8 (Winter 1953): 25–28.

Campbell, Karlyn Kohrs, and Kathleen Hall Jamieson. *Deeds Done in Words:*

Presidential Rhetoric and the Genres of Governance. Chicago: University of Chicago Press, 1990.

Carey, James W. *Communication as Culture: Essays on Media and Society*. Boston: Unwin Hyman, 1988.

Caudill, Edward, and Susan L. Caudill. "Nation and Section: An Analysis of Key Symbols in the Antebellum Press." *Journalism History* 15 (Spring 1988): 16–25.

Charland, Maurice, "Rehabilitating Rhetoric: Confronting Blindspots in Discourse and Social Theory." *Communication* 11 (1990): 253–64.

Charvat, William. *Literary Publishing in America, 1790–1850*. Philadelphia: University of Pennsylvania Press, 1959.

———. *The Profession of Authorship in America, 1800–1870*. Edited by Matthew J. Bruccoli. Columbus: Ohio State University Press, 1968.

Chielens, Edward E., ed. *American Literary Magazines: the Eighteenth and Nineteenth Centuries*. Westport, Conn.: Greenwood Press, 1986.

Condit, Celeste Michelle. "Interpellating Rhetoric, Politics, and Culture: 'Hail' or 'Greetings'?" *Communication* 11 (1990): 241–52.

Connell, Ian, and Adam Mills. "Text, Discourse and Mass Communication." In *Discourse and Communication: New Approaches to the Analysis of Mass Media*, edited by Teun A. van Tijk, 26–43. New York: Walter de Gruyter, 1985.

Crawford, Richard, ed. *Civil War Songbook: Complete Original Sheet Music for 37 Songs*. New York: Dover Publications, 1977.

Croushore, James H., and David Morris Potter. Introduction to *A Union Officer in the Reconstruction*, by John W. De Forest, v–xxvi. New York: Archon Books, 1968.

Cullen, Rosemary L. *The Civil War in American Drama Before 1900: Catalog of an Exhibition, November 1982*. Providence, R.I.: Brown University Library, 1982.

Curtis, Michael Kent. *No State Shall Abridge: The Fourteenth Amendment and the Bill of Rights*. Durham, N.C.: Duke University Press, 1986.

Dann, Martin E., ed. *The Black Press, 1827–1890: The Quest for National Identity*. New York: Putnam's, 1971.

Davis, Angela. "Reflections on the Black Woman's Role in the Community of Slaves." *Black Scholar* 3 (December 1971): 2–15.

Davis, Rebecca Harding. *Bits of Gossip*. Boston: Houghton Mifflin, 1905.

Dekker, George. *The American Historical Romance*. New York: Cambridge University Press, 1987.

DiMaggio, Paul. "Market Structure, the Creative Process, and Popular Culture: Toward an Organizational Reinterpretation of Mass-Culture Theory." *Journal of Popular Culture* 11 (1977): 436–52.

Dobson, Joanne. " 'The Invisible Lady': Emily Dickinson and Conventions of the Female Self." *Legacy* 3 (Spring 1986): 41–55.

Douglass, Frederick. *Life and Times of Frederick Douglass, Written by Himself.* 1881. Reprint. Secaucus, N.J.: Citadel Press, 1983.

Downes, William Howe. *The Life and Works of Winslow Homer.* 1911. Reprint. New York: Dover Publications, 1989.

Eble, Kenneth E. *Old Clemens and W.D.H.: The Story of a Remarkable Friendship.* Baton Rouge: Louisiana State University Press, 1985.

Emerson, Everett. *The Authentic Mark Twain: A Literary Biography of Samuel L. Clemens.* Philadelphia: University of Pennsylvania Press, 1984.

Exman, Eugene. *The House of Harper: One Hundred and Fifty Years of Publishing.* New York: Harper and Row, 1967.

Fairman, Charles. *History of the Supreme Court of the United States.* Vol. 6, *Reconstruction and Reunion, 1864–88: Part One.* New York: Macmillan, 1971.

Farber, Daniel A., and John E. Muench. "The Ideological Origins of the Fourteenth Amendment." *Constitutional Commentary* 1 (Summer 1984): 235–79.

Farmer, David Hugh. *The Oxford Dictionary of Saints.* 2d ed. New York: Oxford University Press, 1987.

Faust, Drew Gilpin. *The Creation of Confederate Nationalism: Ideology and Identity in the Civil War South.* Baton Rouge: Louisiana State University Press, 1988.

Ferguson, Robert A. *Law and Letters in American Culture.* Cambridge, Mass.: Harvard University Press, 1984.

Fiedler, Leslie. *The Inadvertent Epic: From "Uncle Tom's Cabin" to "Roots."* New York: Simon and Schuster, 1979.

Finley, Ruth E. *The Lady of 'Godey's': Sarah Josepha Hale.* Philadelphia: Lippincott, 1931.

Fisher, Philip. *Hard Facts: Setting and Form in the American Novel.* New York: Oxford University Press, 1987.

Fisher, Walter R. "Narration as a Human Communication Paradigm: The Case of Public Moral Argument." *Communication Monographs* 51 (March 1984): 1–22.

Fleming, Herbert E. "The Literary Interests of Chicago." *American Journal of Sociology* 11 (1906): 377–408.

Flexner, Eleanor. *Century of Struggle: The Woman's Rights Movement in the*

United States. Rev. ed. Cambridge: Harvard University Press, Belknap Press, 1975.

Foner, Eric. *Reconstruction: America's Unfinished Revolution, 1863–1877*. New York: Harper and Row, 1988.

Foner, Philip S. *History of Black Americans*. Vol. 3, *From the Compromise of 1850 to the End of the Civil War*. Westport, Conn.: Greenwood Press, 1983.

———. *Mark Twain, Social Critic*. New York: International Publishers, 1972.

Forgie, George B. *Patricide in the House Divided: A Psychological Interpretation of Lincoln and His Age*. New York: Norton, 1979.

Foster, Frances Smith. " 'In Respect to Females . . .': Differences in the Portrayals of Women by Male and Female Narrators." *Black American Literary Forum* 15 (Summer 1981): 66–70.

———. *Witnessing Slavery*. Westport, Conn.: Greenwood Press, 1979.

Fox-Genovese, Elizabeth. *Within the Plantation Household: Black and White Women of the Old South*. Chapel Hill: University of North Carolina Press, 1988.

Frederickson, George M. *The Inner Civil War: Northern Intellectuals and the Crisis of the Union*. New York: Harper and Row, Harper Torchbooks, 1965.

Gaines, Francis Pendleton. *The Southern Plantation: A Study in the Development and the Accuracy of a Tradition*. New York: Columbia University Press, 1925.

Garrison, William Lloyd. "Official Proclamation." *Liberator* (22 December 1865): 202.

Garwood, Irving. *American Periodicals from 1850 to 1860*. Macomb, Ill.: Commercial Art Press, 1931.

Gaston, Paul M. *The New South Creed: A Study in Southern Mythmaking*. New York: Knopf, 1970.

Gillespie, Marcia Ann. "The Myth of the Strong Black Woman." In *Feminist Frameworks: Alternative Theoretical Accounts of the Relations Between Women and Men*, edited by Alison M. Jaggar and Paula Rothenberg Struhl, 32–36. 2d ed. New York: McGraw-Hill, 1984.

Gillette, William. *The Right to Vote: Politics and the Passage of the Fifteenth Amendment*. Baltimore: Johns Hopkins Press, 1965.

Gilmore, William J. "Literacy, the Rise of an Age of Reading, and the Cultural Grammar of Print Communications in America, 1735–1850." *Communication* 11 (1988): 23–46.

Gordon, Robert W. "New Developments in Legal Theory." In *The Politics of*

Law: A Progressive Critique, edited by David Kairys, 281–309. New York: Pantheon, 1982.

Graham, Howard Jay. *Everyman's Constitution: Historical Essays on the Fourteenth Amendment, the "Conspiracy Theory," and American Constitutionalism.* Madison: State Historical Society of Wisconsin, 1968.

Green, Constance McLaughlin. *The Secret City: A History of Race Relations in the Nation's Capital.* Princeton, N.J.: Princeton University Press, 1967.

Griska, Joseph M., Jr. "Uncle Remus Correspondence: The Development of Joel Chandler Harris' Writing, 1880–1885." *American Literary Realism* 14 (1981): 26–37.

Grove, James. "Mark Twain and the Endangered Family." *American Literature* 57 (1985): 377–94.

Hagemann, E. R. "John William De Forest and *The Galaxy*: Some Letters, 1867–1872." *Bulletin of the New York Public Library* 59 (April 1955): 175–94.

Halttunen, Karen. "Gothic Imagination and Social Reform: The Haunted Houses of Lyman Beecher, Henry Ward Beecher, and Harriet Beecher Stowe." In *New Essays on "Uncle Tom's Cabin,"* edited by Eric J. Sundquist, 107–34. New York: Cambridge University Press, 1986.

Hamm, Charles. *Yesterdays: Popular Songs in America.* New York: Norton, 1979.

Harwell, Richard Barksdale. "A Confederate View of the Southern Poets." *American Literature* 24 (1952): 51–61.

Hemenway, Robert. "Author, Teller, Hero." In *Uncle Remus: His Songs and His Sayings*, by Joel Chandler Harris, 7–31. 1880. Reprint. New York: Penguin, 1982.

Hijiya, James A. *J. W. De Forest and the Rise of American Gentility.* Hanover, N.H.: University Press of New England, 1988.

Hooks, Bell. *Ain't I A Woman: Black Women and Feminism.* Boston: South End Press, 1981.

Howe, M. A. DeWolfe. *The "Atlantic Monthly" and Its Makers.* Boston: Atlantic Monthly Press, 1919.

Hubbell, Jay B. *The South in American Literature, 1607–1900.* Durham, N.C.: Duke University Press, 1954.

Hughes, Gertrude Reif. "Subverting the Cult of Domesticity: Emily Dickinson's Critique of Women's Work." *Legacy* 3 (Spring 1986): 17–28.

Hyman, Harold M. *A More Perfect Union: The Impact of the Civil War and Reconstruction on the Constitution.* New York: Knopf, 1973.

Hyman, Harold M., and William M. Wiecek. *Equal Justice Under Law: Constitutional Development, 1835–1875.* New York: Harper and Row, 1982.

Jacobs, Harriet A. *Incidents in the Life of a Slave Girl, Written by Herself.* Edited by Jean Fagan Yellin. Cambridge: Harvard University Press, 1987.

Jacobus de Voragine. *The Golden Legend.* New York: Longmans, Green and Co., 1941.

Kaczorowski, John A. "Searching for the Intent of the Framers of the Fourteenth Amendment." *Connecticut Law Review* 5 (Winter 1972–73): 368–98.

Kaser, David. *Books and Libraries in Camp and Battle: The Civil War Experience.* Westport, Conn.: Greenwood Press, 1984.

———. "Carey and Lea." In *Publishers for Mass Entertainment in Nineteenth Century America,* edited by Madeleine B. Stern, 73–80. Boston: G. K. Hall, 1980.

Keenan, Hugh T. "Twisted Tales: Propaganda in the Tar-Baby Stories." *Southern Quarterly* 22 (Winter 1984): 54–69.

Kerber, Linda K. "The Republican Mother." In *Women's America: Refocusing the Past,* edited by Linda K. Kerber and Jane De Hart-Mathews, 83–91. New York: Oxford University Press, 1987.

Klumpp, James F., and Thomas A. Hollihan. "Rhetorical Criticism as Moral Action." *Quarterly Journal of Speech* 75 (1989): 84–97.

Lamplugh, George R. "The Image of the Negro in Popular Magazine Fiction, 1875–1900." *Journal of Negro History* 57 (1972): 177–89.

Langford, Gerald. *The Richard Harding Davis Years: A Biography of Mother and Son.* New York: Holt, Rinehart and Winston, 1961.

Leisy, Ernest E. *The American Historical Novel.* Norman: University of Oklahoma Press, 1950.

Levinson, Sanford. "Law as Literature." *Texas Law Review* 60 (March 1982): 373–403.

"The Life-Story of a Magazine." *Dial* 54 (16 June 1913): 489–92.

Lincoln, Abraham. *Collected Works of Abraham Lincoln.* Vol. 8, *1864–65.* Edited by Roy P. Basler. New Brunswick, N.J.: Rutgers University Press, 1953.

Lipsitz, George. "'This Ain't No Sideshow': Historians and Media Studies." *Critical Studies in Mass Communications* 5 (1988): 147–61.

Lively, Robert A. *Fiction Fights the Civil War.* Chapel Hill: University of North Carolina Press, 1957.

M., S., Jr. "The Amendment Adopted." *Liberator* (22 December 1865): 202.

Martin, Biddy, and Chandra Talpade Mohanty. "Feminist Politics: What's Home Got to Do with It?" In *Feminist Studies/Critical Studies,* edited by Teresa de Laurentis, 191–212. Bloomington: Indiana University Press, 1986.

May, Ernest R. "Bret Harte and the *Overland Monthly*." *American Literature* 22 (1950): 260–71.

Menendez, Albert J. *Civil War Novels: An Annotated Bibliography*. New York: Garland, 1986.

Minor, Benjamin Blake. *'The Southern Literary Messenger,' 1834–1864*. New York: Neale Publishing, 1905.

Montenyohl, Eric L. "Joel Chandler Harris's Revision of Uncle Remus: The First Version of 'A Story of the War.'" *American Literary Realism* 19 (Fall 1986): 63–72.

———. "The Origins of Uncle Remus." *Folklore Forum* 18 (Spring 1986): 136–67.

Morello, Karen Berger. *The Invisible Bar: The Woman Lawyer in America, 1630 to the Present*. New York: Random House, 1986.

Mott, Frank Luther. *A History of American Magazines*. 5 vols. Cambridge: Harvard University Press, 1938–68.

"National School Celebration of Columbus Day. The Official Programme." *Youth's Companion* 66 (8 September 1892): 446–47.

Nelson [Salvino], Dana. "The Word in Black and White: Ideologies of Face and Literacy in Antebellum America." In *Reading in America: Literature and Social History*, edited by Cathy N. Davidson, 140–56. Baltimore: Johns Hopkins University Press, 1989.

Nickels, Cameron C. "An Early Version of the 'Tar Baby' Story." *Journal of American Folklore* 94 (1981): 364–69.

Nord, David Paul. "A Republican Literature: Magazine Reading and Readers in Late-Eighteenth-Century New York." In *Reading in America: Literature and Social History*, edited by Cathy N. Davidson, 114–39. Baltimore: Johns Hopkins University Press, 1989.

O'Connor, Richard. *Bret Harte: A Biography*. Boston: Little, Brown, 1966.

Olsen, Tillie. "A Biographical Interpretation." In *Life in the Iron Mills and Other Stories*, by Rebecca Harding Davis, 69–174. New York: Feminist Press, 1984.

Oravec, Christine. "The Sublimation of Mass Consciousness in the Rhetorical Criticism of Jacksonian America." *Communication* 11 (1990): 291–314.

Paine, Albert Bigelow. *Mark Twain: A Biography*. New York: Harper and Row, 1912.

Parbury, Kathleen. *Women of Grace*. Boston: Oriel Press, 1985.

Pawling, Christopher. "Popular Fiction: Ideology or Utopia?" In *Popular Fic-

tion and Social Change, edited by Christopher Pawling, 1–19. London: Macmillan, 1984.

Pearson, Justus R., Jr. "Story of a Magazine: New York's *Galaxy* 1866–1878." *Bulletin of the New York Public Library* 61 (1957): 217–37, 281–302.

Peterson, Richard A. "The Production of Culture: A Prolegomenon." *American Behavioral Scientist* 19 (1976): 669–84.

Pettit, Arthur G. *Mark Twain and the South.* Lexington: University Press of Kentucky, 1974.

Pfaelzer, Jean. "Rebecca Harding Davis: Domesticity, Social Order, and the Industrial Novel." *International Journal of Women's Studies* 4 (1981): 234–44.

Poovey, Mary. *Uneven Developments: The Ideological Work of Gender in Mid-Victorian England.* Chicago: University of Chicago Press, 1988.

Potter, David M. *History and American Society: Essays of David M. Potter.* Edited by Don E. Fehrenbacher. New York: Oxford University Press, 1973.

Riley, Sam G. *Magazines of the American South.* Westport, Conn.: Greenwood Press, 1986.

Riley, Susan B. "The Hazards of Periodical Publishing in the South During the Nineteenth Century." *Tennessee Historical Quarterly* 21 (1962): 365–76.

———. "The Southern Literary Magazine of the Mid-Nineteenth Century." *Tennessee Historical Quarterly* 23 (1964): 221–36.

Rose, Jane Atteridge. "The Fiction of Rebecca Harding Davis: A Palimpsest of Domestic Ideology Beneath a Surface of Realism." Ph.D. Diss. University of Georgia, 1988.

Ross, Andrew. *No Respect: Intellectuals and Popular Culture.* New York: Routledge, 1989.

Rubin, Louis D., Jr. "Uncle Remus and the Ubiquitous Rabbit." In *Critical Essays on Joel Chandler Harris*, edited by R. Bruce Bickley, Jr., 158–73. Boston: G. K. Hall, 1981.

Ryan, Mary P. *Cradle of the Middle Class: The Family in Oneida County, New York, 1790–1865.* New York: Cambridge University Press, 1981.

Sanchez-Eppler, Karen. "Bodily Bonds: The Intersecting Rhetorics of Feminism and Abolition." *Representations* 24 (Fall 1988): 28–59.

Sanders, Clinton R. "Structural and Interactional Features of Popular Culture Production: An Introduction to the Production of Culture Perspective." *Journal of Popular Culture* 16 (Fall 1982): 66–74.

Satterwhite, Joseph N. "The Tremulous Formula: Form and Technique in *Godey's* Fiction." *American Quarterly* 8 (1956): 99–113.

Schmidt, Dorey. "Magazines in American Culture." In *The American Magazine, 1890–1940*, edited by Dorey Schmidt, 6–9. Wilmington: Delaware Art Museum, 1979.

Scholnick, Robert J. "The *Galaxy* and American Democratic Culture, 1866–1878." *Journal of American Studies* 16 (1982): 69–80.

Schudson, Michael. "The New Validation of Popular Culture: Sense and Sentimentality in Academia." *Critical Studies in Mass Communication* 4 (1987): 51–68.

Scott, Anne Firor. *The Southern Lady: From Pedestal to Politics, 1830–1930*. Chicago: University of Chicago Press, 1970.

Sedgwick, Ellery, III. "The Early Years of the *Atlantic Monthly*." *American Transcendental Quarterly* 58 (December 1985): 3–30.

Smith, Henry Nash, and William M. Gibson, eds. *Mark Twain–Howells Letters*. Cambridge: Harvard University Press, Belknap, 1960.

Smith, Rebecca Washington. *The Civil War and Its Aftermath in American Fiction, 1861–1899*. Chicago: University of Chicago Libraries, 1937.

Smith, Valerie. *Self-Discovery and Authority in Afro-American Narrative*. Cambridge: Harvard University Press, 1987.

Sollors, Werner. *Beyond Ethnicity: Consent and Descent in American Culture*. New York: Oxford University Press, 1986.

Spector, Robert M. "Woman Against the Law: Myra Bradwell's Struggle for Admission to the Illinois Bar." *Journal of the Illinois Historical Society* 68 (1975): 228–42.

Staples, Robert. "The Myth of the Black Matriarchy." *The Black Scholar* 1 (January–February 1970): 8–16.

Stepto, Robert B. "Distrust of the Reader in Afro-American Narratives." In *Reconstructing American Literary History*, edited by Sacvan Bercovitch, 300–322. Cambridge: Harvard University Press, 1986.

Strickland, William Bradley. "Stereotypes and Subversion in *The Chronicles of Aunt Minervy Ann*." *Atlanta Historical Journal* 30 (Fall–Winter 1986–87): 129–39.

Tassin, Algernon. *The Magazine in America*. New York: Dodd, Mead, 1916.

Tatham, David. "Winslow Homer at the Front in 1862." *American Art Journal* 11 (1979): 86–87.

Taylor, Joseph H. "The Fourteenth Amendment, the Negro, and the Spirit of the Times." *Journal of Negro History* 45 (1960): 21–37.

Taylor, William R. *Cavalier and Yankee: The Old South and American National Character*. New York: Harper and Row, Harper Torchbooks, 1961.

Tebbel, John. *The American Magazine: A Compact History*. New York: Hawthorn Books, 1969.

———. *A History of Book Publishing in the United States*. New York: R. R. Bowker, 1972–81.

TenBroek, Jacobus. *Equal Under Law: The Antislavery Origins of the Fourteenth Amendment*. New York: Collier Books, 1965.

Thomas, Brook. *Cross-Examinations of Law and Literature: Cooper, Hawthorne, Stowe, and Melville*. New York: Cambridge University Press, 1987.

Tompkins, Jane. *Sensational Designs: The Cultural Work of American Fiction, 1790–1860*. New York: Oxford University Press, 1985.

Turner, Darwin T. "Daddy Joel Harris and His Old-Time Darkeys." In *Critical Essays on Joel Chandler Harris*, edited by R. Bruce Bickley, Jr., 113–29. Boston: G. K. Hall, 1981.

Turow, Joseph. "Cultural Argumentation Through the Mass Media: A Framework for Organizational Research." *Communication* 8 (1985): 139–64.

Twain, Mark. *Life on the Mississippi*. New York: Harper and Brothers, 1929.

U.S. Congress. House. Committee on the Judiciary. *Amending the Pledge of Allegiance to the Flag of the United States*. 83d Cong., 2d sess., 1954. H. Rept 1693.

Walker, Barbara G. *The Woman's Encyclopedia of Myths and Secrets*. New York: Harper and Row, 1983.

Walker, Franklin. *San Francisco's Literary Frontier*. New York: Knopf, 1939.

Warnick, Barbara. "A Ricoeurian Approach to Rhetorical Criticism." *Western Journal of Speech Communication* 51 (1987): 227–44.

White, James Boyd. *When Words Lose Their Meaning: Constitutions and Reconstitutions of Language, Character, and Community*. Chicago: University of Chicago Press, 1984.

White, Robert A. "Mass Communication and Culture: Transition to a New Paradigm." *Journal of Communication* 33 (1983): 279–301.

Williams, Raymond. "Communications as Cultural Science." *Journal of Communication* 24 (1974): 17–25.

Wilson, Edmund. *Patriotic Gore: Studies in the Literature of the American Civil War*. New York: Farrar, Straus and Giroux, 1962.

Wilson, James D. *A Reader's Guide to the Short Stories of Mark Twain*. Boston: G. K. Hall, 1987.

Wisbey, Herbert A., Jr. "The True Story of Auntie Cord." *Mark Twain Society Bulletin* 4 (June 1981): 1, 3–5.

Wolfe, Bernard. "Uncle Remus and the Malevolent Rabbit: 'Takes a Limber-

Toe Gemmun fer ter Jump Jim Crow.'" In *Critical Essays on Joel Chandler Harris*, edited by R. Bruce Bickley, Jr., 70–84. Boston: G. K. Hall, 1981.

Wolseley, Roland E. *The Black Press, U.S.A.* Ames: Iowa State University Press, 1971.

Wood, James Playsted. *Magazines in the United States.* 3d ed. New York: Ronald Press, 1971.

Wood, Peter H., and Karen C. C. Dalton. *Winslow Homer's Images of Blacks: The Civil War and Reconstruction Years.* Austin: University of Texas Press, 1988.

Woodward, C. Vann. *Origins of the New South, 1877–1913.* Baton Rouge: Louisiana State University Press, 1971.

Yeazell, Stephen C. "Convention, Fiction, and Law." *New Literary History* 13 (1981): 89–102.

Yellin, Jean Fagan. "The 'Feminization' of Rebecca Harding Davis." *American Literary History* 2 (1990): 203–19.

Zarefsky, David, and Victoria J. Gallagher. "From 'Conflict' to 'Constitutional Question': Transformations in Early American Public Discourse." *Quarterly Journal of Speech* 76 (1990): 247–61.

INDEX